TABLE OF CONTENTS

CONTENTS OF THE INTRODUCTION

CONTENTS OF TRAINING SESSIONS

LIST OF ILLUSTRATIONS

LIST OF TABLES

TO ALL WHO HAVE ENRICHED OUR JOURNEY
IN LOVE, AWARENESS AND COMMITMENT

ACKNOWLEDGMENTS

This material is an integration of some of our experience and learning from innumerable sources.
   Our thanks go to:
Those who set us on the path of praying and loving
The thousands who through sharing their struggles and their joys have helped to form us
Those whose written ideas have shaped our own
Those who listened and gave us the key to listening effectively
Those who allowed Earle to experience the stimulation and rigor of study at Oxford University

   For their contribution toward crystallizing the specific material of this book, we especially thank
Paul Davidson, Earle's friend and supervisor for many years
Gerald May and Tilden Edwards, spiritual directors at Shalem Institute for Spiritual Formation in Washington, D.C.
Staff and participants of Shalem's 1985–86 spiritual guidance extension program
Tutors and fellow seminarians of San Francisco Theological Seminary
Barbara Fouhy for learnings in communication and change
Gloria Grattan, Principal Nurse, Wellington Hospital
St. John's College Trust Board, Aukland
Study Leave Committee of the Wellington Diocese
Participants in our pilot training program and subsequent courses
Dawn Wilson and Jenny Drury, our typists
Harper & Row for permission to use quotations from Gerald May's *Will and Spirit,* 1983
The originators of short quotations and of any exercises which we have adapted, acknowledged in the text as far as we have known them.

Earle and Elspeth Williams
20c Hackthorne Road
Christchurch
New Zealand

Be still and know that I am God.
Psalm 46:10

INTRODUCTION

1. THE TRAINING PROGRAM

Aims, Assumptions and Structure

This training program aims to provide a shared learning structure to enable us as Christian helpers to develop and integrate our spiritual awareness, communication and counseling skills.

Each session devotes time to practicing the deepening of our spiritual life, developing and appreciating our own gifts, and incorporating appropriate techniques into our own listening, discerning and counseling skills, integrating them into our growing spiritual awareness. We share organized experience and learn through one-to-one and group situations.

We each already have a certain ability to help others to cope; in our homes, at work, in social activities, perhaps in formal counseling. This course is designed to help us to develop our present skills and learn new ones to apply in any of these situations, which are often crises of varying magnitude.

Everyone is familiar with crises from childhood on. Some of us surmount them relatively easily, others seem to ricochet from one crisis to another. Whether a crisis is major or minor, when we feel unable to cope we may well go to someone else for help; similarly, others in crisis may turn to us.

But this course is far more than a skills program. As Christians we know that God is active in the world. This course aims to make us more aware of God's presence. Then, when we are helping others in crisis, instead of being drawn into the crisis, or imagining that the responsibility is on us, we recognize God's activity in the situation and may enable others to recognize God for themselves in their own way.

The group provides the opportunity to learn from participating in new experiences, from sharing and making links with our past experience as well as through appropriate input.

It is useful but not essential for participants to have had some formal counseling skills training; this program aims to develop whatever level of expertise and awareness we may bring from our own unique life experience, and each group will be different.

The thirty-three-session program may easily be divided into three eleven-session terms. Two hours without a break is the minimum required for each session; two-and-a-half or three hours with a break provides more adequate time for prayer, sharing and the demonstration and practice essential for incorporating the counseling and guidance skills effectively into our own practice of prayer and ministry.

The session material is in four unequal parts:

1. Discerning God's Spirit in contemplation and crisis in nonverbal awareness skills.
2. Discerning God's Spirit in formal and informal meditation and in verbal listening skills.
3. Discerning God's Spirit in pain, healing, words and concepts, in our own past and present, and in verbal skills for accepting, forgiving and changing.
4. Evaluation and celebration.

Basic assumptions of the program are:

1. God is present and active as a loving, integrative force, at work in the world, in the universe and in the lives of everyone now, whether we recognize God or not.
2. As Christians, we are called to enable people to make effective links between contemporary and historical religious experience and their own unique situation.

3. As Christians we are called to enable people to make discoveries and choices for themselves, with appropriate input, and so come to a deeper acceptance of themselves, and a deeper awareness, commitment to and confidence in God within and beyond themselves.

In the group we are encouraged to reflect on our own life of prayer and practice of ministry in the light of the contemplative spiritual guidance tradition, with its special contribution in the areas of solitary prayer and silence, and appreciation of the potential that impasse, extreme crisis, holds for growth as persons in community.

The program affirms contemporary understandings of crisis, and uses communication and change techniques appropriate to the normally short-term nature of crisis, with its unique opportunity and responsibility for ministry.

By learning to attend and listen to the sharer, and to stay in the sharer's world, we are encouraged throughout as helpers to keep our own factual input to an appropriate minimum. When praying aloud with the sharer, we become used to using the sharer's own words, and are alerted to the temptation of manipulating the sharer, and of retreating into a ritual of prayer or pious talk as an escape. Our approach is exemplified in the session contents, which leave the helper's own input of words and ideas to the last sessions.

There is emphasis throughout on us as participants enlarging our concepts of reality and linking our own experience with the accumulated Christian wisdom of past and present, so that we may become more effective guides in our work of discerning the Spirit in and through our counseling and listening. Discerning is important: we may often have thought that if discerning ministry had been available to someone in a time of crisis, they might have avoided many later crises.

Extensive notes make material accessible from some of the growing body of relevant literature and courses, for participants with limited time and access to such resources. The notes are intended to summarize and complement what may have arisen from the sharing of group members' own prayer practice and experience of skills. So participants are to be encouraged to use, study and amplify them during or after the appropriate

session rather than beforehand, and to recognize that the value of the notes lies in encouraging people to become more trusting, committed servants of God.

It would be a basic misunderstanding of the intention of this program to allow the structure to become a straitjacket that quenched the Spirit and stifled the potential of the group for spontaneous learning. Discerning God's guidance is the essence of this program, and it is essential for leaders to have the flexibility and awareness to use each session according to the needs of the group and its members and to discern the leading of God's Spirit at the time.

The program may be most effective with a small group of six to ten people in which leaders and participants are encouraged to learn and share together as peers. It assumes that the leaders have experience of experiential group dynamics and of facilitating groups. It is essential for them to be familiar with the whole program before starting to lead it, and for them to have incorporated into their own communication and praying skills the basic approach of staying with the sharer's own words and in the sharer's world. Then they may serve as models of the listening, discerning and counseling skills they are aiming to encourage. Two leaders are preferred for the presentation of material, demonstration of counseling skills, monitoring of group process and skills practice, especially if time is short.

Members bring to each group very different experiences and potential; that is part of the reality and interest of our lives as persons in community. Recognizing and using the potential that this variety holds for discovering our unity in diversity is part of the challenge for the group. Members will also bring personal crises. Dealing with crisis is a major focus of this program. So the potential for growth offered by crisis in the life of a member or of the group may be demonstrated in a living laboratory, providing a marvelous opportunity for realizing and demonstrating what crisis is and how it may be dealt with.

Each session needs to be an exercise in discerning and trusting the guidance of God in and through the life of the group and its members, and practicing the skills that facilitate this discernment. So a deeper commitment to prayer and a willingness to change in the light of what is learned through times of prayer in solitude and through honest, loving, responsible interaction with others are prerequisites of the effective use of this program.

Ongoing evaluation of the process and content of each session is part of the leader's preparation for following sessions. Participants' self-evaluation and evaluation of the course is encouraged by journaling, group discussion, verbal evaluations at each session, and written evaluations at the end of each term. Two of the last three sessions are devoted to an in-depth evaluation based on detailed written evaluations of personal growth and of the training program. The program culminates in celebration and Godspeed.

Throughout the program, reflection is encouraged on two questions:

1. What is happening in my life of prayer?
2. In what way am I aware of God's Spirit present in my life and practice of ministry today?

Present Training

Many clergy and lay people have little formal training in pastoral care, and where this has been attempted the church has tended to train its leaders in a psychological problem-solving model which has too narrow a frame of reference.

For many people questions of ultimate concern and opportunities for spiritual growth and response arise from the crisis of being in the hospital. So hospital chaplains, like prison chaplains, have a special opportunity and responsibility to help people to surface these concerns, respond creatively to their own crisis, and connect their unique situation with historical and contemporary spiritual and religious experience.

(Spiritual is taken as being aware and open to ultimate reality, immanent and transcendent; so for Christians, open and responding to the God who calls and guides on all levels of being.)

In counseling situations ministers and chaplains often find themselves in a double bind. They are trained with an inadequate frame of reference in pastoral care; they are faced with an opportunity and an imperative to maintain the spiritual focus, but they are seldom given specific guidelines on how this is to be achieved in their own spiritual development and in their spiritual counseling.

Nouwen recognizes the dilemma: "We need to explore ways to introduce schooling in prayer into pastoral education" (Nouwen 1977, 74). Christian helpers need a vital prayer life for a life of praying and discerning ministry.

This program sets out to take up Nouwen's challenge. It addresses the double bind that, a decade later, many Christian helpers still find themselves in, even though there is growing interest in spiritual direction and its relation to modern psychology. It offers them specific guidelines toward an adequate frame of reference and toward maintaining a spiritual focus both in their own lives and in counseling. Throughout the training program participants are encouraged to interrelate their developing spiritual and counseling awareness.

The bibliography indicates some background reading in the areas of spirituality, pastoral care, and counseling. Books that were especially helpful in the initial stages of developing this program are by Edwards and Leech on the contemplative tradition (Edwards, 1977, 1980; Leech, 1980), May on meditation and contemplative psychology (1977, 1982b), Cameron-Bandler on communication skills (1985), and May, Leech and Thayer on the relationship between spirituality and pastoral care (May 1982a, Leech 1985, 1986; Thayer 1985). Kenneth Leech is a pioneer in the move to integrate prayer, ministry and social action, and has drawn up an important manifesto for a renewed spirituality.

We go further than either Thayer or Leech in indicating the potential of a contemplative approach to crisis, especially crisis that leads to impasse. The great guides of the contemplative tradition have some crucial insights which have not been explicitly drawn out in any other authors we have read, although the indications are there. We make the overt link between crisis counseling and a contemplative approach to reality as the basis of an effective approach to life and the helping relationship. This program aims to integrate contemplative insights into Christian counseling and practice of ministry; pointing beyond spirituality and pastoral care to an effective spiritually aware pastoral caring.

2. THE SEARCH FOR MEANING AND WHOLENESS THROUGH EXPERIENCE

Seeking

In our society today there is widespread yearning for meaning, purpose and fulfillment. People are seeking experiential answers to ultimate questions. The search takes many forms, some of which lead people up misleading and spurious paths, and this indicates the need for guidance and direction for the seekers and for the guides.

The Goal of the Seeking

What is it that people seek?

May sums up the search as "a seeking for our deepest roots . . . our roots as creatures of and in this cosmos. . . . Somehow, at some level we are all one with all creation" (May 1982b, 89). The widespread seeking is an attempt to realize this deep-rooted connection with ultimate reality.

Many indigenous people look to the land to realize this deep connectedness with their roots. Western disconnectedness with land and roots is exemplified by the readiness to treat land as a commodity which can be bought or sold. Connectedness, belonging, cannot be bought or sold.

Having lost this sense of deeper connectedness, people often look in the wrong direction for this yearning for belonging to be satisfied, not realizing that ultimately it can only be satisfied by the divine.

The problem is not new. St. Augustine wrote in the fourth century: "You have made us for yourself, and our hearts find no peace until they rest in you" (Augustine of Hippo, *Confessions* 1.1).

Jung writes: "Among all my patients in the second half of life—that is to say, over thirty-five—there has not been one whose problem in the last resort was not that of finding a religious outlook on life" (Jung, 1933, 229).

In spite of the many forms that spiritual seeking can take, most people would agree that fundamental spiritual longing is for unconditional love; the need for belonging and union; and the desire to be ourselves.

A difficulty often encountered is that, having forgotten their relationship with God and who they are, people fail to realize in their searching that God is already present. This lack of realization is related to an important feature of the search for guidelines: a reluctance to accept most forms of authoritarian direction. Increasingly people want to accept the authority of their own experience rather than the experience of others.

Thayer and Merton insist that lived experience is the center of spirituality and the base for effective pastoral care (Thayer, 1985, 22,57; Merton, 1973).

All this prominence given to experience underlines the need for an appropriate approach in the helping relationship, an approach grounded in the experience both of the helpers and those seeking help. Today people are searching for wholeness, health, a way to develop, that includes all aspects of themselves.

In the twentieth century, science has too often restricted people to what can be seen and proved; the church has alienated them by emphasizing God's transcendence and distance. Both have tended to neglect the creative, intuitive side of life. When people turn to mental health professionals they may find little or no spiritual help. When they turn to the Western church they find a church conscious of its spiritual calling but caught up in its culture, largely training its leaders in an inadequate frame of reference.

Western churches as part of the Western world have tended to emphasize the intellectual content of knowledge; with the effect of confusing faith, the commitment of a whole person, with beliefs, the intellectual component of faith.

This confusion is exemplified in many churches which see preaching, didactic teaching, acts of worship and a paternalistic approach to visiting and pastoral care as fulfilling their role of spiritual guide, while neglecting individual needs and the intuitive side of human nature. Some church leaders, continuing the paternalism of the past, have followed a model of spiritual guidance with little understanding derived from depth psychology; others have embraced the new psychology without relating it to their role as spiritual guide. So some are attempting to offer spiritual guidance without reference to the actual situation of the person concerned, others are attempting to offer care that is psychologically grounded without the spiritual dimension.

An illustration is the not uncommon experience of a woman terminally ill in the hospital. Ella was a lapsed member of her church who was being visited by a chaplain of her own denomination. She complained in deeply emotive language that this minister, attempting to offer spiritual guidance, simply trotted out the stock answers to questions in his mind which bore little relationship to her own struggle as the dying mother of teenage daughters and the wife of a devoted husband.

We Christian helpers may sincerely offer time-honored counsel, unaware of escaping into pious quotations and untimely prayer ritual in self-defence. Modern psychology has exposed this mechanism and highlighted the importance of meeting people at their personal point of need.

Ella's experience illustrates related aspects of the church's failure to meet people's deeper needs: failure to recognize that pastoral care and spiritual guidance need to be grounded in and related to a person's actual situation; and failure to recognize that the way we learn is not by being told by someone else how it is; that the way to spiritual maturity is through a self-knowledge that leads us to discover our own answers to our own situation.

Certainly many churches in recent years have moved away from an exclusively catechetical approach, and are using a far more dynamic and experientially-based approach. The church is starting to reembrace the Eastern emphasis on the unity of all being, but many effects of the narrower approach remain.

Clinebell sounds the clarion call:

The response of the pastoral counseling movement to our society's spiritual crisis should be a more explicit, robust, and imaginative theological thrust in all that we do. We must recover our largely neglected heritage of spiritual direction, and integrate it fully with insights from the human sciences and with psychotherapeutic methods from both tradi-

tional and contemporary psychotherapies (Clinebell, 1983, 182).

The church, then, in its pastoral caring today needs a concept and practice of pastoral care and of knowledge which is spiritually aware, wide open to reality, and which encourages the integration of the rational and the intuitive, of body, mind and spirit, in the development of the whole person.

3. A BASIS FOR SPIRITUALLY AWARE PASTORAL CARE—THE CONTEMPLATIVE TRADITION

Contemplation

Contemplation is fundamental to pastoral caring that is spiritually aware.

"Contemplation is . . . a secret and peaceful and living inflow of God, which, if not hampered, fires the soul in the spirit of love" (John of the Cross, *Dark Night* 1.10.6, about 1582).

The contemplative way has been lived and taught down through the centuries by great spiritual guides, such as the Desert Fathers Evagrius and John Cassian, Bernard of Clairvaux, Teresa of Avila, John of the Cross, Ignatius Loyola, and twentieth-century Thomas Merton.

These Christians have much to teach about the relevance today of contemplation in action, about discerning God's presence, and working in line with God's will in everyday life and in the helping relationship.

In *Will and Spirit* (1982b), May provides a theoretical and experientially-based framework for a spiritually aware pastoral care. Both Thayer and Leech in their separate books *Spirituality and Pastoral Care* (Thayer, 1985; Leech, 1986), like May, link prayer life with the quality of attending to others. But May goes further in making the overt connection of will with a spiritually-based pastoral care.

An assumption behind our program is that the role of will is crucial to an understanding of Jesus' ministry, and foundational for effective pastoral care. It is also central to a contemplative response to living in the tradition of the great spiritual guides.

The contemplative tradition of prayer appreciates the importance of our concepts being appropriate for effective living, yet recognizes that concepts have no ultimate significance. Appreciating the significance and limitations of concepts and images lays the foundation for a postmodern consciousness of reality, with its implications for freeing people. In becoming less attached, less driven, people may allow themselves and others simply to be, to grow, to become what they are not yet in God.

Thayer (1985, 21–24) sees an emerging postmodern response to reality as recognizing the limits of a scientific attitude; as affirming new understandings of the human propensity for projection and delusion; as yearning for meaning and deep union with the whole of being; and emphasizing the centrality of experience in both the interior and transcendent dimensions of the person in community.

A contemplative response is concerned with the neglected intuitive form of knowing. Intuition in this sense is not the same as the popular notion of a hunch, sixth sense or gut reaction. Intuition is a way of knowing, a state of apprehending or appreciation that occurs before the filtering process of thinking takes place (see Edwards, 1980, 114). In other words, the source of this attitude is in the heart, rather than the mind, the heart understood as the center of our being, the intuitive faculty in us that makes it possible to communicate with God.

It is because intuition is our mode of knowing in which appreciation or apprehension of the divine is most likely to occur, that the great spiritual guides of the past consider the intuitive form of knowing so important.

Yet intuition is the neglected faculty in much of the modern search for meaning. This program is concerned with contemplative disciplines as the way to encourage awareness and the possibility of encounter with God, because it is the awareness and experience of the divine that may lead to transformation at the level of action.

The contemplative guidance tradition already appreciated many of the basic understandings recognized anew by Freud and his successors. The value and meaning of dreams is an obvious example. Again, the modern understanding of self-deception and of human development is

rightly attributed to these modern psychologists, but the propensity for self-deception is well-known to the great spiritual guides, and the idea of sifting through motives is central to their discernment process (John of the Cross, *Dark Night* 1.1.3).

John of the Cross and Teresa of Avila also have a dynamic developmental concept of human being that precedes and agrees with modern psychology (FitzGerald, 1984, 93–116). They go further than much modern psychology in their understanding of interior experience, and in acknowledging the importance of brokenness and of the transcendent in the search for meaning, purpose and direction which Frankl sees as the distinctive feature of being human (John of the Cross, *Dark Night* 1.4.; Teresa of Avila, *Interior Castle*; Frankl, 1979).

The Relevance of Contemplation Today

For many people today, the word contemplation conjures up something remote and alien to the practicalities of life. Social concern and action has become for many a substitute for private prayer.

In the church, clinical models of pastoral intervention have tended to be dominant, as in Clinical Pastoral Education (CPE). Despite all its benefits:

> . . . it is widely recognized within the CPE movement itself that the combination of the comprehensive antireligious bias of psychoanalytic theory and the success of the clinical model directed attention from the traditional practices of formation such as prayer, meditation and Bible study. . . .
>
> . . . It denies no credit . . . for what they accomplished to point out that the accomplishment has been won to the exclusion of much that has been profound in the history of the Christian experience of God, and the exclusion of dimensions of one's own being. The epidemic of midlife crisis, burnout, and the experience of meaninglessness in ministry suggests that we neglect the interior firming of our connectedness and relationship with the Ultimate only at great risk to ourselves (Thayer, 1985, 76).

Thayer's timely warning encourages people to rediscover for themselves the value of contemplative prayer.

Mother Teresa, in a moving television documentary on her life, puts it this way: "Holiness is not for the few. Holiness is the simple duty of us all."

The search on the part of so many today for new directions, depth of understanding, meaning and purpose indicates that contemplative prayer cannot happily remain marginal. Growing numbers of people are discovering that spiritual disciplines are needed for spiritual maturity and for recovering the balance between contemplation and Christian service. Edwards speaks of this balance in terms of the basic rhythm of life, sabbath and ministry; Thayer refers to the rhythm of withdrawal and engagement. Reed talks of extra- and intra-dependence. (Edwards, 1980, 69–89; Edwards, 1982; Thayer, 1985, 82; Reed, 1978 quoted in Edwards, 1980, 77).

The suspicion that true contemplation is an escape into pietism, that it is an ivory tower defense against the world is unfounded. The great spiritual guides insist that recovering a contemplative attitude clears blocks and releases the energy needed for our effective involvement in the world; furthermore, that our involvement is a test of a valid spirituality. The social service record of the Society of Friends (Quakers) is an outstanding example.

So contemplation is highly relevant today and is basic to recovering the core of Christian ministry and pastoral care. It may do much to restore a needed balance. It may help to satisfy spiritual as well as mental and emotional needs, including an appreciation of God as both immanent and transcendent. Far from alienating people, it may challenge them to a deeper and more responsible personal and social involvement.

Pastoral Care and Society

The emphasis of much of the training in pastoral care and practice addresses the needs of the individual for growth and awareness without necessarily including any social involvement. But the concept of pastoral care divorced from community is a contradiction; it is a denial of the church's call to a prophetic stance in relation to social structures, and it denies the individual the perspective of community relationship.

The heavy emphasis on self-actualization and self-realization often puts institutions, the community and the family into the role of "blocking the growth" of the individual, where individual growth is identified as the goal, the good. At best the family or community is in tension with the individual (Turner, 1987).

A truly pastoral care needs to see the individual in community. Some of the individualism that has crept into pastoral care may be traced directly to a failure to appreciate that the biblical concept of the person is in community in relation to God. The ancient biblical world was far more community-minded than our present European one. Because the words of the old Bible translations have lost or changed their meaning, while the words of new translations do not fully convey the original concepts either, the failure to recognize the personal and corporate nature of pastoral care has been compounded.

In contrast, a spiritually aware pastoral care, grounded in prayer and the tradition of the great spiritual guides, confronts people again and again with the need for a spirituality that expresses and validates itself in responsible social action, the need not simply to adapt to the environment but to work for more just and humane social structures.

The Christian's role is to represent the truth that God is both strengthener and disturber of the structures of society.

The Role of Will

May considers that the difference between secular and spiritually aware pastoral care rests largely on their differing view of the role of will. Will is "the sense of volition, how we manage ourselves and our lives; our perceptions of what we can and cannot control in ourselves and in the environment" (May, 1982b, 104). Will is the function we use to align soul with spirit.

Secular psychology may use the exercise of the will as an important factor in building autonomous ego-strength, self-worth and power. But "Self-will . . . is pride. It is the will to power which acknowledges no other master than itself" (Abbott, 1963, 23).

Pastoral care based on such a psychological approach alone is insufficient. Spiritually aware pastoral care sees the right use of our will as a willingness to surrender our will for power, surrender our will for staying in personal control, to the loving willingness of God.

Our will for power, to be in control, is so strong that it is very difficult for us to give it up, to stop deceiving ourselves that we can go it alone. Sometimes we are driven by our own will for power until it breaks us, and we are then ready to give up the struggle.

Alcoholics Anonymous recognizes the strength of the familiar will to be in control in their view that alcoholics need to be willing to give up the illusion that they are personally in control before they find the incentive and discover the power to transcend their dependency.

From a contemplative perspective, we may discover that when we surrender to God our will for power, the power to transcend our will for power is released, and that God is indeed real. God's power comes to us through our accepting God's loving, willing acceptance of us as we actually are in our powerlessness. The contemplative aim is the union of our willingness with the loving willingness of God.

This contemplative view of the role of will is far from the breaking of the will, which may even lead to the breaking of the will to live. But it has often been tragically distorted in the name of religion. The demonic confusion of the distinction between a healthy will in human development and the misdirection or self-destructive use of the will to power, is highlighted in the advice of John Wesley's mother, Suzanna. It illustrates the philosophy behind a whole Western way of child-rearing which has had disastrous consequences for individuals and society, and is far removed from the teachings of the gospel:

> I insist upon conquering the will of children betimes, because this is the only strong and rational foundation of a religious education; without which both precept and example will be ineffectual. . . .

> As self-will is the root of all sin and misery, so whatever cherishes this in children, ensures their after-wretchedness and irreligion: whatever checks and mortifies it, promotes their future happiness and piety. . . . Religion is nothing else than the doing the will of God, and not our own; that the one great impediment to our temporal and eternal happiness being this self-will, no indulgence of it can be trivial, no denial unprofitable. Heaven or hell depends

on this alone. So that the parent who studies to subdue it in his child, works together with God in the renewing and saving a soul: the parent who indulges it does the Devil's work, makes religion impracticable, salvation unattainable, and does all that in him lies to damn his child, soul and body, for ever (Wesley, 1732).

Today those with a secular approach may look to their own strengths, and look to others in reinforcing their strengths and exercising their will for power, their desire for autonomy, whereas those with a contemplative psychological approach may look beyond their own and other people's ability to surrender, to transcend their own will to power, their own desire for autonomy. And in surrendering their own power and accepting the willing accepting love of a love that transcends all human loves and desires, they find an ability, a power, an energy, which is beyond both themselves and others—the reality that is God.

Jesus is the supreme example of surrendering the will fully to doing the loving will of God, and so receiving power. "My food is to obey the will of the one who sent me and to finish the work he gave me to do" (Jn 4:34).

Developing a strong will and the ability to make healthy choices is crucial in our growth towards Christian wholeness.

The Concept of Spirit in the Helping Relationship

Our will and spirit are closely linked. Energy, power, and the ability in and beyond ourselves to transcend ourselves and others may all be ways of referring to spirit:

> . . . spirit has something to do with the energy of our lives, the life force that keeps us active and dynamic. Will has more to do with personal intention and how we decide to use our energies. Spirit, for me, has a quality of connecting us with each other, with the world around us, and with the mysterious source of all. In contrast, will has qualities of independence, of personal freedom, and of decision making (May, 1982b, 2–3).

Different understandings of spirit affect the goals of psychotherapy, counseling and spiritual guidance, and confirm the need for an inclusive contemplative psychological approach rather than a narrowly secular one.

Fairchild discusses the contrasting and overlapping functions of these three types of helping relationships, highlighting the differing views of persons, relationships, and the role of will (Fairchild, 1985, 32). These views roughly correspond to the three views of spirit outlined by Thayer (Thayer, 1985, 31–53).

The first category, psychotherapy, focuses clearly on the person, on the reduction of confusion and conflict, on ego control and on the desire of the therapist to solve mystery. There is recognition of the need to relate, which leads to some personal transcendence, but the individual person remains the center of attention. The will for power, the need to be in control, is paramount, and mystery is seen as a gap in self-understanding and knowledge, needing to be filled.

This first category, psychotherapy, corresponds by and large with Thayer's first understanding of spirit as the higher human capacities in a person, especially the ability to assert one's will and to choose. While there is some idea of spirit in psychotherapy, in its usual denial of a reality transcending our empirical world, traditional depth psychology alone does not provide an adequate understanding of spirit.

The second category, counseling, and especially pastoral counseling, is based on a broader understanding of the transcendent dimension of human being. In counseling the sharer is called on to make choices about life situations and relationships, and the need for values is recognized.

Many transpersonal psychologists and counselors would accept Thayer's second understanding of spirit as the human capacity to respond to a transcendent dimension beyond our ordinary everyday reality (Erikson, 1963, 23–25).

As the counselors become more inclusive in their understanding of human being, their appreciation of transcendence and spirit comes closer to Thayer's third understanding of spirit. But there is one important respect in which both the psychotherapist and the counselor generally differ from the spiritual guide: in their attitude to the role of the helper and of will. It remains an important focus of both these disciplines to work collaboratively with clients to help them to achieve self-direction and self-assertion. The aim is to strengthen their will and ability to manage and to stay in control.

In the third category, spiritual guidance, the goal is different: it is personal meaning, and union or communion, especially the union of the seeker's will, with the loving will of God transcendent and immanent, ultimate reality. The seeker surrenders the will for power through willing acceptance of God's loving acceptance of them as they are. In other words, the goal is reducing ego dependence rather than enhancing ego strength. Yet the goals of counseling and spiritual guidance are not necessarily in conflict; a healthy sense of self-worth or ego strength is needed before it may be surrendered.

Having union as a goal means a different attitude to mystery: the spiritual guide is a companion with the sharer in acknowledging rather than attempting to solve mystery.

For the spiritual guide, spirit is understood as the human desire to participate in a source of power, meaning and mystery in and beyond the human, the capacity for union with the ground of all being, with ultimate reality.

In the progression from psychotherapy through counseling to spiritual guidance, then, there is an increasingly comprehensive understanding of human being and of recovering the human experience of immanence and transcendence.

The biblical experience embraces and develops these understandings of spirit. In the Yahwist creation story the very being of the human is permeated by the breath of God, the fundamental life force (Gen 2:7). In Hebrew, the breath or spirit that enlivens the divine is the same breath that is the source and sustainer of human life. The soul is the totality of a person. "Man does not have a soul. He is a soul" (Squire, 1976).

> We can take soul to mean the fundamental essence of a person, and spirit is the aspect of that essence that gives it power, energy and motive force. Thus soul and spirit are not "things" in which one may choose to believe or not to believe. They are simply descriptive aspects of our existence, the one referring to our essence and the other to our fundamental energy (May, 1982b, 32).

It is important to avoid identifying God with soul. "The center of the soul is not God, but it is so intimately grounded in God it can be sometimes mistaken for God himself" (McNamara, 1975).

Another danger lies in compartmentalizing people into body, mind and spirit, a concept developed from Greek thought and still current in much Western church teaching. Modern scientific thinking tends to ignore spirit and reduce humans merely to body and mind. Popular phrases such as "a person is a bio-psycho-social being" indicate some reaction to this dichotomy but still do not include the spiritual. Today the growing holistic movement represents a trend towards the recovery of the Hebrew and Eastern concept of the essential unity of all humans and of all creation with the ultimate reality and source of being.

A spiritually aware pastoral care is based on encouraging in contemplation our willingness to open ourselves (soul) to the essential energy (spirit) which is understood as the gracious gift of an all-loving God.

Mystery

Spirit, fundamental life force, is closely connected with mystery.

It was noted earlier that just as the attitudes of psychotherapists, counselors and spiritual guides to their role as helper tends to correspond to their concept of spirit, so it tends also to correspond to their concept of the role of will and of mystery.

The person with a modern scientific view of reality is likely to deny the place of mystery and the transcendent dimension in human being. A psychotherapist or psychologist who sees a human as needing to be in control, needing a will for power, leaves little room in their perception of reality for mystery, for the inexplicable, regarding it as a gap to be filled.

Counselors and spiritual guides who have a transcendent view of spirit relate more closely to the Christian tradition which affirms that "our human knowing and experience carry us ultimately into mystery" (Thayer, 1985, 67). Jung insists that each person is a profound mystery.

How people use will and regard mystery is crucial to which kind of helping they choose. What do those who choose to acknowledge the mysterious offer us? A basic paradox: "A funda-

mental contribution of the contemplative tradition is their constant affirmation that mystery can be known without being solved, mystery can be experienced, sensed, felt, appreciated, even loved, without needing to be understood" (May, 1982b, 30).

The way of knowledge is the way of darkness, for God is unapproachable and hidden (Leech, 1980, 155). The way of knowing is through unknowing (Greek: *agnosis*).

The prerequisite for this kind of knowing is encouraging in ourselves the ability to be aware, open to reality, on all levels of our being. Committing ourselves to the unknown can be a risky and frightening business, but the willingness and the courage to open our self to mystery is the essence of contemplative spirituality, and our key to its contribution to living and to helping others.

> Mystery . . . will not allow itself to be packaged, harnessed or collected. Only images of spiritual reality can be mastered; the real thing constantly eludes capture (May, 1982b, 34).

An attitude of humility, which may be reassuring or even more frightening, helps us to realize that it is not for us to understand, control or use mystery but for us to surrender to it.

Job is the epitome of humility when confronted by great mystery:

> I know that you are all-powerful: what you conceive, you can perform. I am the man who obscured your designs with my empty-headed words. I have been holding forth on matters I cannot understand, on marvels beyond me and my knowledge. . . . I retract all I have said, and in dust and ashes I repent (Job 42:1–3,6, *The Jerusalem Bible*).

The ability and desire to surrender humbly to mystery are determined by the use of will.

Consciousness, Awareness and Attention

Another important factor in both contemplation and in spiritually aware pastoral counseling is the quality of our consciousness and the related aspects of our awareness and attention.

If we are to encourage a Christian consciousness of reality, what do we mean by consciousness? While recognizing many interpretations of

Locke's definition of consciousness as "the perception of what passes in man's own mind," Thayer writes:

> Consciousness refers to how we construct, experience, and respond to our world. . . . The process of constructing our consciousness is identical with constructing our sense of "reality." We cannot know "external" reality in itself; we can only know it through the contents of our own consciousness. Robert Ornstein has described the process this way: "Sense organs gather information that the brain can modify and sort. This heavily filtered input is compared with memory, expectations, body movements . . . until, finally, our consciousness is constructed as a 'best guess' about reality. These 'best guesses' . . . offer stability at the cost of exclusion."[2]

The exclusion occurs because our brain filters out information that has no survival value (Thayer, 1985, 77).

[2] Robert Ornstein, *The Psychology of Consciousness* (New York: Harcourt Brace Jovanovich, 1977), 44.

We are constantly bombarded by our sense impressions; our brain tends to filter out information that has no survival value.

This filtering process has been studied by Bandler and Grinder in their *Neuro Linguistic Programming* (Bandler and Grinder, 1979). The universal processes of deleting, generalizing, and altering or distorting are essential to our survival, essential to understanding our experience of reality and to forming our concepts (see Cameron-Bandler, 1985, 223–33). Our experience helps to form our concepts and our concepts help to form our experience, so that we each develop a unique and changing concept of our own world. These concepts are essential, but they have no ultimate significance; that is, they are symbols of reality, not reality itself.

Often our concepts are too restricting; they may limit us and deny us flexibility, they may diminish our ability to make effective choices and changes. We are only conscious at any given moment of a fraction of what our senses are processing and how we are reacting. Because our conscious mind is deeply affected by our unconscious mind, by the concepts and reactions that are linked there, when we as helpers aim to encourage a Christian consciousness of reality, we are aiming to encourage a greater integration of the conscious and unconscious mind, an integration of the whole person. We are aiming to help people become more aware and to realize that they have freedom to choose more appropriate concepts and ways of relating to their own and other people's reality, and to the reality they understand as immanent and transcendent; that is, God.

The state of our consciousness is related to the quality of our awareness and attention. Attention is awareness that is both restricted or focused and also alert. We have eliminated distractions; we are wide-awake and interested. Being aware and attending are important features of a contemplative attitude to reality. Water provides a beautiful and ancient analogy of awareness and the factors that enhance or distort it. In the East awareness is often likened to clear water which ideally reflects all there is around it, clearly and without distortion. A favorite Zen example is that of water reflecting the moon with total accuracy.

But the conditions that pertain to clear uninterrupted perception rarely obtain in everyday life. As May points out, in normal daily life the water is often turbulent and muddied. It becomes turbulent if we are preoccupied or distracted or work hard to pay attention, because our will causes disruptions that interfere with, rather than improve, our perception. The water is muddied or clouded so that only vague, hazy reflections are possible, when we slip into a dulled, lethargic or somnolent state.

Without doubt, we often need to intervene actively for effective living, and willingness may at times call for determined action. But we are so used to willful interference in the course of events that we are seldom prepared to let things be.

Our willfulness blocks the clear perception which we need in order to know and become aware intuitively. The goal of our contemplation (our intuitive approach to knowledge and awareness) is to reach beyond the discursive thinking phase of meditation, beyond concepts, to a state of openness and awareness in which our comprehending gives way to apprehending. Apprehension is openness to being embraced by, rather than embracing, reality. This is the "knowing through unknowing" of the contemplative tradition.

An intuitive contemplative attitude is essential to a truly spiritually aware pastoral care; praying in solitude cultivates this attitude and encourages our awareness and openness in life generally. The quality of the awareness and attention we develop in solitary prayer is directly related to the quality of attention we give to the sharer in the helping relationship and is the key to its effectiveness.

Unitive Experience

In a contemplative approach to reality as demonstrated in the pool example, we open our self to the possibility, though never the assurance, of a conscious encounter with God.

There are many kinds of religious experiences. Examples include charismatic, visionary, conversion, psychic and unitive experiences. All of them except unitive experience retain some sense of self. Unitive experience leads to a loss of self-definition.

Unitive experience has three main characteristics: being at one—the unitive quality itself; a change in our awareness in which our attention ceases to be focused, but we are alert; and an experience of wonder, awe and reverence which leaves us feeling that what we have experienced is the way things really are (May, 1982b, 53).

A test of whether the experience is pathological or creative, according to May, is its result. The pathological gives people grandiose ideas of their own self-importance, a desire to manipulate and convert people, and so distances them from others. The valid creative experience increases our sense of humility and the desire to serve humanity, leading us to be compassionate and concerned for others.

Attempts to engineer unitive experience do not work. Any attempt to still the ripples only creates more ripples. Christian contemplatives see unitive experience as a gift from God. Although we cannot make it happen, we may dispose ourselves toward the possibility of unitive experience by such disciplines as quiet open prayer, which may lead us to a heightened awareness of God.

Unitive experience is not an end in itself; the goal of Christian spirituality is a union of will, resulting in our willingness to do the loving will of God. "Not my will but your will be done," prayed Jesus (Lk 2:42).

It is this union of our will with God's will that releases power.

Fear and Self-Image

Unitive experience and this union of wills, however, involve our surrendering our self-definition or self-image.

Because losing our self-definition is frightening, our fear is a major obstacle to the openness leading to our union with God.

We have two ways of dealing with this threat to our self-image. One is to defend ourselves against such threats, the other is to repress them.

The fundamental problem in our fear of losing our self-image is that self-surrender feels like dying, because in unitive experience our self-image is suspended. Our inevitable strong identification of our self with our self-image produces the basic fear that, with the suspension of our self-image, our entire self will be wiped out. In his impressive *Denial of Death* (1972), Ernest Becker has shown how pervasive is our fear of dying, our fear of being obliterated.

Although self-image seems to be such an obstacle to our spiritual realization, it is essential for living. It is being trapped in our self-image that is the problem. As with any excessive dependency, over-attachment is the obstacle to our becoming aware of our true self.

In the psychotherapeutic approach to emotional and mental health, the development of an effective self-image tends to be regarded as synonymous with health, without reference to the spiritual issues of meaning and purpose, a stance that Frankl has been challenging for more than forty years.

A spiritually aware view of self-image sees a healthy self-image as important for effective living in this world, but maintains that this healthy self-image is not an end in itself, but a means to our self-surrender, leading to discovering our true self and God. Many of the great spiritual guides insist on the need to know ourselves if we are to know God. And knowing ourselves is to value our self-image for what it is, an image; to recognize the fear of losing it and to see beyond this fear to love.

Self-Realization

A feature of the current search for meaning, purpose and direction is the emphasis on self-realization. Self-realization is the discovery of our potential.

As psychology rightly reminds us, we may need to experience willful self-assertion, especially if it has been denied us in early childhood, in order to develop a healthy self-image, a prerequisite for our spiritual maturing. However, the self-assertion of religious pietism, or of some distorted assertiveness courses which encourage attitudes and behavior that effectively block true self-discovery, have no more place in true self-realization than a medieval denigration of self in the name of self-denial.

True self-realization lies beyond attachment to our ego and self-image, at the point of knowing and realizing our true self which lies beyond our self-image. It is particularly at this point of being in touch with our real self that we may be aware of God. For our deepest wanting is what God wants.

"The kingdom of heaven is within you" (Lk 17:21). "When we are in touch with our own deepest orientation and desire, we have found God's direction for our lives. . . . What God wants for us and what we are are consistent with each other" (Hart, 1980, 75)

Or again, James: "God is the natural appellation, for us Christians at least, for the supreme reality. . . . We and God have business with each other; and in opening ourselves to his influence [prayer] our deepest destiny is fulfilled" (James, 1902, 516–17).

We realize the true direction of our lives and achieve self-realization at the level of our deepest desire, when our own wills are aligned to the loving will of God.

Love

Our attitude to love is central in a spiritually aware pastoral care.

Love is the answer to fear; "Perfect love casts out fear," states the epistle writer (1 Jn 4:18). What is the perfect love to which John refers?

God is love and all love originates from the energy or life force which is spirit; love emanates from God. There are broadly three interrelated human expressions of God's love. Narcissistic love is a receiving, inward-looking love which gives self the priority over the welfare of others, and is concerned mainly with self-preservation, like an infant sucking its thumb. Erotic or romantic love is sexual love for another. The love of friends or family commits people to the welfare of others.

The origin of love in all its forms is *agape*, the divine love which, like the other forms of love, may be expressed through humans, and originates in God.

It is God's agape that is perfect and capable of casting out the deepest fears. For only agape is constant, cannot be taken away. All love, like life itself, is a freely given gift from God; but the various human expressions of God's love are necessarily conditional. Agape is unconditional. Agape is God's love in all its fullness.

A major difficulty is that again and again we expect the various human expressions of love, which are expedient and good in themselves, to satisfy our deepest yearning for love and belonging which only God can satisfy. We attach ultimate significance to the expressions of love which derive from and are affirmed by **agape** love.

It is in disposing ourselves to God's unconditional love that we find ourselves, and discover a new joy in God given love expressed through friendship, sex and self-love. By being open to agape, we come nearer to the union and self-realization that we seek, nearer to the freedom and to the release of energy which results in loving, Christian service. Agape, like wind, breath, spirit, is active; constantly impressing and needing to be expressed in and through people to others. So we need to maintain the openness essential for agape to impress us, to be expressed in and through us.

This need to maintain openness is the basis of a spiritually aware pastoral caring. Our role as Christian helpers is to allow God's love to be expressed through us to enable the sharer's potentialities to grow towards maturity.

As Frankl writes:

Love is the only way to grasp another human being in the innermost core of his personality. No one can become fully aware of the very essence of another human being unless he loves him. By the spiritual act of love he is enabled to see the essential traits and features in the beloved person; and even more, he sees that which is potential in him; which is not yet actualized but yet ought to be actualized. Furthermore, by his love, the loving person enables the beloved person to actualize these potentialities. By making him aware of what he can be and of what he should become, he makes these potentialities come true (Frankl, 1964, 113–14).

It is also the case that, when we begin to appreciate the real worth of another person, we ourselves sense a deeper connection and love. Love evokes love.

"Willingness to be open to the divine love and decreasing our opposition to it . . . in the last analysis may be the most significant thing in life" (May, 1982b, 42).

Feelings and Emotions

In having a loving attitude we are bound to take seriously people's feelings and emotions.

Feelings and emotions are an integral part of being human, and we need to recognize, accept and affirm them instead of denying or repressing them. Yet there is still fear and embarrassment in acknowledging them, and resistance to introspection is widespread.

Feelings and emotions are an important road to self-discovery. It is in acknowledging our feelings alongside our thinking that we may become aware of our broad potential for growth, self-understanding, ability to be open to others and to God and, contained in this breadth, our potential for evil through repression, suppression or expression of feelings. Through feelings and emotions we may discover our self at a deeper level; hence the need for taking them seriously in the helping relationship.

In accepting and dealing with feelings and emotions, we have to choose whether we will follow the direction of God's loving will or our own willful desire for autonomy and power. However much hereditary factors and social conditioning may affect the potential for growth and the ability to choose, the God-given choice of whether we recognize and how we deal with our feelings and emotions remains our individual responsibility.

Most contemplatives advocate a relaxed attention to feelings, agreeing that we have a real possibility for choice. Our will is paramount; we may choose to express our feelings, suppress them or leave them alone and just feel them. If we choose either to express or suppress feelings it may be counterproductive, in that the energy so absorbed may reduce our awareness, openness, and ability to act appropriately.

Although excessive attachment to feelings may preoccupy, cloud or confuse our judgment, yet through feelings and emotions we may discern how God may be moving and guiding us.

Modern psychology has led us to a reappraisal and renewed appreciation of the positive attitude to emotions in the writings of such spiritual guides as Julian of Norwich, Teresa of Avila and John of the Cross. Long ago John believed that the process of transformation occurs, not through killing or repressing desire, but through a gradual process by which we are transformed through what we cherish and through what gives us security and support (John of the Cross, *Dark Night* 1.13).

Encounter with Evil

Just as fear of losing our self-image diminishes our ability to be open to God, self and others, so fear of our own capacity for evil and of evil outside our self also leads to defensive behavior.

> Jung's individuation process provides a context for the assessment of good and evil as traditionally understood. To be involved in the individuation process is to be moving towards a psychic totality, a completeness called the self. The presence of this self is judged good. Not to be involved in the individuation process results in an absence, a lack of self-knowledge which is properly understood as evil. From this lack of consciousness flow actions and effects which themselves are evil. The evil of not going on the individuation journey is a privation, an absence of self, but it is also the destructive reality which Jung observed in his psychology (Welch, 1982, 198).

Describing attitudes to evil, James writes:

> There are people for whom evil means only a maladjustment with things, a wrong correspondence of

one's life with the environment. Such evil as this is curable . . . merely by modifying either the self or things or both at once. . . . But there are others for whom evil . . . is more radical and general, a wrongness or vice in his essential nature, which no alteration of the environment, or any superficial rearrangement of the inner self, can cure, and which requires a supernatural remedy (James, 1902, 134).

The latter group may find special meaning in John's teaching on impasse, considered later in more detail.

Any opening to reality, intentional or spontaneous, inevitably exposes us to the reality of evil. The reality and mystery of evil around and within us may take hold through our overattachment and will for power, and through our unconscious or deliberate disregard of other people's rights to freedom and self-realization.

Here, as in all other aspects of the contemplative way, we need guidance to survive the inevitable encounter with evil and the risk of distortion and misdirection in the spiritual quest. Guidance, therefore, is essential not only in the form generally provided by the church in its preaching, teaching, worship and pastoral care, but also in sharing in what Edwards calls the oral tradition of the great guides, in one-to-one and peer group situations where the expressed purpose in meeting is to seek God's guidance.

Guidance may help us on our spiritual journey to survive the inevitable encounter with evil, and to discover for ourselves the link between contemporary and historical religious experience and our own unique experience and situation. As Teresa believed: "Evil is present and yet transformed in the symbol of the crucified" (Welch, 1982, 199).

Prayer in Solitude

Central to this program is the conviction that spiritual awareness is the basis of an effective pastoral caring and that prayer is the cornerstone. Praying is learning to be open in our depth to receiving and responding to the immanent and transcendent in our own and others' reality and to the reality that is God.

The way to encourage this crucial awareness is through time for prayer in solitude, and attention to our quality of consciousness during this time (see section on awareness and attention).

Prayer in solitude is an essential part of a disciplined religious life. As Cobb says about prayer in solitude, there is "no other way to achieve adequate self-knowledge, self-control and stability of commitment. . . . With others there are always intervening variables to honesty, but thinking of oneself as alone before God enables and causes us to take a deeper responsibility for ourselves" (Cobb, 1974, 24).

Praying in solitude recovers the prophetic or confrontational dimension of the call to self-discovery in a form that is more potent than other prayer, because what we are confronted with in solitary prayer may be our true self without pretense, without delusion, without possibility of blaming another, which may be more devastating than any confrontation by others.

It is the experience of great guides of the contemplative tradition that the quality of our prayer life in solitude determines whether or not our daily life is a life of prayer. Each reinforces the other, and is augmented by communal Christian acts such as worship, preaching, teaching, study and shared experience.

So prayer, especially praying in silence and solitude, confronts us with truth. It is an indispensable aid to the honesty, openness, trust and ability to listen which are our means of knowing ourselves and God, prerequisites of our being there for others in honesty, openness and attentiveness.

Centering Prayer

The way to this attentive awareness is through all our senses, including the intuitive; its deepest point of registration is in our depths, at the center of our being. Centering prayer is a means for our time apart to become a time of deepening consciousness of reality.

Various forms of centering prayer have been practiced through the ages. Most of them use an object, words or some sound, scent, touch, activity and/or mental symbol as a pivot or base to center our attention in the present, in order to free our awareness for the open alertness that may lead us to a deeper appreciation of reality.

Some people find it helpful to use the ancient

practice of reciting the Jesus Prayer to the rhythm of their breathing. In full it is: "Lord Jesus Christ, Son of God, have mercy on me a sinner," often shortened to "Lord, have mercy," or to breathing in the name of Jesus and breathing out either what is not considered of God or of breathing out God's love.

Some people find it most helpful to use here and now as a base. There is no limit on what we may use.

Distractions may be regarded negatively as impairing the quality of attention and ruffling the water in the pool. But we may also use them positively. Time alone to become aware of what preoccupies and distracts us may provide an opportunity to acknowledge who we are, where our real interests lie, and so what may block our open attentiveness to the sharer in the helping relationship. Distractions, too, in a process allied with transcending emotions and feelings, may become a base for freeing awareness. And acknowledging what distracts us may itself be the means of releasing the energy needed to effect the response and change which is prompted by the encounter with reality on all levels of our being.

In the process that leads from solitary prayer to a life of prayer (Greek: *hesychia*—perpetual inner prayerfulness) there is a two-way movement between prayer grounded in human dependency on the use of symbolism and images (known to contemplatives as kataphatic prayer), and imageless prayer, prayer that breaks free of such dependence (apophatic prayer). Either may lead us to an experience of union or communion of will with the loving will of God, a fleeting unitive experience.

Because we are symbolizing creatures, the moment we experience God in immanence and transcendence our minds automatically work on the experience to make it understandable. So we are thrown back into labeling, deleting and altering to form concepts, and in the process reality eludes us again.

But prayer without words and images leaves us open to knowledge about our self and our relationship with others and with God in a way that the use of words and images may shelter us from. There is a sense in which even saying prayers, and reading the Bible and other devotional material, may stand in the way of our knowing self and others, which a more complete exposure to reality, to God, may provide.

"Regular apophatic prayer . . . frees us to recover the symbolic language of our tradition as symbolic" (Thayer, 1985, 103).

Praying in Words

Although silent, solitary prayer with or without symbols remains the cornerstone of the spirituality which is the foundation of an effective spiritually aware pastoral care, yet words, too, are needed in praying.

"Because we are persons that require relationship, . . . verbal prayer—conversation—is crucial" (Thayer, 1985, 106). The operative word is "conversation"; the relationship is two-way. We need to be honestly open and present, listening as well as talking.

Writing and later evaluating verbatim dialogue with God is a form of journaling which encourages conversational openness (refer Anderson, 1978). In our relationship with God, as with human relationships, words both lead us toward God and into and out of ourselves. "We discover ourselves with our own words" (Thayer, 1985, 104). This process has profound significance for a helping relationship, in which an important aim is to help the sharers discover themselves with their own words (see Introduction section 4, spiritually discerning listeners in crisis).

In praying, we may use our own words or draw on contemporary and traditional expressions of experience such as books of devotion, hymns, poetry and the Bible. These words may lead us conversationally toward God and into and out of ourselves, or they may be used as a base for contemplative openness.

Praying the Bible

Praying the Bible, along with the intellectual emphasis encapsulated in the term "Bible Study," is familiar to contemplatives and is implicit in a spiritually aware approach. John of the Cross' notion of immersion, the need for engaging one's whole self in the Christ of the gospels, has been revived in Wink's modern approach to transforming Bible study.

This form of Bible study focuses on experiential learning of the whole person, encouraging us to explore and relive an experience in relation to the written word of the Bible. Experiencing the biblical situation in this way may lead us to discover the living Word which is God's word for us now.

Prayer and Transforming Desire

John of the Cross knew that immersing our whole self in the Christ of the gospels leads to our will and desire being educated and transformed. As we saw earlier, John considers that, rather than killing or repressing our desires, we need to acknowledge, accept, and offer them to God; the first step in transforming our will. We cannot ourselves transform our will and desires into the love of God; God may transform them by leading us with a more powerful desire, the educating power of the love of Christ.

Christ may become our focus of meaning, and our desire may be transformed by our consciously referring to Christ's stronger love, a process that takes place through prayer.

Here prayer is not something only done at certain times: praying and life are one. Praying is the process of transferring and transforming our desire, of changing our own image in and toward the image of Christ (John of the Cross, *Ascent of Mount Carmel* 2.13,14). The influence of Christ is crucial.

Pain, Impasse and Dark Night

Finding our focus and center in Jesus Christ confronts us immediately with the reality of pain, suffering and crisis.

Pain, in its many manifestations, is real and we may not healthily deny it permanently. Great pain is debilitating. It may wipe out our customary ability to cope. Modern medicine has done wonders in developing painkilling drugs. There are also less common ways of coping with pain, which recognize that our pain is not necessarily to be killed or denied. Some people turn to meditation as a way to bypass pain. However, meditation is not a panacea; it makes us more sensitive and aware. "Genuine meditation involves a whole series of deaths and rebirths. . . . It hurts" (Wilbur, 1987, 43).

Indeed, pain may be treated as an opportunity for growth, and in being accepted and experienced as meaningful, our pain may diminish. Frankl's experiences in a concentration camp led him to such a conclusion (Frankl, 1946).

Pain, crisis and death are inevitable experiences of life; extreme crisis is impasse. Some people interpret impasse as death, as perhaps the death of a relationship, rather than as the way to a richer, more meaningful life.

Indeed, for some people, impasse does lead to death. Even in impasse we have a choice: either to choose to sink into utter despair and physical annihilation, as in suicide, or to choose the way of hope, believing that somewhere there must be some meaning and potential in the impasse.

All of us are familiar with crisis, which occurs when we perceive a gap between the situation and our ability to meet the situation adequately. Most crises are short-lived. After the initial shock we mostly rally the resources we need.

Impasse is different. In genuine impasse, the more we try to escape, the worse it becomes.

Although impasse, and its potential for change and growth, is known to many in a helping relationship, it is mystics and those who are familiar with the mystics' theological and prayer orientation who appreciate more fully its significance. It is one thing for us to have an intellectual or theological understanding of the meaning of pain and suffering and of the potential that death has for resurrection. But great spiritual guides such as John also bring personal experience of journeying through impasse that resembles death, and in retrospect they know its potential for new life.

It is those of us who have some experience of this journey and of the spiritual guidance traditional practice of one-to-one guidance relationships who may bring a transforming understanding to those who are immersed in impasse. Our own experience, intellectual and practical, qualifies us to stay with the sufferer in impasse, with support, understanding and hope, as the sufferer works through the inevitable pain that such an experience brings.

FitzGerald explains:

When I am able to situate a person's experience of impasse within the interpretive framework of dark night, that person is reassured and energized to live, even though she feels she is dying. The impasse is open to meaning precisely because it can be redescribed (FitzGerald, 1984, 97).

The teaching of John of the Cross on impasse and dark night is the crown of the contemplative understanding of the potential that impasse has for human development and its relevance for a spiritually aware pastoral care.

Dark night, knowing through unknowing, is the image that John uses. Impasse is the darkest part of the night because impasse usually seems like a dark night that will never end, and which has no way through it. John's teaching on dark night is an integral part of his teaching about the transformation of desire, and is given in the context of God's love. John sees impasse as crucial. He believes that breakdown and failure are a necessary and vital stage of our development.

In the process of our desire becoming transferred and transformed in union with Christ, we go through many struggles, doubts and questioning of ultimate values. So there is a dark side to our desire, an experience of joylessness and suffering. But it is within this dark night that the change is occurring; what we interpret as death is already resurrection (John of the Cross, *Dark Night* 1.1–8).

The dark of midnight is not a sign of death but of our life and growth, a sign for us to move on to the dawn of new hope, vision and experience in our everyday life and its relationships. The universal rhythm of change, decay and renewal means that breakdown and failure hold as much possibility for new growth and resurrection, as the discarding of an outgrown skin has for a snake, as the splitting open of a seed case for a seedling, and the breaking open of a pupa to release the caterpillar, newly transformed into a butterfly.

In FitzGerald's synthesis of John's signs, the first sign is a breakdown of communication with God: we lose our usual concepts, and are powerless to do anything about it.

The second sign is dryness, boredom, emptiness, deadness. FitzGerald writes:

It is in the throes of this crisis that people abandon God and prayer, a marriage, a friend, a ministry, a community, a church, and forfeit forever the new vision, the genuine hope, the maturity or love and loyalty, dedication and mutuality, that is on the other side of darkness and hopelessness. Darkness is the place where egoism dies and true unselfish love for the "other" is set free (FitzGerald, 1984, 102).

Our real fear is of disintegration, annihilation. But if we choose hope, our desire is not being destroyed, only transformed, deepened and integrated. This is especially the point at which a helper's presence may provide reassurance.

Soelle describes it:

All extreme suffering evokes the experience of being forsaken by God. In the depth of suffering people see themselves as abandoned and forsaken by everyone. That which gave life its meaning has become empty and void: it turned out to be an error, an illusion that is shattered, a guilt that cannot be rectified, a void. The paths that lead to this experience of nothingness are diverse, but the experience of annihilation that occurs in unremitting suffering is the same (Soelle, 1975, 95).

The third sign is initially our suspicion, blaming and fearing that our own failure and mistakes have caused our loss of ability to cope, have created our own dark night.

"The only way for us to break out of this desperate circle of insoluble self-questioning is to surrender in faith and trust to the unfathomable Mystery that beckons onward and inward beyond calculation, order, self-justification and fear" (FitzGerald, 1984, 103).

As we open ourselves to the mystery of God, we gradually experience a new, deeper, richer loving understanding, vision and hope.

A distinctive contribution of a spiritually aware pastoral care is to bring to the helping relationship the contemplative perspective on impasse, the triumphant understanding of the dark night. God's love, infusing the mystery of our pain, suffering and death and its potential for resurrection, is the good news of the gospel of Christ, and so must be central to a spiritually aware pastoral care.

To Sum Up

In considering the basis of a spiritually aware pastoral care, it is evident that the widespread search for meaning may be fulfilled more effectively with a contemplative psychological, rather than with a secular approach.

A spiritually aware pastoral care affirms the real contribution of psychology to human understanding, and aims to integrate psychological insights into a contemplative attitude to reality. The contemplative attitude is highly relevant today to satisfy our deeper needs and to build community, because it recognizes the intrinsically spiritual nature of reality and our search for meaning, while affirming that the test of a valid spirituality is whether it results in Christian service.

A spiritually aware pastoral care aims to take account of the whole range of relating and responding to the reality of our self, of others, and of God in self and beyond. It is based on traditional concepts of the role of will and spirit held by great spiritual guides and outlined by May in *Will and Spirit* (1982b. See also Abbott, 1963).

In opening ourselves to the divine, we are also open to the possibility of evil, which means that we need guides, as great spiritual guides have found for themselves. Spiritual guidance and solitary prayer are an essential path to the self knowledge and experience we need as helpers, to give more adequate support to a sufferer in crisis and impasse. It is those of us with personal experience of the journey who may be able to help others. Whatever joyful or sorrowful situation the sharer may present, our growing spiritual awareness may help us to provide discernment and maturing pastoral care.

But if spiritual guidance is essential, which of us is to be the guide today? And who is to guide and train us as guides? The wheel has come full circle. Often the present church pastoral training in skills and prayer is inadequate. There may be some exposure to psychological teaching but there is still a general lack of grounding in the art of contemplative prayer and spiritual guidance, and in integrating the two.

We Christians need training, encouragement and practice in developing an effective spiritually aware pastoral care.

4. SPIRITUALLY AWARE PASTORAL CARE IN CRISIS

Pastoral care embraces the whole of life from birth to death, the whole range of human response through joy and sorrow, struggle and surrender, the crises and milestones, with all the potential they hold for human development. "Pastoral care is also care taken for the nurturing, guidance and growth of persons in relationship to themselves, others, nature and God as an ongoing part of ministry unrelated to whether the person experiences himself or herself in crisis or in trouble" (Thayer, 1985, 70).

The Crisis of Hospitalization and Imprisonment

Crisis, however, is an inevitable part of being human; the very need for helping implies that people are not self-sufficient and may be in some degree of crisis.

For many of us, a clear-cut example of a crisis situation is finding ourselves in the hospital. It may be a crisis of minor or of catastrophic proportions. And this often raises for us questions of ultimate meaning, value and purpose.

The crisis of being in the hospital or prison may suspend our connection with all that has meaning most of the time, in terms of our loss of freedom and relationships, cessation of the usual activities and involvements that give us meaning and purpose; and it gives many of us some space to reflect on our lives and all the now-suspended connections.

Some of the most important lessons we may learn in the hospital, perhaps even in prison, stem from the caring of staff and other people. The very crisis of being isolated from the familiar may be the catalyst for us to discern and experience community at a deeper level, by heightening our awareness and connecting us, at least temporarily, in a new realization of community relationships.

The crisis of being in the hospital may become, especially for middle-aged business and professional men, a time of discovering new values and recovering old ones—the importance of people, community and caring. Some do not remember or may never before have experienced caring such as they receive from staff and other people in a hospital. In short, the crisis of being in the hospital becomes for them a time of unexpected discovery, a grace time for which they are deeply grateful.

The Christian helper may well be a catalyst in this time of discernment.

Crisis Intervention Theory

It is the recognition of the special features of crisis as a normal reaction that has led to the development of crisis counseling as distinct from general longer-term counseling modeled on the needs of a sick person.

Contemporary crisis intervention theory began with Erich Lindemann and Gerald Caplan:

> Lindemann observed that grief is a natural and necessary reaction following a death and that there are a series of phases in the grief process. . . . Caplan postulated that there are both adaptive and inadaptive ways of responding to the emotional hazards in one's life. How adaptively a person copes with these hazards will determine whether he or she will be likely to have emotional problems later, or will be better equipped to handle future crises (Stone, 1976, 3–4).

Caplan's theory of crisis is useful in spiritually aware pastoral counseling. Though not underestimating the pathological, Caplan begins by assuming that we are dealing with people at a normal level of their functioning, that is, with people who are capable of a healthy level of response. His method of treatment focuses on supplementing and strengthening the individual's personal resources. His view is a radical departure from a "disease model,"

> . . . which assumes that a breakdown of emotional function is a manifestation of an underlying disorder, the method of treatment based on the disease model is to "cure" psychological illness by changing the defective personality. Caplan on the contrary assumes that the person's resistance to stress is finite and that under some circumstances any individual's coping methods may become inadequate to sustain his or her psychological balance (Stone, 1976, 75).

A crisis occurs within the person when "usual problem-solving activities are blocked or ineffective" (Clinebell, 1966, 158).

The most important contribution of the crisis intervention movement is its recognition of the emotional vulnerability of a person in crisis. It is a crisis because the balance can go either way, towards a positive response or towards a negative destructive one. As Caplan puts it, "A relatively minor force, acting for a relatively short time can switch the whole balance to one side or to the other—to the side of mental health or to the side of ill-health" (Caplan, 1964, 293). (See diagram, session 3.)

A minimum effort on the part of helpers at the right moment may affect the whole course of a person's life. That opportunity may never come again. If the opportunity is missed, however, the unfinished business of an unresolved crisis does not disappear. It may continually resurface, sometimes in an altered but recognizable form, or perhaps as a physical symptom, seemingly unrelated to the disease. It may later take many sessions for us to establish the rapport that could have been established quickly at the point of crisis. These two factors, the heightened psychological accessibility and its relatively short duration, indicate the need for us to recognize the crisis and to be available.

Some crises arise through attempts to relate in inappropriate ways. If people are attempting to deal intellectually with a situation with a high emotional content such as sadness, then the crisis is compounded. The intellectualizing, separating the subject and object instead of using a more symbolic intuitive approach, may lead to denial or repression of the emotional content.

In most crises people can, with appropriate help, rally the coping resources that they need. But anyone may unexpectedly, in seconds, be in a state of deep shock, even impasse. In extreme crisis a person may feel that neither they themselves nor any of their resources or possible solutions are adequate. Even God may seem to have deserted them. Because their resources seem so inadequate, they perceive themselves as powerless; their fear compounds their fear. They withdraw, clam up, their senses grow numb so that they do not feel their pain and growing fear of annihilation (Becker, 1973, 115–23). Their numbness paralyzes them, they are petrified. This paralysis, this utter powerlessness, is impasse.

Helpers with a contemplative view of life's meaning and purpose, those with spiritual awareness, may offer the necessary support without themselves being drawn into the crisis.

When impasse overtakes those who have a contemplative psychological view and have embraced spiritual values, as Frankl found in the concentration camp, they are the ones more likely to be the survivors.

> The prisoner who had lost faith in the future—his future—was doomed. With his loss of belief in the future, he also lost his spiritual hold; he let himself decline and become subject to mental and physical decay.

> Yet, in reality, there was an opportunity and a challenge. One could make a victory of those experiences, turning life into an inner triumph, or one could ignore the challenge and simply vegetate, as did a majority of the prisoners.

> Suffering ceases to be suffering in some way at the moment it finds a meaning, such as the meaning of sacrifice (Frankl, 1964, 74,72,115).

Suffering in impasse is no exception. Impasse's dark night of unknowing and senselessness starts to lift once the dawn of meaning begins to be discerned. Frankl writes again:

> The meaning of life always changes, but . . . it never ceases to be. . . . We can discover this meaning in life in three different ways: (1) by doing a deed, (2) by experiencing a value, (3) by suffering (Frankl, 1964, 113–14).

The meaning that comes to us from action, (1), is linked with our urge to relate to others in Christian service, the sign of a mature and healthy spirituality. The value that we experience, (2), may be a work of nature or culture, or a person, that is, love.

Frankl has much to say on (3), suffering:

> The way in which a man accepts his fate and all the suffering it entails, the way he takes up his cross, gives him ample opportunity—even under the most difficult circumstances—to add a deeper meaning to his life.

There are situations in which one is cut off from the opportunity to do one's work or to enjoy one's life; but what can never be ruled out is the unavoidability of suffering. In accepting this challenge to suffer bravely, life has a meaning up to the last moment, and it retains this meaning literally to the end. In other words, life's meaning is an unconditional one for it even includes the potential meaning of suffering (Frankl, 1964, 67,116).

For those who have found meaning and spiritual values, pain and suffering, impasse or a lesser crisis situation may be a growing time, a turning point which becomes one of life's treasures.

Spiritually Discerning Listeners in Crisis

Pastoral care is deeply involved in meaning; in the need to help people find meaning, individually and corporately, in a continuous process of connection and reconnection. And, as we have seen, crisis threatens the ordered, value-laden world of the individual or the community.

Clinebell and Stone, following Boisen, a pioneer in pastoral counseling, insist on the strategic advantages of a minister in crisis work, and of the crucial need for spiritual growth in coping constructively with crises. As Stone puts it, "all crises are religious at their core; they involve ultimate issues with which one must come to terms if one's life is to be fulfilling" (Stone, 1976, 8).

Being with people in crisis is part of the daily experience of hospital and prison chaplains; much of the counseling work of a parish minister is also short-term and crisis oriented. They are strategically placed for discernment. Because their concern with the spiritual provides them with a unique contribution and responsibility, the crisis situation offers a unique opportunity. In their crisis counseling they may enable the sharer to listen to themselves and to discern with increased awareness the movement of God in and beyond themselves. And the aim is to evoke this reality from within the sharer.

All Christian counselors are called to be discerning listeners, often in a crisis situation. Three of our most important functions as Christian helpers in crisis are often seen separately as crisis counseling, listening and discerning the Spirit. In reality a Christian is called in crisis to one process of discerning the Spirit through listening.

Discerning, discernment (Greek: *diakrisis*, through crisis), is understood by the Desert Fathers and other great guides of the contemplative tradition, as a "seeing through" to what a person needs for their spiritual nurture (Edwards, 1980, 57).

The primary focus for our Christian crisis counseling, discerning the presence and guidance of God in the life of the sharer, is realized through our ability to listen, to discern and to encourage the sharer to do likewise. Since "God is redemptively at work in the whole of humanity . . . the church must listen to others before she may speak to them" (Baum, 1970, 81).

To enable the guide and the sharer to become more discerning, listening is crucial. The importance of listening is realized by most people in the helping professions. Great guides of the contemplative tradition also emphasize it. It is an art, a gift for us to develop.

But how well are we trained for this opportunity and responsibility?

Christian counseling involves some skill in problem solving, including strengthening self-image and self-esteem. However, the danger of providing skills alone in counseling training is two-fold: relegating the spiritual, God, to the fringes of one's awareness and practice; and then acting as if the ultimate source of help lies not in God but in the counselor or in the relationship of the helper and sharer.

Such writers as Clinebell, Stone, Whitlock, Morley, Jacobson, and Switzer offer valuable guidelines for the Christian helper involved in crisis intervention (Clinebell, 1966; Stone, 1976; Whitlock, Morley, Jacobson, Switzer, all 1970). Yet the authors of this book have found inadequate specific help in any of their writings as to how Christian helpers may maintain a spiritual focus. This training program addresses this basic need.

Unexpected Benefit of Spiritually Aware Pastoral Care

A spiritually aware pastoral care diminishes the danger of providing skills while forgetting God as our fundamental source of help.

Cogent reasons for us to be spiritually aware are offered by a group of hospital chaplains and pastoral counselors who were spiritual directors for one another in a seminar. May instructed them to seek God's guidance in this relationship.

When they attended to the Holy Spirit, were aware of seeking grace, and recalled as often as possible that true healing comes from God's work through the relationship, they were surprised at the lack of the weight of responsibility which they generally felt in their work. Usually, although they recognized God as the ultimate guide, they acted as though they themselves were the source of guidance.

Despite Carl Roger's emphasis on leaving the client's share of responsibility with the client, in practice many in the helping professions, whether or not they have a religious orientation, do feel weighed down.

The effect is not only on the counselors. When we as counselors become weighed down we may unconsciously reinforce the sharer's negative behavior and attitudes. So we may continue to alienate the sharer from others, and in a broader sense from society, from God and from their own true self.

A proven way of becoming more aware of God is through intentional spiritual discipline: personal attention to our own prayer life, continually remembering God's presence, and being in spiritual direction ourselves.

Need for a Training Program

When we remember God as our ultimate source of guidance, trust in God, and become aware of God's activity in the situation, we as helpers may be saved from going into crisis with those already in crisis, and so may be more effective. The inevitable wonderful result of our trusting to the movement and guidance of God in the sharer's situation is an increasing experience of the love of God also in our own life.

As we have seen, guidelines are widely needed on how to maintain our spiritual awareness.

Leech rightly comments on training courses:

I am sure that the great spiritual guides of the past would have been horrified at the modern idea of training spiritual directors through courses, institutes of spiritual leadership, cassettes, and the like. They would have seen the spiritual director as one who emerges as an almost accidental side effect of the life of prayer and recollection (Leech, 1986, 25).

But Leech also believes that modern spiritual directors must be competent in relating theology to the needs of the individual, and that they need head knowledge as well as prayer.

It is the lack of effective available training on how to maintain a spiritual focus in Christian ministry that has led to this training program in spiritually aware discerning, listening, communicating, and counseling in crisis.

5. TRAINING RESOURCES

Resources for a spiritually aware pastoral care training program require a balance of didactic and experientially-based material. The bibliography indicates some of the extensive written material investigated and used in researching and developing this program.

Experiential Contemplative Resources

Because an evocative approach to learning—that is, learning from experience—is fundamental to this program, it is essential for leaders to be equipped through personal experience to lead such a course and to avoid obvious pitfalls.

We have already considered how the experience of sharing, in the oral tradition of the great guides, has long been considered central for those involved in spiritual guidance. This means that those of us involved in spiritual guidance, especially in long-term one-to-one and group guidance or training programs, also need a spiritual guide, variously called a soul friend, spiritual friend, spiritual companion (Leech, 1980; Edwards, 1980; Holmes, 1982).

At the present time there seem to be few persons with much experience as spiritual guides. So peer-group evaluation of our work by others who are also learning is an important complement to the guidance we may receive in a one-to-one relationship. The latter focuses specifically on our own spiritual formation; the peer group focuses on our growth as it relates to our work as spiritual friend or leader to others.

Programs such as those run by the Shalem Institute for Spiritual Formation in Washington, D.C., and General Theological Seminary in New York, and more widely by the Catholic Church, provide useful background training and opportunities for spiritual development.

Experiential Psychological Resources: Discerning Through Listening and Change Skills

Just as in formal praying our discerning develops from our contemplative listening, rooted in silence and attention (Leech, 1986, 24), so in effective caring our attention is equally significant in encouraging discerning listening. The question is, how may we learn to attend more effectively?

Psychological listening skills can be valuable tools for the listening that leads through and beyond the sharer's thinking and feeling to hearing the spiritual significance of the sharer's experience. Books abound on the art of helping, listening, and interpersonal relating, and many emphasize the need to reflect the feeling content of the sharer's words. But many miss a vital factor.

Commonly we are advised to use our own words, but the effect may be to shift the sharer's attention from their own world to ours. The profoundly significant factor is staying with the sharer to the point of discreetly reflecting the sharer's own key words and images, which are a royal road to psychological and spiritual self-discovery. By staying with the sharer's actual feeling words and images, we may encourage the sharer to move through and beyond the words to their spiritual meaning, purpose and significance. Because none of us can hold anyone else responsible for our own words, they have more power than other people's words to confront us with reality.

Attending to the sharer's words in this way reduces the danger, inherent in other approaches, of not only missing the significance of what the sharer is sharing, but even of our becoming a stumbling block, deflecting the sharer from discovering its significance for themselves. In a time of acute crisis, with its unique but brief opportunity for self-discovery and discovery of God and others, such deflection may even contribute to a tragic outcome, which in suicide is irretrievable.

"We discover ourselves with our own words" (Thayer, 1985, 104); and others discover themselves with their own words. Through awareness and effective listening-skills practice the listener may greatly enhance this ability to be there for the sharer and for God.

The subtle structure of basic communication which Bandler and Grinder made explicit in their Neuro Linguistic Programming is invaluable in improving the quality of our attending in pastoral care (Bandler and Grinder, 1979; Cameron-Bandler, 1985).

People discover themselves, not only with their words, but through a multitude of nonverbal means. If we match the sharer nonverbally and verbally, we are using a potent means of establishing rapport and of staying with the sharer in their journey of self-discovery. Matching heightens our awareness of how both we and the sharer may unwittingly be linking people into negative patterns and so be alienating ourselves from others and our own deeper selves.

Some useful models for helping the sharer to achieve the effective and lasting changes that they want to make are offered by Neuro Linguistic Programming and Psychosynthesis (Bandler and Grinder, 1979; Cameron-Bandler, 1985; Lankton, 1980; Assagioli, 1973, 1975; Ferrucci, 1982). Because these techniques quickly enable the sharer to attend to the heart of the matter, they are particularly relevant for us in crisis counseling, through optimizing the possibilities in the short time that the sharer may be open to change.

When the sharer attends to what they want (even if they are initially confused about what they do want), instead of to the problem (which is what they don't want), there is greater possibility of discovering and so achieving what they really desire, which may be what God wants for them. The possibility of projection and delusion likely in a more negative, problem-solving approach, is reduced. Here again, when the sharer is confronted by their own significant feeling words, images, movements and desires, they are more likely to accept them.

One of the roles of a pastor is as prophet, and being a prophet involves confrontation. In spiritually aware pastoral care, by gently enabling the sharer's confrontation with their own reality, the Christian helper is exercising a gently prophetic role for the individual. The resulting discernment, based on what the sharer desires deep down, may allow the sharer to discover how God is present and moving them to self-realization in community.

Change, Transformation, Growth

In spiritually aware pastoral care, contemplative and psychological resources are not ends in themselves; they may all be used to lead us to greater openness and response to the reality which is God, with the resulting discovery of ourselves in community.

Change is inevitable; we may perceive change, transformation, growth, as desirable or as a threat. Change is a risk and requires us to trust. Techniques for enabling positive change and widening choice are useful tools in making more real the Christian good news of wholeness, salvation, freedom to trust and choose life.

Our task as Christian helpers is to discern God in the situation, God who is already active in it, and in turn to help the sharer to become more aware and open to God in and through their own experience. Often there may be no mention of God; such talk may be counterproductive and inappropriate. But if the context is the sharer's healthy experience of traditional religious language, naming God may encourage trust and Christian growth. Helping the sharer to recognize and name what is happening in their experience as God or the Holy Spirit or grace may be a powerful way of linking it with their own and the church's past and contemporary experience.

What is essential is for us to stay with the sharer's own sense of growth and discovery; allowing any labeling to be not something we lay on the sharer, but a spontaneous extension of the experience itself.

This attitude of discerning openness, of respect for the sharer's unique experience and growth pattern, permeates the way contemplative and psychological resources have been integrated into this training program.

6. IN SUMMARY

Pastoral care which recovers the centrality of the spiritual dimension is sorely needed to address the widespread longing and searching in our society to experience meaning and fulfillment in depth.

Spiritually aware pastoral care is in line with people's search for a truth and an approach to learning that resonates on all levels of their experience. Some of its contemplative insights lie in developing our use of will in relation to mystery, and our awareness in opening ourselves to God as ultimate reality. Encountering a loving God may fill our deep longing for connectedness and meaning and so release energy to be used in responsible action.

Effective discerning and responding to loving reality requires us to be alert and listening, practicing the ancient way of prayer in solitude, praying in our hearts as well as with our minds. This links our own experience with the accumulated experience of the past and the present, and leads us to be concerned for persons and structures.

Spiritually aware pastoral care incorporates crisis counseling skills. Crisis commonly raises questions of ultimate concern and so provides opportunities for spiritual response and growth.

This program links modern understandings of crisis with the wisdom of great spiritual guides such as Teresa and John of the Cross, especially with their understanding and experience of the potential of impasse for spiritual growth and maturity.

Our present ignorance or neglect of this contemplative tradition in Western Christianity, combined with the limitations of a modern psychological approach such as is found in much church-based counseling and counselor training, indicates the need for Christian helpers to have access to experientially-based training in discernment, listening, communication and crisis counseling. Long-term one-to-one spiritual guidance may make an important contribution in training helpers in ways to enable sharers, especially those in crisis, to listen and to discern God moving in and beyond their lives.

This training program aims to enable Christian helpers to recognize their opportunities, and to respond to the imperative to maintain the spiritual focus in their counseling of people in crisis.

It draws especially on the contemplative tradition and practice of the church and on the positive contribution of the crisis intervention move-ment, and of the work of Bandler, Grinder, Cameron-Bandler and Assagioli for the understanding of crisis, listening, communication, and change. The specific techniques practiced have been selected as appropriate for us in the short-term counseling of crisis situations. The program is geared toward optimum effectiveness in a short time; learning how to enable the sharer to get quickly to the heart of whatever matter may be deeply appropriate for them, and offering them ways to help achieve the changes they desire on many different levels.

Its originality lies in integrating into one training program a triple realization:

1. The contemplative tradition's practical contribution to the counseling situation of an attitude of perpetual inner prayerfulness, which lightens the load on us as counselors in our responsibility to be there for the sharer and for God whom we realize is already active in the situation. The quality of the awareness we develop during our times of praying in solitude may well correlate with the quality of our awareness and our degree of freedom in the helping relationship.
2. The power of incorporating into crisis counseling's understanding of the unique opportunity and responsibility of crisis the contemplative realization of the potential of impasse for growing in Christian consciousness and response.
3. The profound spiritual significance of gently reflecting the sharer's actual feeling words, images and nonverbal communication, in attending to, and enabling the sharer to attend to, their own concepts, choices and inner world.

Spiritually Aware Pastoral Care may be seen as complementary to programs such as Clinical Pastoral Education. Session notes give some idea of the outer packaging and contents, but because the learning is experientially based, it is the interaction, contribution and developing discernment of all the participants in the program that constitute for them its treasure.

The beauty of spiritually aware pastoral care, integrating insights from both contemplative and psychological resources, is that we as helpers do not have to tell what seems to us to be the appropriate truth, do not have to play at being God. Instead, by attentive awareness to God and the sharer, we may enable the sharer to experience the grace and wonder of making her or his own discovery, and so to grow toward and in God.

The challenge and journey facing the Christian helper and the sharer is summed up by Christopher Fry at the end of his play, *A Sleep of Prisoners:*

The human heart can go to the lengths of God . . .
Thank God our time is now when wrong
Comes up to face us everywhere
Never to leave us till we take
The longest stride of soul men ever took.
Affairs are now soul size,
The enterprise
Is exploration into God.

(Fry, 1951, 48–49)

NOTES

Note 1. For greater clarity and in keeping with the shared nature of the learning program, Christian helpers and group members are usually referred to as "we," "us," "the helper"; the person being listened to and helped is "the sharer."

The nonsexist conversational "they," "themselves," is used throughout to denote the singular, to avoid the undue emphasis caused by such combinations as she/he, him/herself.

Note 2. Cassette players are used in groups and with individuals to analyze details of the listening skills practiced.

Note 3. Bible references, unless otherwise stated, are from the *Good News Bible: Today's English Version* (1976).

Note 4. This book has grown out of Earle's thirty years' ordained ministry in country and urban parishes, in industry, and in hospitals, at home and overseas.

It is based on work presented for his Doctorate of Ministry from San Francisco Theological Seminary. The introduction is a shortened version of the dissertation, *Spiritual Counseling,* and the training program has been developed from the project component, *Contemplation in Crisis.*

Sharing of any similar training experience and suggestions for improvement are welcome.

Our hope is that through this training program many will be helped in their journey toward meaning and awareness of ultimate reality.

PART ONE

*Discerning God's Spirit
In Contemplation and Crisis
In Nonverbal Awareness Skills*

SESSION 1

Introducing People and Material: Opening Ourselves to God's Spirit

Note: The basic material for discussion needs to be circulated to intending participants well beforehand.

Group members need to bring an exercise book or looseleaf folder for personal journaling and evaluation.

A. BECOMING AWARE OF WHERE WE ARE

WELCOME
Welcome and apologies.

RECOLLECTING
Let us be still in the presence of God.
Hymn: e.g., "Immortal, invisible."
Let's take a couple of minutes to reflect quietly on the hymn. The leader will conclude the silence, and anyone else is welcome to pray briefly.

TODAY'S THEME
The purpose of today's session is to introduce us to each other and to the aims, assumptions and plan of the program which we are embarking on together. The whole course is based on opening ourselves to the Holy Spirit, discerning God's Spirit, and we shall think briefly about what this discerning may mean for us as helpers.

B. BECOMING AWARE OF EACH OTHER

PRACTICE
Move around the room introducing ourselves to each person present and finding out at least one thing about them.

SHARING
In the whole group we introduce ourselves, saying a little about what we bring to the group —our background, training and experience, what interests us about the program, and what we hope to get from it.
Share how we feel about what we have learned from each other.
It is important to remember that whatever is shared in the group is CONFIDENTIAL, and needs a person's express permission to be repeated or referred to.

C. BECOMING AWARE OF THE PROGRAM

INTRODUCTION
The leader may need to give any housekeeping details such as the layout of the building, refreshments, etc.

SHARING
Together go through the basic material, stopping after each section to offer constructive input and criticism either in the whole group, or first in couples and then in the whole group as seems appropriate.

Basic Material

Questions in Preparation for the Program

We may find it helpful to bring to the first session written answers to questions such as the ones below. These are to stimulate our own prayerful thinking and reflection and do not have to be shared.

1. What constitutes a crisis?
2. How is crisis counseling different from other types of counseling?
3. At the end of a demanding counseling session how do I feel?
4. What do I understand by the term "spiritual guidance"? How is it offered?
5. What sense do I have of God's presence and guidance in my counseling work?
6. How does this affect my work as helper?
7. What gifts and experience do I expect to contribute to the course and what do I hope to get out of it?

Aims and Assumptions

Aims

The aim of this program is to develop a set of guidelines for Christian helpers in listening, discerning God's Spirit, and counseling, through developing a spiritually aware approach to life and to helping people.

We shall draw on and share a variety of spiritual and psychological resources that will encourage us to increase our awareness and to improve our skills.

What is Involved

The program will involve:

1. Reviewing our own prayer life and developing our ability to discern God's action and guidance in our own lives.
2. Developing our ability to minister, drawing on appropriate religious, cultural and psychological insights.
3. Considering the meaning of crisis and how it constitutes a unique opportunity and responsibility for ministry.
4. Linking our learning and experience in these three areas and putting them into practice.

Basic Assumptions

Some basic assumptions are:

1. God is present and active as a loving, personal, integrative force, at work in the world, in the universe and in the lives of all of us, whether we recognize God or not.
2. As Christians, we are called to enable people to make effective links between contemporary and historical religious experience and their own unique situation.
3. We are called to enable people to make discoveries and choices for themselves, with appropriate input from us, and so come to a deeper acceptance of themselves and a deeper commitment to and confidence in God within and beyond themselves.

The journey inward and outward toward God and others may be scary, but it can be one of life's most exciting enterprises. In covenanting to share our experience, ideas and learnings and to pray and work individually and as a group, we shall inevitably experience rewarding learnings and relationships for ourselves and a deeper awareness of God with us.

Session Material

The program is divided into four parts:

1. Discerning God's Spirit in contemplation and crisis in nonverbal awareness skills.
2. Discerning God's Spirit in formal and informal meditation and in verbal listening skills.
3. Discerning God's Spirit in pain, healing, words and concepts; in our own past and present; in verbal skills for accepting, forgiving and changing.
4. Evaluation and celebration.

Contents of Training Sessions

PART 1
DISCERNING GOD'S SPIRIT:
   IN CONTEMPLATION AND CRISIS
   IN NONVERBAL AWARENESS SKILLS

1. Introducing people and material
   Opening ourselves to the Holy Spirit
2. Learning awareness from our hands
   Crisis: an internal reaction
3. Who am I? Being truly ourselves
   Contemplating: opening ourselves to God in everything

4. Where am I in formal praying and in crisis helping?
   Time, space, silence, touching

5. Posture: opening our inner space
   Associating
   Noticing vs interpreting

6. Relaxing and distractions
   Sensory-based information: eye and body messages

7. Breathing praying
   Distractions while helping
   Nonverbal matching: mirroring

PART 2
DISCERNING GOD'S SPIRIT:
   IN FORMAL AND INFORMAL
      MEDITATION
   IN VERBAL LISTENING SKILLS

8. Resumé of part one
   Formal, informal and mini-meditations
   Verbal matching (1): reflecting the actual word

9. Centering
   Centering with a visual base
   Verbal matching (2): using the same thinking mode

10. Centering with sound as a base
    Questions

11. Centering with breathing as a base
    Recording and evaluating a practice listening session
    Group centering with ceremony as a base

12. Centering with the body as a base
    The hearing heart
    Revision and progress evaluation
    Verbal listening skills practice

13. Centering with touch
    Verbal listening skills practice

14. Centering with words: planting the seed
    Verbal listening skills practice
    Choice

15. Centering in the here and now
    Processing our sense experiences, i.e., forming and changing our concepts
    Congruity and incongruity

PART 3
DISCERNING GOD'S SPIRIT:
   IN PAIN, HEALING, WORDS AND
      CONCEPTS

IN OUR OWN PAST AND PRESENT
IN VERBAL SKILLS FOR ACCEPTING,
   FORGIVING AND CHANGING

16. Centering with pain as a base
    Crisis, pain and impasse
    Identifying and owning our feelings

17. Accepting pain
    Opening ourselves to love
    Basic emotions and resources

18. Discerning God's presence in crisis through reliving a peak faith experience
    Some ways of changing
    Reassessing and changing our reactions to our past and our future

19. Discerning God's presence: the journey inward and outward: Surrender
    Overlapping to increase our discerning
    Separating negative feelings from a memory

20. Practicing discerning
    The role of spiritual guide-friend
    An A.B.C. crisis method
    Discerning God's love for us

21. What is healing?
    A way of healing early relationships and memories with Jesus

22. Healing through awareness of our unconscious messages and touch
    Releasing and transforming fear, grief, anger and guilt

23. Contributing words and ideas
    Praying in our own words and in tongues
    Forgiving others

24. Praying aloud
    Our self-concept and sin
    Forgiving ourselves

25. Praying and singing from the written word
    Beyond the written word
    Changing by separating the purpose from our behavior

26. Praying for ourselves and others
    Practice in separating the purpose from our behavior

27. Praying with one other or a group
    What do others understand by our words?
    Developing new behavior

28. Reading the Bible
    Metaphors

29. Understanding the Bible: a living two-way
    relationship
    A relating pattern
    Strengthening a fulfilling relationship
30. Praying the Bible
    Reevaluating relationships

PART 4
  EVALUATION AND CELEBRATION

31. Contemplation in crisis: maintaining our
    awareness of God
    A summary of the program
    Evaluation and personal progress
32. Evaluation and personal progress
33. Celebration and Godspeed

Basic Session Plan (brief)

GREETING
A. BECOMING AWARE OF WHERE WE ARE
RECOLLECTING: Silence, formal praying,
                 and/or hymn.
RECAP: Reminder of previous ses-
                 sion.
SHARING: Reflections, reactions &
                 progress.
TODAY'S THEME:
       B. BECOMING AWARE IN
          FORMAL PRAYING
INTRODUCTION:
PRACTICE:
SHARING: In group and with part-
                 ners.
EXTENSION: Additional material and
                 applications.
       C. BECOMING AWARE IN
          COUNSELING SKILLS
INTRODUCTION:
PRACTICE:
SHARING:
EXTENSION:
          D. CONCLUDING
RECOLLECTING: Quiet reflection and jour-
                 naling.
EVALUATION: Brief evaluation and com-
                 ment on session.

HOME PRACTICE: Reminder from this ses-
                 sion.
LOOKING AHEAD: Theme of next session.
AFFIRMATION: Silent or vocal formal pray-
                 ing in group.

Basic Session Plan (with comments)

GREETING
  It is important for us to have time before the
session starts to greet each other, exchange imme-
diate concerns, and/or look at the book table.
A. BECOMING AWARE OF WHERE WE ARE
RECOLLECTING
  Being still in the presence of God.
  Praying silently or aloud.
  Hymn as desired.

RECAP
  A brief summary of the previous session.

SHARING
  Sharing our reflections on, reactions to, and
progress since the last session.

TODAY'S THEME
  A brief outline of the present session.
       B. BECOMING AWARE IN
           FORMAL PRAYING
INTRODUCTION
  The leader introduces and explains the prayer
theme.

PRACTICE
  The whole group participates in the chosen
form of praying.

SHARING
  Sharing of our prayer experience may take
place in the whole group or in smaller groups of
two, three or four people.
  Couple sharing of our journal entries, and in
turn sharing our celebrations and concerns and
praying and being prayed for, may become a pattern with one chosen prayer partner or with
various group members as seems appropriate.
  Brief sharing in the whole group usually follows couple or small-group sharing.

EXTENSION

The leader may sum up and add any relevant comment or material which has not been raised in the group discussions.

C. BECOMING AWARE IN COUNSELING SKILLS

INTRODUCTION

The leader introduces the skills topic.

PRACTICE

All practice the chosen skill, usually in couples or small groups. Choosing different partners and small-group members is a useful way of getting to know each other.

SHARING

Sharing our reactions to the group experience may take place first in the small group, followed by appropriate sharing in the whole group.

One of the aims of this sharing is to gain some understanding of how the skill may be useful in our own relationships.

There may be several group experiences and sharing in the same session.

EXTENSION

The leader may sum up and add relevant material that has not emerged in the discussion.

D. CONCLUDING

RECOLLECTING

A time for quiet reflection and journaling on the session.

EVALUATION

Brief evaluation and comment on the session.

HOME PRACTICE

A reminder of what prayer and counseling skills to practice.

LOOKING AHEAD

The themes of the next session.

AFFIRMATION

We affirm each other by joining together, often holding hands, in silent and/or vocal formal praying.

It may be appropriate to sing a hymn and to join in the grace.

Note: There will be occasional intentional interruptions for us all to check whether the skills are being used and also to create possible crises to learn and assess how we react in crisis.

The leaders may plan to be available for about half an hour after each session.

Suggested Covenant

This covenant is a suggestion and discussion point to help each of us to examine our own commitment.

"I commit myself to full involvement in this Spiritually Aware Pastoral Care program."

This means that I will do my best to:

1. Attend every meeting.
2. Share as honestly and compassionately as I can.
3. Keep what is shared confidential.
4. Pray every day for my course companions.
5. Prepare for each meeting by praying and keeping a journal.
6. Accept responsibility for contributing to the direction, input, loving atmosphere and outcome of the course, including sharing reflections on any appropriate reading and handouts.
7. Relate new learnings to my ministry and share my current progress and insights both verbally and in written or recorded form.
8. Give ongoing and final written evaluations.

D. BECOMING AWARE OF THE HOLY SPIRIT

INTRODUCTION

In Part One of our program we prepare ourselves to discern God's Spirit in contemplation and crisis in nonverbal awareness skills.

Opening Ourselves to the Holy Spirit

Our course aims to encourage simple openness to the Holy Spirit.

Everything we do together as a group may be used as practice in discerning the presence and movement of the Spirit by asking: "How is the

Spirit present and working in and with us here now?"

There is a difference between aiming to help with . . .

1. Secular psychological skills, and
2. Spiritual as well as psychological insights in which the Holy Spirit is recognized as the prime source of help.

In the second approach there is a lightness in the interaction and the outcome, which may be lacking in a secular approach where the consciousness of God may be present but is not central.

As helpers we need to enable the person to move simply to some effective resolution of the crisis. We need to learn how to keep it simple so that we lower the tension, strain and weight on ourselves as well as on the other person.

The key to such a helping relationship is in learning simple surrender and openness to the Holy Spirit as helper, i.e., "Let go and let God" (cf. May's notion of willingness and willfulness, 1982b). It is not a question of doing nothing, not passively acquiescing, nor of acting as if the Holy Spirit were not there already. It is a question of achieving a balance, of actively cooperating with the Holy Spirit, in harmony with the reflection and action, engagement and withdrawal, the ebb and flow of the universe. God, healing love, forgiveness, acceptance, is active in the situation. We, too, are to be actively involved, cooperating and in harmony with God's action.

Christian ministry is different from "going with the flow," going wherever the current carries us. It is different from our determinedly rowing a boat against the current as though everything depended on our effort alone.

It is more like sailing a yacht. We need to put ourselves into a position to cooperate with the wind, the source of power. We need to maintain a delicate balance between all the elements of the situation—the tide, the wind, the direction of the boat, and the sail—a skillful activity requiring relaxed yet alert attention. Then even when the wind seems to be in opposition, it can move the boat forward.

This course aims to help us to come to terms with the difference between this willing surrender and cooperation with the Holy Spirit and the usual way of many of us, i.e., going into action as though everything depends on our own skills, ability and sensitivity. These qualities are important, but if we concentrate on them we tend to raise our own level of tension, frustration and heaviness, and so deaden the whole process. To change the metaphor, we need to be out of the driver's seat, out of the constraint of trying to move the sharer in a certain direction.

The aim of this program is to encourage us consciously to use our skills in a wider frame of reference.

PRACTICE AND SHARING

With the whole group, take about five minutes to become aware of the Holy Spirit. Recollect one experience which we are prepared to share, in which we have had an awareness of God's presence, greatness, strength and/or guidance.

If time, in threes, share our experience.

Share in the whole group as appropriate.

E. CONCLUDING

RECOLLECTING

A time to reflect quietly on the session, remembering the presence of God in all we do and are.

EVALUATION

Any further comment and evaluation of the session.

HOME PRACTICE

Prayerfully go through the material from this session.

LOOKING AHEAD

Practical details: suitability of dates, time, length of meetings, venue; commitment to participate; payment to cover expenses; any other business.

Next session we shall have a meditation on learning awareness from our hands, and then consider what we mean by crisis as an internal reaction.

AFFIRMATION

Closing praying.

Holding hands to say or sing the grace.

Learning Awareness from Our Hands
Crisis: An Internal Reaction

A. BECOMING AWARE OF WHERE WE ARE

WELCOME
Welcome and apologies.

RECOLLECTING
Let us be still in the presence of God.
Hymn: e.g., "Praise to the living God."
Praying silently or aloud.

RECAP
Last session we met each other and the program. We considered what it may mean for us as helpers to be more open to the Holy Spirit.

SHARING
In twos, briefly share any comments on the last session, and how we have got on since then. Use our journals to jot down anything we need to.
In the whole group, share anything arising, as appropriate.

TODAY'S THEME
Today we shall practice learning awareness from a part of us that we often take for granted—our hands. We shall think about living simply, and what we mean by crisis.

B. BECOMING AWARE IN FORMAL PRAYING

INTRODUCTION
After hearing how Saint Paul describes the Christian community as the body of Christ, we shall have a meditation on part of our own body, our hands, and how they can help us to become more aware of the Holy Spirit.

PRACTICE
Choose one person to read aloud 1 Corinthians 12:12–27: You are the body of Christ and individually members of it.
Make sure we are all comfortable and relaxed. A useful position is to be sitting upright with both feet on the floor. A few deep breaths, and tightening and then letting go of our muscles, help us to relax and free our minds.
The leader then slowly reads the meditation, as a background for our own meditating.

Meditation on Hands

Look at your hands.
What is your immediate reaction?
Looking at front and back;
Putting them in different positions;
Holding them up, down;
Closed and open;
Together, apart;
Cupped, taut.
Taking your time to be aware of your hands.
Perhaps feeling the tingling in your palms;
If you are wearing any rings, looking at them;
Thinking of so much your hands do, and have done for you.
What faithful servants they are.
How little we stop to think about them,
Perhaps only when they are hurt or stop working for us.

Let's take a moment to get ourselves comfy

again. Breathing deeply. You may like to close your eyes.

Your right hand can be thought of as your giving hand;

Your left hand as your receiving hand.

There is a German story of the hands of God.

Let the words flow over you. The logic doesn't matter. Let the meaning speak to you as it will.

God decided to materialize God's right hand in the world in human form.

That hand held all truth.

But God was not fully satisfied with what God learned from the right hand,

So God continues to materialize God's left hand in the world as humans. The left hand is empty, it has space for search and growth.

We as humans have to begin as the left hand.

We search for the full truth of the right hand of God which is already present.

But we can only receive the fullness of the right hand in the space of the left hand.

So to receive God's fullness we must become more and more empty.

A full left hand has no room to receive anything. It is cluttered and satiated and too complex.

As the left hand empties, it becomes simpler and clearer.

As the left hand slowly unites with the right hand we come closer and closer to Jesus' prescription for life. "Be perfect (seek your fulfillment) as your Heavenly Father is perfect" (Mtt 5:48).

Our fulfillment, perfection, lies in uniting openness and fullness.

Lord, as we bring our emptiness to you, we hold open our hands. Fill us with yourself.

Quiet meditating.

Then, remaining quiet, standing up if necessary, holding out our hands to the people next to us, giving with our right hand and receiving in our left, and continuing to be quiet.

Let's use our hands to remind us to live simply through the day, becoming aware of God's giving to us.

Now may be the appropriate moment to jot in our journals anything arising from the meditation.

Note: This story of the hands of God is adapted from Tilden Edwards' book *Living Simply Through the Day*. "This is a composite of two German stories from Rilke and Lessing by the theologian John S. Dunne in *The Way of All the Earth* (Macmillan, 1972), pp. 93–95" (Edwards 1977, 7).

SHARING

When it seems appropriate, perhaps after a slight break, we may want to share something of what has arisen for us, first with one or two others in a small group, and then in the whole group.

EXTENSION

When we think of our hands, we so often think of them as "doing" hands. And in crisis we often think we must be "doing." But a subtitle of this course might be "Contemplation in Crisis"; we are aiming to maintain in crisis the attitude of awareness that we develop in our formal praying.

As we see our hands through the day and in times of crisis, let us remember that they are receiving hands as well as doing and giving hands.

C. BECOMING AWARE IN COUNSELING SKILLS

INTRODUCTION

Our theme is spiritually aware pastoral care. Much of the time when we are called on to help someone else it is because they are in some degree of crisis. So in this part of the session we shall explore a little of what we mean by crisis.

PRACTICE

Sit quietly, breathing deeply and relaxing.

Then remembering a situation which really "threw you," i.e., a crisis situation, getting inside the situation, and experiencing it again. Smelling and tasting and feeling and hearing and seeing the situation from inside yourself. Taking time to experience it again fully.

Then asking yourself:

1. What was it about it that "threw you"?
2. What helped you to cope?

Jot down anything you need to.

SHARING

Divide into groups of three or four. Each in turn briefly share as much as is appropriate.

In the whole group share briefly.

The leader may have the following questions on crisis written up. Discuss them in the whole group, using the notes as appropriate:

1. What is crisis?
2. What makes crisis a unique opportunity and responsibility?
3. What is the Christian helper's role in crisis?

EXTENSION 1

The following notes on crisis as an internal reaction outline some assumptions underlying this course.

Crisis: An Internal Reaction

What is Crisis?

A crisis is an internal reaction to an external hazard, not to be confused with the precipitating event (Fig. 1).

1 →	2 →	3 →	4
Precipitating Event	Assessment	Resources and Coping Methods	Crisis
or external situation (e.g., death loss)	what one makes of this situation	if assessed as inadequate this leads to . . .	one's internal reaction to external hazard

Fig. 1. Four stages of crisis (based on Stone, 1976, 12)

Crisis may arise at any time in life from any feature in life. An event precipitates the crisis because the person perceives it as a hazard. Another person may perceive the event differently. The crisis arises in the person from their sense of inability to cope because their usual coping methods seem to fail them, and may indeed be inadequate (session 16). Crises may range from minor and fleeting to severe.

What Makes Crisis a Unique Opportunity and Responsibility?

In crisis all of us must find some way of coping. The question is how we face the challenge: in a way conducive to sickness or to health (i.e., do we adapt?)

A crisis represents both a danger and an opportunity. It is a danger because adequate ways of coping are not readily available, but it is also an opportunity to find new adaptive ways and so permanently enrich our coping ability (Jacobson, 1970, 25). Lindeman and Caplan saw crisis, not as evidence of disease or emotional disorder (even though it may be), but as a normal behavioral response to a threatening situation (Caplan, 1964).

Persons in crisis are in a state of heightened psychological and spiritual sensitivity, i.e., they are less defensive, more vulnerable and more open to change and intervention. So a crisis may well be a turning point in life, emotionally, mentally and spiritually.

Many people in crisis ask ultimate questions of meaning, purpose and value; e.g., "What is the meaning of life? Is it worth this pain to continue living? Why did this happen to me? Why did God allow it?" This period of heightened accessibility generally peaks quickly and lasts briefly (the acute phase perhaps for four to six weeks), though the aftereffects, as in grief, may last for years.

The brief period when the person is in crisis, when in Figure 2 the triangle is tipped up, is so significant because:

1. Their emotions are strong.
2. Their usual way of thinking about themselves, their world and their interpersonal relationships is challenged and seems inadequate.
3. They are more vulnerable.

A person in crisis usually most wants to reestablish balance. This is what makes them receptive to an inside or outside influence to help to resolve the crisis; so change may be achieved with a minimum of help from the helper. Frequently we do not help soon enough.

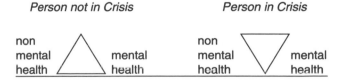

Fig. 2. Balance (based on Morley, 1970, 16)

What Is the Christian Helper's Role in Crisis?

Our aim is to be more effective and faithful ministers of the gospel by helping others to cope creatively with the crises of life; to help people in crisis at least to regain their prior level of functioning and hopefully to grow in the process.

Rather than uncovering by breaking down defense mechanisms or delving into the past, we seek to support: to build and develop existing strengths. However, the crisis may well expose inadequacies in supposed strengths, and so lead a person to examine them.

What we as Christians see as strengths may be different from those a non-Christian sees. Because our crisis counseling is done within a spiritual perspective, i.e., it is concerned with ultimate questions of meaning, purpose and value, we may often perceive in the sharer's words a different struggle and end point. This does not give us permission to impose our values. We need to help the sharer to focus on what their immediate struggle means to them.

EXTENSION 2

How are we to help the sharer to explore for themselves what their crisis means for them?

Our natural reaction may well be to tell them what we think they should do. So in order to curb this natural reaction, and to help the sharer to make their own discoveries, we need to practice more effective skills.

These skills, which we shall practice in our course, have been summarized as an A.B.C.

A.B.C.: A Three-stage Method of Dealing With Crisis (based on Stone, 1976, 32–43)

A. Attuning Self and Achieving Rapport
B. Basic Listening to Extract the Essentials
C. Creative Changing to Cope with Crisis

A.1. *Attuning Oneself to God and Self (Aligning, Being Aware)*

Especially in crisis there is a danger that we may become too heavily identified with the person in crisis and so go into crisis ourselves. If we get hooked into the other person's crisis we become tense and our attention is too narrowed to discern what is happening.

What are our own spiritual and psychological resources? If we have already reflected on our own handling of crisis and are cultivating a simple, open, contemplative approach to the whole of life, we can pause to become more aware, to attune ourselves to God and to center ourselves. As Christians, we know we are already in the presence of the Spirit of God who is our helper. So we are aiming to become more open to God's Spirit, the ultimate source of help in all crisis situations.

A.2. *Achieving Rapport with the Person in Crisis*

Genuine care and concern for the other person is a prerequisite. Just being there is important and may be all that is needed. We need to achieve rapport, and we shall learn skills to help us to establish and maintain rapport.

B. *Basic Listening to Extract the Essentials*

We need to listen to the Holy Spirit and to the person in crisis. By effective listening to what constitutes the crisis, we may enable the person to work through the situation and encourage responsibility, growth and effective action. We shall study and practice basic listening skills.

C. *Creative Changing to Cope with Crisis*

In a physical crisis we may need to take responsibility for direct action; e.g., calling the fire department. In a personal crisis we aim to encourage the person in crisis to take responsibility for growth and effective action; i.e., to change. We do this by helping them to marshall and deploy relevant spiritual and psychological resources.

So in this program we are developing our own spiritual resources, and learning ways of changing.

In crisis we need to divide the situation into manageable-sized pieces; i.e., to "chunk" it. We need to do this in our sessions too.

The Spirit of God, our great Helper, Comforter, Disturber, Lover, is present always and everywhere. The main aim of this program is to become more aware and open to that fact as we go about our work of helping others.

To help us to be more open, after each session we may ask, "What may you, Holy Spirit, be teaching me in this session?"

SHARING

Discuss anything arising from the A.B.C. method of dealing with crisis.

D. CONCLUDING

RECOLLECTING

Quiet reflection, asking the Holy Spirit, "What are you, Holy Spirit, teaching me in this session?" Jotting down in our journals anything that comes to mind.

EVALUATION

Any comments on the session.

HOME PRACTICE

Using our hands as reminders of God's presence. Becoming aware in our own lives of how crisis is an internal reaction, and reminding ourselves of the A.B.C. method of dealing with crisis.

LOOKING AHEAD

Soon we may want to pair up for a while with one other group member as a prayer partner, or we may decide to keep changing around each session. So keep the idea prayerfully in mind.

Next session we shall be asking ourselves "Who am I?" and considering how we may be more open to ourselves and to God.

AFFIRMATION

Closing praying, holding hands to say or sing the grace, making eye contact with each person before breaking up.

Who Am I? Being Truly Ourselves
Contemplating: Opening Ourselves
to God in Everything

A. BECOMING AWARE OF WHERE WE ARE

WELCOME AND APOLOGIES

RECOLLECTING
Let us be still in the presence of God.
Hymn: e.g., "Breathe on me, Breath of God" (choose tune first).
Silent and vocal praying.

RECAP
To ensure we know everyone's name, each say our own name clearly. Make eye contact with each person and check on their name if necessary.
Last week our theme was openness and crisis; God's hands and our hands; crisis as an internal reaction and an opportunity; the A.B.C. method of dealing with crisis.

SHARING
In the whole group share our comments on last session; on how we have got on since then; journals; thinking about prayer partners.

TODAY'S THEME
Today we shall practice opening ourselves to God's Spirit in silent contemplation, and then in a led meditation, as we each ask ourselves who we really are.

B. BECOMING AWARE IN FORMAL PRAYING

INTRODUCTION
Choose one person to read.
Make ourselves comfortably relaxed and alert, e.g., with our backs straight, and feet on the floor.
Take deep breaths and in turn tense and relax our muscles.

PRACTICE
Reader slowly and meditatively reads Psalm 8: God's glory and man's dignity. Praising God and asking what is man.
Meditate silently.

SHARING
Share as appropriate in the whole group our experience of this type of praying and awareness.

EXTENSION

Contemplating

Contemplating, or contemplation, is opening ourselves to God in the whole of life.

The Relevance of Contemplating

In crisis work, indeed in all counseling and interactions with other people, we face the inherent danger of becoming too identified with the person and their problem. If we become too identified, we lose the ability to relate in an alert, relaxed manner and to be open to alternatives.

This tendency may be true of our general attitude; we may tend to become too narrow, too focused or analytical, i.e., too attached. A scientific training, with its emphasis on facts, may encourage us in this narrow attitude, though the recent renewed emphasis on emotions and feelings has partly regained the balance. But our search for reality, for God, needs to go beyond facts and feelings to include our spiritual dimension.

It is in opening ourselves to the spiritual that contemplating becomes relevant because it helps us to discern God's presence. To be effective spiritually aware crisis counselors we need to loosen our attachment to everything, including our concept of God.

There are ways to encourage an open attitude to our life and to God, to help us to be more effective faithful ministers.

*Three Ways to Become More Open to God,
to Others and to God's World
(based on Edwards, 1977, 49–50)*

Committing ourselves to becoming

1. Simple
2. Accepting
3. Confident and trusting

1. *Simple.* We must want God if we are to overcome our fascination with facts and feelings. Then everything is like a stained glass window which has different colored glass but which is filtering the same light: God's loving grace. Our life is simplified when we become aware of God's grace, God's action, as an unexpected gift available everywhere. We are able to relax and be less manipulating.
2. *Accepting.* We need to be kind to ourselves, to accept ourselves deep down as we are. Then we may recognize our need for grace and begin to recognize more clearly God's grace working in us.
3. *Confident.* We need to trust daily in God, to be confident that God will never give us more than we can bear.

SHARING
Comment as appropriate.

C. BECOMING AWARE IN COUNSELING SKILLS

INTRODUCTION
Being open to God also involves being open to and accepting ourselves, knowing ourselves.

Let's spend time now each reflecting on who we are. The leader will slowly suggest a framework. Use it when it is appropriate for you, letting it fade into the background or surface, whatever is most appropriate for you.

It is important to reexperience our varied situations from the inside, seeing, hearing, feeling, smelling and tasting them as though we are actually experiencing them NOW.

You may prefer to sit quietly with your eyes closed all the time or you may like to jot something down as we go along. There will be plenty of time at the end to make jottings. Afterwards we will share in small groups.

PRACTICE
The leader goes very slowly through the meditation, "Who am I?"

Meditation on "Who am I?"

As you are thinking over your life and asking yourself "Who am I?" instead of looking at yourself from the outside as though you are looking at a photo or a movie, experience yourself as if you are inside yourself at whatever age you are thinking about, experiencing being yourself, feeling and hearing and seeing and smelling and tasting for yourself.

Perhaps first imagining yourself way, way back, still in your mother's womb, feeling all cozy and warm. Part of your mother's body. Now you are being born. You are taking in breath for yourself. Breathing. You are breathing in and out. You are yourself. And now asking yourself "Who am I? What makes me me? Who am I? What does make me me?"

You are far more than the words you use. But asking yourself "What am I like?" Remembering yourself perhaps in the days before you start school. Your first days at school. How you feel in your early school days. What people are important to you. And now perhaps moving on to your later school days. Your holidays. Your home. Exploring the world around you. Realizing you are part of the universe. How you feel as a young adult. What is important to you. Who is important to you?

And now perhaps thinking of important times in your life since then, turning points you are reaching, important decisions you are making. And now, coming up to the present time, asking yourself again "What makes me me?" "What am I?" "Who am I?"

And as you are ready, writing in your journal whatever is appropriate for you.

SHARING

In small groups, e.g., in threes, preferably with different people from last week's groups, sharing whatever is appropriate for you. Remember that what is shared is confidential.

Then share as appropriate in the whole group.

EXTENSION

After each section take time for comments.

The Key to Learning to Be Who We Really Are

Accepting ourselves involves learning who we are and learning to be who we really are.

The key to learning to be who we really are, to becoming aware, is to relax and let go, to empty the left hand so it may receive the fullness of the right hand.

Fear makes relaxing difficult; fear of pain, fear of losing control, fear of death, fear of becoming nothing. Ernest Becker developed this theme in his book *Denial of Death* (Becker, 1973). We try to defend ourselves against these fears by leaving our mark everywhere, including ourselves. But it is only by giving up this struggle, by giving up our need to impress, and by letting God impress us, that we become who we really are.

Becoming our true selves is a matter of having something done to us rather than a matter of our doing something; it is apprehension rather than comprehension.

Being true to ourselves in the helping relationship is becoming a person open to apprehension,

to being influenced. To be open, to become aware, to relax in this sense, as the image of the yacht suggests, still affirms the importance of action and doing. Contemplation is a call for balance between doing and being, a call to be so that we can do effectively.

How to Be: Becoming Who We Really Are,
Aware of God's Presence

Our aim is to be; to be open, aware, relaxed, contemplating. Meditating is something we may do to help us to be.

Two basic styles of meditating, formal and informal, may lead us into contemplating, may help us to be more open to reality, more aware of God's presence.

Formal Meditating

In formal meditating we set aside a special time and place to practice letting our minds relax. We may use an object, image, activity or words as a base to center our attention and to still our minds, but this centering is only an aid to becoming alert and open to what is, here and now, to becoming aware of God.

Informal Meditating

In informal meditating we use what is happening around us and in us to increase our awareness in the midst of our daily living; e.g., we may use our hands to remind us.

At any time we may use any action, object, situation or our own sense of identity as the means of freeing us into contemplative awareness of the reality of God present and working in the situation.

We may use both formal and informal meditating to lead us to contemplative openness, but at any time we may be given unexpected moments of contemplation when we spontaneously become aware of God. When we begin to reflect on what happened in this moment of contemplative awareness, we are meditating on it.

In contemplating we are freed from the limitations caused by over-identifying with our thinking processes, which are necessary and appropriate for effective living, but which may stifle our intuitive awareness. In encouraging the spiritual side of our nature, we are aiming to be open and ready for God's unexpected gifts at any time.

Sometimes this openness allows a more intense experience, an experience of greater realization, union, apprehension to take us by surprise. We do not engineer it; it comes unexpectedly as a gracious gift.

Contemplating maintains the balance in the withdrawal-engagement rhythm which is essential for us to live effectively.

SHARING

Share our own experience and comments as appropriate.

Five Ways of Encouraging Awareness
(based on May, 1977, 20–21)

1. Perceiving. For example, watching all the things we are involved with as if they are passing by like clouds in the sky. Then taking a deep breath, blinking our eyes and seeing what our eyes see.
2. Doing things differently; e.g., changing a habitual way of doing something.
3. Keeping something in our heart; e.g., carefully picking a silent mantra, sound or image, planting it deep inside us and letting it go on working by itself, nourishing us. We do not need to repeat it or to work on it. Then during moments of peace during the day we may listen to it.
4. Working with desire; e.g., taking something we like doing and practicing doing a little less of it.
5. Getting into now; e.g., tuning in to whatever is happening, stressful or otherwise. Avoiding

labeling, judging, stifling or turning away anything. Just being open to what is happening: to sights, sounds, colors, smells, textures, forms and activities in the world around us, and to the perceptions, feelings and thoughts within. Accepting everything as completely as possible.

Note: Getting into now, without interfering with the present moment, practiced in a set place and time, i.e., formal meditating, is a simple way to nurture informal meditating during the day. And as we become more aware, improvement, growth and healing take place.

D. CONCLUDING

RECOLLECTING
Reflect quietly and journal on the session.

EVALUATION
Briefly evaluate and comment on the session.

HOME PRACTICE
Practice opening ourselves to God in silent relaxed alertness so that we become more open to God in everything (contemplation), becoming more aware of who we really are.

LOOKING AHEAD
Next session we shall ask "Where am I?" considering time and place, space, silence, and touching in formal praying and in crisis helping.

AFFIRMATION
Let's hold hands and stand silently together, becoming more aware of God's presence as we prepare to go out in God's Spirit.

Perhaps end by saying, "Thank you, God."

SESSION 4

Where am I in Formal Praying and Crisis Helping?
Time, Space, Silence, Touching

A. BECOMING AWARE OF WHERE WE ARE

WELCOME

RECOLLECTING
Let us be still in the presence of God.
Praying silently and aloud.

RECAP
Last session we explored the two questions: "What is contemplation?" "Who am I?" using a guided meditation.

SHARING
Briefly share anything arising out of last session.

TODAY'S THEME
This session, "Where am I?" we shall consider aspects of time and space for formal praying, different kinds of silence and the importance of touch.

B. BECOMING AWARE IN FORMAL PRAYING

INTRODUCTION
Last session we meditated on "Who am I?" Let's take time now to consider "Where am I?"
Someone be ready to read Psalm 139:1–16a, 23–24: You saw me before I was born.

PRACTICE
Hymn: e.g., "Be still and know that I am God". Singing it slowly, remembering God's love for us, "I am the Lord that healeth thee," and our response, "In thee, O Lord, I put my trust."
Read the psalm slowly.
Silent meditating.
Journal as appropriate.

SHARING
Share in whole group anything arising out of the questions "Who am I, and where am I?"
In the whole group share experiences and useful tips on when and where for formal praying; e.g., on making time and space for formal meditation and journaling.

EXTENSION

Time, Space, Silence

Time and space set apart for formal meditating at a particular time or place are opportunities for us to practice being open and relaxed, so that we may achieve similar openness at other times. Through formal meditation we aim to heighten our own awareness of the God of love who is present and active everywhere, and to enhance our ability to be aware of alternative ways of dealing with another person's problem.

Time

It is the quality of our time rather than the quantity that is important; i.e., how free our awareness is. Each of us needs to plan to set aside a definite amount of time to practice improving its quality.

Space and Silence

A fantasy of our place apart being quiet and uninterrupted may be unrealistic; but it may be our mistake to think we need a quiet environment. Sometimes we distract ourselves by being too selective about what we want to attend to, and so we consider noises as interference. We carry within ourselves the ability to be silent and quiet; we carry within ourselves the ability to be distracted. It is our attitude to internal and external stimuli that determines whether we are distracted. In being open and aware of the spaciousness of God, we become aware that God is active in and through the noise. Hearing is itself a gift. We need to be aware of the noise and let it pass through us instead of expending energy keeping it out.

C. BECOMING AWARE IN COUNSELING SKILLS

Space and Silence

INTRODUCTION

Emotional and spiritual silence and space may be more necessary than physical space for us to hear the still small voice within. However, we need to give ourselves time and space to realize the spaciousness of God and we need to give others the time and physical and emotional space which is essential to their realizing who and what they are. As helpers in crisis we need to be aware of suitable times and timing, the arrangement of the physical space and personal space needs.

PRACTICE

1. In twos, try out the effect of varying physical arrangements in space; e.g., sitting at different heights, different chair arrangements, across a desk or table, one person facing into a window with the other having their back to the light, being at different distances.

2. Attending and nonattending. In twos . . .

A. shares; e.g., what you have been doing or thinking this morning or recently.

B. actively nonattends, then actively attends.

Discuss the difference, then change roles. Take about five minutes each.

SHARING

In the whole group share briefly on the effect of different space arrangements, attending and nonattending.

EXTENSION

Creative Silent Listening

"Be still and know that I am God" (Psalm 46:10).

It is not easy to listen to someone else if we are talking at the same time, either aloud or inside ourselves. Our whole program is aimed at helping us to listen to God's Spirit in our own inner depths where God's Spirit may be heard, to listen to the other person, and to enable them to listen to God's Spirit in their own inner depths. All the techniques we learn are only aids to help us to achieve this listening and openness. Listening requires a certain silence in ourselves, a stilling to draw on our own depths; an emptying of the left hand so it can be filled by the right hand. In the helping relationship it is important to offer creative silence, setting aside our own experiences, suggestions, judgments, advice and interpretations (Table 1).

SHARING

Comment briefly about different silences.

PRACTICE

Touching

To experience touch let's move around greeting each other, being aware of each person's differing needs and reactions to touching and being touched. Greeting each partner in three ways if appropriate:

(a) Shaking hands and saying "hello"

(b) Touching their arm

(c) Putting our hand round their shoulder or waist

Then moving to next person and doing the same. Be sure to experience initiating the greeting and being greeted.

SHARING

In threes, thinking first of a small incident or time in our own life when touch was or would have been helpful. Sharing as seems appropriate:

TABLE 1
POSSIBLE EFFECTS OF DIFFERENT TYPES OF SILENCE

Silence	Listener	Sharer
Isolating	Not listening	Feels lonely, unwanted, valueless, unable to concentrate
Destructive	Antagonistic	Feels hated, put down, embarrassed, defensive
Creative	Attending, expectant, accepting, comfortable	Feels accepted, free to move and develop in own way
	Listening	Has time to think out own thoughts
	Instead of comforting with words, giving sharer time	Is free to feel the feeling which may be strong and has not had a chance to be expressed

(a) What effect did touch or lack of touch have on me?

(b) What does this say to us as helpers of others in crisis?

When we are listening to others in the group, remembering the importance of attending to the sharer, giving them time, space, and creative silence.

Sharing in the whole group.

EXTENSION

Touching

Touching is a basic and powerful form of communicating. We read often of Jesus touching people to heal them. We all have had many experiences of the power of being touched and not being touched. We as helpers may benefit from the way touching in our society has become more socially acceptable, and has freed many people from thinking that this has a solely sexual meaning.

In crisis touch is particularly powerful, as the person in crisis may be blocked to more usual communication channels, such as words. From our infancy we have known the soothing power of touching and stroking to comfort and relieve distress and pain; we have held our head in our hands when in despair. Now touch is being used increasingly and systematically to diagnose troubled areas and restore balance to our bodies and minds; e.g., massage, touch for health, therapeutic touch, stress release, reflexology, polarity, acupressure, muscle testing. Some of these ways of touching may be useful for us in crisis situations.

D. CONCLUDING

RECOLLECTING
Let us be still again in the presence of God.

EVALUATION
Journal if we want to, and make any comments or suggestions.

HOME PRACTICE
Where and when: acting on improving our time, space and silence in our formal praying time; becoming more aware of the importance of time, space, silence, and touch in our helping.

LOOKING AHEAD
Next session we shall be considering how we may use our body posture to help us to open our inner space; how we are all the time linking up our different experiences, and what this linking may mean for the sharer and for us as helpers.

We shall need to wear loose clothing suitable for lying on the floor.

AFFIRMATION
Let's stand touching the person next to us. Let's sing one verse of "Be still and know that I am God." Then be silent for a while before singing God's promise, "I am the Lord that healeth thee," and silent again before accepting God's promise for ourselves, and committing ourselves to God, "In thee, O Lord, I put my trust."

Posture: Opening our Inner Space
Associating; Noticing vs. Interpreting

Note extra materials needed: e.g., books for heads; cassette player; electric cord; music cassette, e.g., Eno, *Music for Airports* (Ambient 1). Polydor 310647, 1978.

A. BECOMING AWARE OF WHERE WE ARE

RECOLLECTING
Being still in the presence of God.
Praying silently or aloud.
Hymn; e.g., "Stand up and bless the Lord."
Short time of silence and recollection.

RECAP
Last session we considered the importance of time and place, silence and touching.

SHARING
In twos share and pray:
(a) Anything from journal
(b) How have we been aware of God present and active in our lives this week?
(c) How are we linking this to our awareness of our own and other people's crises?
In whole group share as desired from couple sharing.
How are you finding the program as a whole?

TODAY'S THEME
Today we consider our physical posture: opening our inner space with various exercises and a meditation in movement; then associating, and noticing versus interpreting sensory information.

B. BECOMING AWARE IN FORMAL PRAYING

Physical Posture: Opening our Inner Space

INTRODUCTION

Physical Posture in Prayer

Our body is our basic prayer environment
Discuss what postures we find helpful when we pray

Positive Effects of Relaxed Posture

"Don't you know that your body is the temple of the Holy Spirit, who lives in you . . . so use your bodies for God's glory" (1 Cor 6:20).
If we allow our bodies to relax, our minds are more likely to relax. Tension is what is left over from the previous unbalanced activity.
We are aiming to achieve openness, balance, space. A relaxed posture helps us to maintain our inner physical space and our openness to the spaciousness of God. It helps us to make positive links with God, God's world and others, and so enhances our ability to help others. Poor posture, on the other hand, may link us and other people into negative, ineffective behavior patterns and so drastically reduce our ability to help.
There are many traditional postures for meditation; e.g., kneeling, sitting cross-legged, sitting on a chair. In all our postures it is important to maintain our inner space, which is determined by our skeleton.

Today we are going to experience various postures to practice becoming more relaxed. The instructions are based on the Alexander Technique (Alexander, 1974).

PRACTICE

Your Length

Standing: your spine needs to be upright; i.e., reaching up and away from your legs, like a spring, not a rigid stick.

Your head needs to be balanced, with the neck not cramped, so that it can send clear information to the rest of your body. Turning your head left and right, up and down. What do you notice about your neck? When turning, allow your whole head to move up and away from your body. Letting your body follow. Keeping your eyes open.

An upright spine maintains your physical space from the crotch to the top of your head. It may be helpful to imagine your head being attached to an upward spring. Two common postures to be avoided are:

1. Punched in the stomach
2. Stabbed in the back

Lying down on your back with your head on a book about five centimeters (two inches) thick, with knees up at hip width. This position allows gravity to straighten the spine at the waist and stretch the neck. Maintaining this relaxed straightness when you get up slowly.

Width and Breadth

Your space from front to back and side to side is maintained by your ribs and pelvis.

1. *Ribs.* Your space is maintained by your ribs and by a balance between collarbone and shoulder blades. Now relaxing your shoulders, allowing the weight of your arms and what you are carrying to be taken by the shoulder blades and to go down your back, taking it off the chest.

Lying down: To be aware of width, while lying down take in a deep breath and let it out through your mouth saying "ah."

2. *Pelvis.* Lying on your back, keeping the hip joints balanced and loosening the tension in your abdomen muscles. Slowly bringing the soles of your feet together and allowing your knees to drop outward. When ready, bringing your knees up slowly.

Performing all the movements slowly with the minimum of effort required, maintaining body balance.

Sitting Down

To maintain inner physical space when sitting, first of all regain it when standing; i.e., balancing your head and lengthening your neck and the rest of your spine without exerting any tension. Unlocking your legs at hips, knees and ankles. Slowly bending your knees and keeping them going forward. Keeping your head up; i.e., in the direction of the rest of your spine. Bringing the weight of your buttocks up. Allowing your body to support you till it touches the chair. Still keeping the whole of your back straight; i.e., maintaining your space, bringing your body up till you are sitting straight with your hands in your lap.

Getting Up

Have your hands at your side, your back straight, your head balanced on your neck, your feet slightly behind knees, hip width apart. Avoiding a tendency to collapse forward or to throw yourself forward, by maintaining the space between the bottom of your breastbone and your bottom. Coming forward without folding up and gradually rising.

Practicing the movements slowly helps the new movements to be substituted for old habits and gradually become automatic. We may check on our physical openness during the day when we are getting up, eating, drinking soup, driving a car, or on the toilet, as well as when meditating.

Feet flat on the floor helps to earth us into the flow of the universe; if we are sitting on the floor we may cross them in various ways. If we are kneeling back on our heels it may be helpful to put a cushion on our legs to support our bottom.

Hands

Our hands and arms are very expressive; e.g., making fists and holding them up in front of us;

opening them up palms outstretched facing up; bringing them back palms facing away.

Four useful hand positions for relaxed alertness in praying are:

1. On knees or legs, palms up or down
2. On knees or in lap with index finger touching the pad of the thumb
3. Palms up in lap, fingers of one hand resting on fingers of the other
4. As in 3, with tips of thumbs touching

Other Hand and Body Positions in Praying

It may be useful to vary body and hand positions; e.g., experiment with different postures for praise; confession; accepting into ourselves God's forgiveness, healing and love; lifting others to God; reaching out to others.

The Feldenkrais method of Awareness Through Movement has also explored dissociating us from our habitual patterns of moving, feeling, and thinking (Feldenkrais, 1977).

SHARING

Sharing our own experience of those positions and of what postures we find helpful in formal praying.

Meditation in Movement

Neutral background music such as Brian Eno's *Music for Airports* is most suitable.

INTRODUCTION

Our meditation today is meditation in movement with music, to experience and experiment with different postures as we open ourselves to God in various kinds of prayer.

GROUP EXPERIENCE

Meditation in movement, like all meditation, is slow, gentle, reflective. The suggested movement, which may be led by one group member, is a starting point. Let's use it as we want to, feeling free to make it our own, holding the posture, moving into it, developing it or substituting whatever seems appropriate for each of us.

1. Creator God, I bring together the diverse facets of my being (Standing, bringing palms together). Be still and know that I am God.
2. I open myself to you. Give me a hearing heart (Arms stretched up. Hands to center).
3. I draw back the veil that blocks my vision (Crossed hands with back of hands to eyes, moving outwards).
   I am dazzled by your radiance (Cover eyes).
4. But you open my eyes wide to behold the glory of your creation (Turning head and really seeing).
5. Glory to you, O God most high (Arms up and outstretched).
   Praise the Lord, O my soul, and all that is within me praise God's holy name.
6. What am I that you are mindful of me? (Standing, head bowed).
7. Search me O God and know my mind;
   Test me and discover my thoughts;
   Find out if there is any evil in me and guide me in the everlasting way (Hands crossed on breast).
8. I have sinned against heaven and before you (Sink slowly to the floor enfolding chest and upper arms with opposite hands and shaking head or head down to floor with hands on floor in front).
9. My unforgiving thoughts, my burdens, my obstacles; I release them all; all my sins and pain. I cast them at the foot of your cross (Kneeling upright and casting them).
10. I take your forgiveness, O God.
11. I hold it to myself.
    It flows into my innermost being (Hands to one's center).
12. Loving Creator, I accept myself as you accept me.
13. You embrace and comfort the unhappy parts in me.
    You cradle me as a child in your arms (Rock arms as though rocking an infant).
14. I am at peace.
15. I thank you God with great thankfulness (Slowly standing).
    My life is risen with your risen life.
    Like a tree I grow and flourish.
    I am grounded, rooted in you.
    I receive your life-giving energy of love.
    I respond to the seasons. I change.
    I put forth buds. I shed leaves.

I withstand the storms of life.
Your strengthening love flows through me.
(Move around as desired).

16. And there are others, joyful, loving, sad, confused, in pain. You know their hearts, their minds, their needs. I lift them up to you (Raised hands).

17. I receive your lifegiving power of love flowing through me to others (Hands up receiving and moving down front of body and forward at waist level, one palm resting on the other, arms outstretched).

18. For we are all one in you, in our ups and downs, in our pain and joy. We join in giving and receiving your lifegiving power and love.
(Join hands with others in a circle, giving with the right hand and receiving love with the left. Stand silently).

19. Amen.

Journal if desired.

SHARING
Brief sharing as appropriate.

C. BECOMING AWARE IN COUNSELING SKILLS

Associating

INTRODUCTION
When we attend to time and place, silence and touching, we help to make the present experience more pleasant or positive for the person helped, and so help the present experience to become a more pleasant past experience. Our present experiences are linked with our past experiences and because our unconscious mind does not keep chronological time, our past experiences are part of our present.

Random Associating

A powerful way of bringing a specific past experience into the present is by a definite stimulus associated with the situation and the attached feelings; e.g., we hear a familiar tune and immediately we remember a certain experience. The stimulus may be an object, a sound, touch, smell, word, tone of voice, gesture, posture, facial expression, etc. Associating is a constant mental process which is often unconscious and random.

Being Aware of Associations

As we become more aware and open, we may realize how much associations with the past are affecting the lives and relationships of ourselves and others now; e.g., we may use a gesture, which in the other person unconsciously produces a reaction to a past experience, when someone else used that gesture. If the original past gesture was friendly, they may react in a friendly way to us; if it was hostile, they may react to our friendly gesture in a hostile way. We probably do not anticipate a hostile reaction, and in turn we may react to a sudden hostile experience of our own past. Which time are we in, past or present?

We need to become aware of how often people are locked into past negative, ineffective or destructive ways of behaving, and also how they may unconsciously be linking their present experiences with their past negative ones, through their associations with our tone of voice, looks, etc. But we may also enable them to categorize their present experiences as positive and desirable, and help them to link them into their desirable past creative experiences, so that they may be able to recall them and use them as creative resources in the present.

Part of our task as Christian helpers is to enable people to link up their present situation with the positive aspects of their present and past religious experience, which is their experience of the values, meaning and purpose of life.

Some of the patterns we have established in our group are probably familiar links with our own past religious experience; e.g., hymn singing, closing our eyes to pray. Others, like the arrangement of the room, may be becoming familiar for us. Although we are constantly associating randomly, we may also make systematic links.

Systematic Associating

To associate systematically and constructively, we consciously apply a definite stimulus as a link; e.g., a specific touch, when another person or we ourselves are fully in touch with a present or a remembered experience. Then when the same stimulus is used, the situation is likely to be experienced again; e.g., when the touch is repeated in exactly the same place with the same pressure, when the exact gesture is made again, or when the word is said with the same tone and volume. So if we want to have specific positive feelings available to us; e.g., feelings of confidence, love, trust, we may consciously link in a present or remembered experience of the feelings we want, and recall it at will by using the specific link, just as we may hum a tune or smell a red rose.

To link our chosen stimulus with one of our desirable past experiences, we need to imagine ourselves inside the positive meaningful experience, not looking at ourselves from the outside as if we are looking at someone else. We need to be experiencing it ourselves now, in the present, from the inside. The experience may be a peak experience, exciting, beautiful or harmonious, such as looking at a sunset, feeling really loved, confident, etc. At the most intense part of the experience we may use our link; e.g., we may press our thumb on the pulse of our wrist. When we repeat the pressure in the same way, we are likely to experience the same feelings. It is more effective to touch a place not normally touched in that way, to avoid using other unconscious links. To be effective, the gesture, word, whatever we choose, needs to be a special one without continual random associations.

Touch is a useful link because we may use it unobtrusively whenever we need it. We may also use it at any time or place to make more positive links for ourselves.

PRACTICE

Practicing Systematic Associating

Let's practice associating systematically now, attending to the leader's voice as appropriate. Timing will be different for each person. Putting your thumb near your pulse in readiness. Closing your eyes, with feet on the floor, taking deep breaths, releasing any tension, starting at your feet and working up your body. Re-experiencing from the inside a satisfying experience for you; one that is meaningful, a peak experience. It may

be exciting, beautiful, harmonious, full of love, whatever it is for you. It may be feeling really confident, feeling loved, seeing a beautiful sunset, whatever it is for you.

Becoming aware of the sounds, the sights, the feelings in your experience, the smells and perhaps the taste. And as you reach the intensest part of the experience, associating it by pressing the thumb on the pulse of your wrist, maintaining the pressure for several seconds. Taking whatever time you need. And when you are ready, returning to this room.

SHARING

Discuss the experience in the whole group.

EXTENSION

Associations as Bases to Free Our Awareness

A relaxed open posture and creative associations between contemporary and past religious experience and our present situation help to free our awareness, to open us to God on all levels, especially in the inner depths of our being, so enabling us to be more open to others. Many of the basic skills we shall be considering help us to be more aware of what we are linking into other people and how to help them to use their own links to get in touch with their own satisfying resources.

Noticing vs. Interpreting Sensory Information

INTRODUCTION

Each of us is linked into many kinds of unconscious reactions. The very word reacting implies reenacting, acting out the past again.

Our essential need to organise the enormous amount of information we receive through our senses involves us in interpreting and categorizing what we receive, i.e., associating it with what we already know (sessions 15 and 16). We take shortcuts and often put the information straight into categories without adequate awareness of the individual situation; e.g., stereotyping. When someone else presents us with a link which is familiar to us, though neither of us may be aware of it, we may well react to all the experiences we

TABLE 2
EXAMPLES OF NOTICING AND INTERPRETING

Sensory-Based Information (noticing)	Nonsensory-Based Information (interpreting)
shouting	angry
frowning	puzzled
sudden flush in skin	embarrassed
foot tapping	impatient
legs crossed	uptight

have put into that category. Sometimes the present experience may have seemingly tenuous links with the category, and the other person may not understand our reaction. So it is important to become aware of the difference between the information our senses are receiving and how we are interpreting that information. Table 2 gives some examples.

When we become free from some of our unsatisfactory automatic behavior and thought patterns, some of our old associations, we become aware that we have greater choice and openness of attitude and action.

Bandler, Grinder and Cameron-Bandler in their Neuro Linguistic Programming extracted and summarized basic skills behind many therapeutic disciplines which may enable us to communicate more effectively and to achieve changes that we want. In this program we are drawing on their work, especially Cameron-Bandler's *Solutions,* as we develop and integrate our personal contemplative and counseling skills (Bandler and Grinder, 1979; Grinder and Bandler, 1981; Cameron-Bandler, 1985; also Lankton, 1980).

GROUP EXPERIENCE
Practice in threes:
A adopts posture.
B describes, then interprets the posture, e.g., "I notice that you . . ."; "I imagine that you . . ."
C observes and then checks. Reverse roles.

SHARING
Share in your group how you got on.

D. CONCLUDING

RECOLLECTING
Quiet reflection and journaling.

EVALUATION
Brief evaluation and comment.

HOME PRACTICE
Opening our inner space to the Holy Spirit. Associating. Noticing without interpreting.

LOOKING AHEAD
Next session we shall practice relaxing, dealing with distractions, and becoming aware of the sensory-based information that we continually receive from other people, especially from eyes and body posture.

AFFIRMATION
Standing in a circle. Hymn: e.g., "Stand up and bless the Lord," v.1.
Learning gestures for the grace, ending up holding hands either to say or to sing it.

Relaxing and Distractions Sensory-based Information: Eye and Body Messages

A. BECOMING AWARE OF WHERE WE ARE

RECOLLECTING
Being still in the presence of God.
Praying silently or aloud.

RECAP
Last session we tried out various physical postures to achieve physical openness and interior space, and openness to the spaciousness of God; we meditated in movement with music; and considered associating, and noticing vs. interpreting.

SHARING
Comment briefly on the last session and our progress since.

TODAY'S THEME
In thinking about relaxed awareness and how to deal with distractions, we shall use the story of Martha and Mary. Then we shall consider ways to become more aware of the sharer's own world through their sensory-based signals, their eye and body messages.

B. BECOMING AWARE IN FORMAL PRAYING

INTRODUCTION
Let's first use a hymn to help us to let go of our stress, and to open ourselves to God's stilling voice.
Then let the gospel story about the two sisters make its own impact on us. Let's hear, reflect quietly and journal on it, being aware of our feelings and any new learning. Then in threes, act out the story as Jesus, Martha and Mary.

PRACTICE
Hymn: e.g., "Dear Lord and Father of mankind," sung slowly.
Reading: Jesus visits Martha and Mary (Luke 10:38–41).
Reflecting silently on the story. Then noting down our reactions to it, and what we think God may be wanting us to realize.
In threes, act out the story, and discuss anything we have learned from the acting and from the quiet reflection. Journal as appropriate.

SHARING
Share in the whole group.

Relaxing

SHARING
In the whole group discuss ways which we find help us to achieve relaxed awareness.

EXTENSION

Relaxed Awareness

When we are meditating or praying we need to be relaxed and aware. Last session we thought of our bodies as our basic prayer environment and that when we allow our muscles to relax our minds also relax. So we aim to let go of the tension and restriction, to stop struggling and allow ourselves to be; to be open, accepting, allowing things to be. When we relax we are not sleepy or befuddled. "Free relaxation means a very bright, clear and open awareness" (May, 1977, 69).

Our mistake often may be to associate awareness with tension. When we say "pay attention" we usually mean to restrict our attention; i.e., shut out stimuli and not be distracted. Restricting our attention requires energy and causes conflict and tension. Relaxing means that we free our awareness; we do not shut out distractions, we open ourselves to everything that enters awareness. In this way we free our energy, diminish conflict and tension and move towards just being.

INTRODUCTION

Stretching as a Way to Relax

Stretching is one of the best ways to relax. We do something which requires effort and then let go, e.g., an arm and leg shaking relaxation exercise, which releases tension, allows limbs to be what they are and produces a feeling of well-being.

PRACTICE
Stand up and stretch, and then relax.
Still standing, shake both arms and then relax; then shake each leg and relax it.

SHARING
Comment briefly.

EXTENSION
In formal meditation most of the things we do, e.g., repeating words or prayers, are mental stretches which allow our minds to relax, and like a muscle, to return to their natural state. There are many ways we can stretch: active prayer, reading the scriptures, the liturgy. The essential is to stop and listen after the stretch; the stopping is the relaxation point.

Emphasizing relaxing does not deny the necessity of physical and mental work and muscular tension; we are not expected to be limp glove puppets, or spineless blobs. The purpose of relaxing is to rid ourselves of the tension that is left

over from the previous unbalanced activity (session 5), and unclutter our bodies and minds so that we can live more in the present rather than being locked into the past.

Distractions

SHARING
In the whole group briefly discuss how we deal with distractions.

INTRODUCTION
Distractions occur when we are trying to concentrate on one thing and shut others out. We often deal with distractions by stifling our awareness of them, which may take a great deal of energy.

We may learn how to use our energy more constructively by considering the difference between a traditional western and oriental approach to conflict. The western way is confrontation or attack, going like a bull at a gate, which ends in a smash. The oriental approach, typified in martial arts, is relaxed centered calm or balance. Relaxation, not power, is what counts. And in this centered calm there is an important clue to dealing with mental conflict and distractions, so-called obstacles to meditating and praying.

The key to handling distractions is to acknowledge and accept them, and gently let them come and go, to let stimuli flow past freely rather than to struggle with them. This is our aim in the exercise on acknowledging and accepting what is going on in and around us. Our senses are taking in information all the time and registering everything we can see, hear, feel, taste and smell. It has been calculated that our conscious mind can only attend to seven bits of information, plus or minus two, at any one moment. Our purpose in contemplating is to open ourselves to allow whatever is most appropriate to be what surfaces into consciousness or attracts our attention. What we are receiving either through our present sensory experience or what we are recalling from our past experience becomes a distraction when we allow our minds to concentrate on it instead of becoming aware of more appropriate information.

A factor in manipulating the automatic flow of incoming information and dragging it into consciousness is often that the information is linked to past experience, and we are reacting to a past experience instead of to the present. If we can recognize this link, we may be able to detach our present from the particular past experiences which we are reacting to automatically, and realize that we have a choice in our reactions to these stimuli. For example, if we hear continual banging of workmen outside, instead of reacting to it negatively and letting it intrude into our consciousness, we may go inside the noise, translate it into the beat of a favorite piece of music, and let it provide a pleasant background of which we are not consciously aware. Relaxing, and recognizing that we have choice in what we attend to, may help us towards the aim of spiritually aware pastoral care, i.e., contemplation in crisis, achieving openness and awareness that leads to more appropriate action.

PRACTICE

Identify some present noise which could be distracting, or the leader may make some noise such as repetitive knocking. Each decide what we want to attend to, then choose music suitable as a background and a color that fits in harmoniously.

Now, superimposing the music and the color on the distraction, hearing and seeing them from inside ourselves. Gradually letting everything fade into the background as we become more aware of God's presence.

SHARING

Comment in the whole group.

C. BECOMING AWARE IN COUNSELING SKILLS

Sensory-based Information: Eye and Body Messages

INTRODUCTION

Different Thinking Modes

In helping someone to achieve the changes which bring freedom of choice and greater openness we need to be as aware as possible of how they are thinking and feeling. We may enter their world further by:

1. Becoming more aware of the sensory-based information they are sending us; i.e., their body and eye language and their choice of words;
2. Distinguishing between the information and our interpretation of it; i.e., noticing rather than interpreting (session 5).

All of us experience the world through our five senses, and process our experiences (think) in one or more sensory channels: we see, hear, feel, smell, and taste.

Most of the time we are concerned not with our present sensory experience, e.g., the weight of our feet on the floor, but with our internal responses to the present or to past or future events. Particular internal processes tend to be linked to certain body changes and movements. By becoming more aware of the sensory-based information which the other person is sending us we may develop our ability to know which sensory mode they are using to perceive and assess their experience, and we can use this information to establish rapport with them. This is stage A of the A.B.C. method of dealing with crisis (session 2).

Eye Positions to Indicate Thinking Modes

The direction and pattern in which our eyes move when we are bringing into consciousness past or future remembered or constructed experience is definitely linked to the sensory channel we are using.

PRACTICE

In twos while the leader asks two questions of each type, take it in turns to watch each other's eyes, nose and mouth. A watches B; then for the next question B watches A.

Some Eye Accessing Questions

Seeing Remembered:
 What does a kingfisher look like?
 What color clothes did you wear yesterday?
 Can you see all the colors of a rainbow?
 What color roses do you like?
Seeing Creating:
 Can you imagine the bottom half of a horse connected to the top half of a chimpanzee?

Can you imagine the sea turning bright yellow?

Can you see yourself dressed up as a giraffe?

Can you see yourself climbing Mount Everest?

Hearing Remembered:

Can you recall the sound of your mother's voice?

Can you hear a favorite tune?

Can you remember a really loud noise?

What is something you say to yourself?

Hearing Creating:

Can you hear the sound of a waterfall changing into a symphony orchestra?

Can you imagine the sound of a whisper with the sound of a dog barking?

Can you hear the sound of a fire engine and a church organ at the same time?

Can you hear a baby crying while someone is playing the bagpipes?

Feeling:

When you are embarrassed, how do you react?

How does it feel to be enfolded in something gorgeously soft?

How does it feel to be bumped around in a vehicle on a winding road?

When you stroke a cat, how does it feel to you?

Tasting and Smelling:

What is the smell of carnations?

What is the taste of lemon?

What does garlic (taste/smell) like?

Combine the taste of honey with the smell of manure.

Combine the taste of something bitter with the smell of newly-baked bread.

SHARING

Discuss what we noticed.

EXTENSION

For right-handed people across many cultures, the link is usually as in Figure 3. Left-handed people may be partially or totally reversed.

A way of learning the eye positions in Figure 3 is:

Left = what we "left," in the past, i.e., remembering.

Right = creating possibilities, + feeling.

We may consciously put our eyes in the appropriate position to help us to think in a specific way, e.g., to imprint a mental picture of the diagram above, hold it high to our left. To recall it

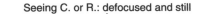

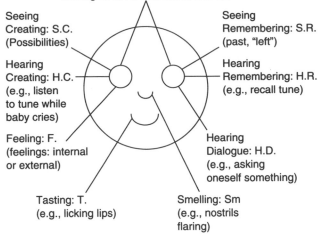

C = creating, possibilities: what, how etc. would . . . ?
R = remembering: what, how, etc. did . . . ?

Fig. 3. Eye positions and thinking modes (based on Bandler and Grinder, 1979, 25)

visually, again put our eyes up left. This seeing remembering position is useful for example, for spelling, getting a picture of something mislaid.

When we are observing the sharer, we need to remember that their eyes go to their left, which is our right.

PRACTICE

In twos watch each other's eyes again, while the leader asks two more of each kind of question.

SHARING

Discuss it briefly in the whole group.

EXTENSION

Most of us develop favorite thinking patterns which we tend to use in different situations, sometimes inappropriately. Eye movements may be a clue to these habitual patterns.

Other Body Messages Linked to Thinking Modes

Other parts of our bodies also respond to our sensory thinking modes. Here are some common patterns:

Seeing: High

High eyes, head, breathing, shoulders, voice; quick speech; tense abdomen; paling skin.

Hearing: Level

Level eyes, head, breathing; voice and movements even and rhythmic; even skin color.

Feeling: Low

Low eyes (down right), head, breathing; voice low and slow; muscles relaxed with sudden, abrupt movements; increased skin color.

In our daily lives let's practice noticing the clues which our bodies are giving us to the way that we and other people are thinking.

Changing our Associations

INTRODUCTION

We have been experiencing how the way we think affects our bodies' reaction.

The way we think and react is also influenced by our past habits and experience, i.e., how we link our present to our past experiences, as we considered last session. Although these links may be automatic, they may not be permanent. If we are dissatisfied, we may work on changing our associations, so that we are able to react in a more satisfying way.

The following exercise provides one way to substitute satisfying feelings and reactions for negative ones that we want to replace.

Negative and Positive Links

In the whole group each decide what you will use as reachable negative and satisfying links; e.g., for the negative one pressing one spot on your right thigh with your right index finger, and for the satisfying link pressing your left thigh with your left index finger.

When you are comfortable and relaxed, the leader may use the following as a guide:

Thinking of a time when you were mildly upset with someone's behavior. Not looking at it as though you are looking at someone else, but being inside the situation, experiencing the situation now. When you get to the most intense part, pressing your right index finger as a negative link. What are you seeing, hearing, feeling outside and inside yourself? What can you smell and taste?

Then releasing the pressure, and returning to the room. Testing the link by pressing again in the same spot with the same pressure and noticing how much the negative feeling returns.

To disengage yourself, do something different such as moving or clearing your throat.

Then asking yourself what internal resources you would have needed for the negative experience to have ended more satisfactorily, giving yourself time to choose really satisfying experiences and actions.

Now choosing a situation when you have felt or can imagine feeling and acting and hearing and seeing in this way.

Remembering to stimulate your satisfying left hand link at the intensest point, experiencing now this satisfying situation; feeling, seeing, and hearing yourself using your satisfying resources. Associating any other resources that you want.

Then releasing the pressure, and returning to this room.

Test your satisfying link by pressing your left finger on your left thigh in the same place with the same pressure, and notice how far the satisfying feelings return.

Press both links at once.

Press the negative link again. Notice how far the negative experience is less intense. If need be, mobilize stronger satisfying resources and repeat the exercise from where you choose and associate satisfying resources, satisfying sights and sounds and feelings and actions.

SHARING

In the whole group share as appropriate.

EXTENSION

Emotional Stress Release, with Eye Movements (based on Topping, 1985, 56–58)

Eye positions may be used to increase the relaxing effect of touch, and this may be useful in crisis.

We may use touch in many ways to reduce stress and restore balance to the body. One way is to put our fingers on the prominent bumps on our foreheads, one hand on each side. Think of the stressful situation and keep our fingers there until the pulses become the same on both sides, or if we are doing it for someone else, until they have had enough. This is thought to balance the body energy, and act as a positive link, balancing out or disconnecting the automatic link with negative reactions.

A development of this common act of putting our head in our hands is to incorporate eye positions. Again, we may do it for ourselves or for someone else. With another person it is better to be behind them, and it is easier to see their eye movements if they are lying down relaxing.

1. Identify the problem state and the state they want, e.g., I am frustrated, powerless > I am in control; I am embarrassed > I am confident.
2. Put fingers on the bumps on the forehead. When doing this with someone else put the fingers of one hand on their forehead and use one finger of your other hand to lead their eyes slowly for the first few times.
3. While remembering the problem state, either silently or while repeating it quietly, slowly rotate the eyes in a large circle, first one way and then back the other.
4. Escape from the problem state by some distraction.
5. Experience the desired state either silently or while repeating it quietly, and once again slowly rotate the eyes in a large circle, first one way then the other.
6. Associate the positive state with the future by thinking of a future situation and experiencing the desired state.

D. CONCLUSION

RECOLLECTING
Time for us to reflect quietly and to journal.

EVALUATION
Any brief comments and evaluation of the session.

HOME PRACTICE
Becoming aware of what distracts us and how we may alter our attitude. Becoming aware of our present links into our own past, and how we may make new more satisfying links.

LOOKING AHEAD
Next session we shall be considering ways of using our breathing to increase our awareness, and how we as helpers may minimize our own distractions and unhelpful past associations, staying in the sharer's world by mirroring it.

AFFIRMATION
Softly sing the last verse of the hymn by J.G. Whittier: ''Dear Lord and Father of mankind'':

Breathe through the heats of our desire
Thy coolness and thy balm.
Let sense be dumb, let flesh retire,
Speak through the earthquake, wind and fire,
O still small voice of calm.
The grace.

SESSION 7

Breathing Praying
Distractions While Helping
Nonverbal Matching: Mirroring

A. BECOMING AWARE OF WHERE WE ARE

RECOLLECTING
Being still in the presence of God.
Praying silently or aloud.

RECAP
Last session we began with Martha and Mary as examples of dealing with distractions, and practiced dealing with distractions by letting them flow past us and by changing them into something more pleasant and then letting them fade. We changed some of our own unpleasant reactions into ones that we preferred by associating systematically, and then thought about how the sharer's eye and body movements may help us to stay in their world.

SHARING
Brief comments.

TODAY'S THEME
In session 5 we thought about how our body posture affects our whole attitude and openness. Last time we considered how our particular way of thinking affects our eye and body movements.

Today we consider how one of our most basic automatic activities, breathing, may help us to be more aware of God's Spirit. Effortless effort like breathing is needed in the helping relationship too. We shall think about how we can minimize distractions when helping by mirroring different body messages which the sharer may be sending us unconsciously.

B. BECOMING AWARE IN FORMAL PRAYING

INTRODUCTION
Let's choose a partner now, then after the hymn and breathing praying and silence, when the leader gives the signal, move into twos to share and pray together.

PRACTICE
Hymn: e.g., "Breathe in me, Breath of God."
The leader leads into the breathing praying:

Breathing Praying

Breathing praying helps us to open ourselves in the depths of our being to God's forgiving love and acceptance of us as we are. When we accept that God accepts and loves us as we are, then we find the heart to become what we truly are.

A Way of Breathing Praying

Have your body in an open posture. Tense up your muscles and then let them relax. As you breathe in, breathing in everything that is of God; becoming aware of God's breath (Spirit) filling you, from your toes up; God's gift of life and love flowing through your whole system. As you breathe out, breathing out everything you want to let go; being aware of your breathing without altering it. Keeping on breathing steadily, breath-

ing in God's love, and breathing out everything that you want to let go.
Silence.

SHARING

Move into twos. Share:

(a) anything from the silence

(b) how we got on with the last session and since

(c) any thanks or needs

Each of us in turn shares and is prayed with.

Share in the whole group, e.g., how we got on being aware of our breathing without altering it.

EXTENSION

The Jesus Prayer

A traditional breath prayer, the Jesus Prayer is the central discipline of some Eastern Orthodox Christians (Hesychasts). They learn to pray in the rhythm of their own breathing so that on the in breath they say, "Lord Jesus Christ (Son of the living God)," and on the out breath, "Have mercy on me (a sinner)." After a while this praying goes on and on unconsciously, and so becomes a prayer of the heart, a state of perpetual inner prayerfulness.

Breathing is used as a base for meditation in many different traditions. Why is it considered so important? The word spirit and our words for breathing—inspiration respiration, expiration—all come from the same root, meaning breath. Our breath goes deep down inside us; it affects every cell in our body, it reflects and alters our feelings. Breathing has been found to be one of the best things to use to help us to achieve a balance between control and free awareness. When we have learned to be aware of our breathing without controlling or influencing it, we are closer to freeing our mind which, like our breathing, works by itself when left alone.

C. BECOMING AWARE IN COUNSELING SKILLS

Effort and Relaxing

Effort may help or ruin meditation; it may help or ruin the helping relationship.

In Meditation

A bulldozing approach destroys meditation. But effort while meditating is useful in three ways:

1. *As a stretch.* It prepares us to relax.
2. *To occupy the conscious mind.* Our minds are so used to being busy that we get restless doing nothing. So a simple action like looking at something may occupy our minds initially, i.e., stretch it, so that we may then let go, stop trying, and be free to contemplate.
3. *As effortless effort, the paradox of meditation.* A gentle, accepting effort, like blinking or sighing, may help to bring us into immediate awareness, but our bodies and minds may still be restless because our wills want to be in control. So we may need an incredibly gentle effort to remain open and stay aware, an effort as gentle as a falling snowflake (May, 1977, 88).

In the Helping Relationship

Effortless effort is our aim also as helpers. In the helping relationship, as in meditation, techniques and skills may be useful. It takes effort to acquire them, and to incorporate them into our total spontaneous response. But it is the same reality we are responding to both in formal meditation and in helping others, and the aim is the same: after learning the technique, after the stretch, our aim is to be aware of God, to relax, to free awareness, and to enlarge our capacity to make effective choices.

Distractions While Helping

We ourselves are one of the major distractions when we are helping others, as when we are meditating formally. Our aim as helpers is to be aware of the other person and to enable them to become more aware in their situation. We need to keep our attention on them, not on ourselves. We need to keep our thoughts and feelings from intruding into their world, and from distracting us. We distract ourselves:

1. When we get hooked into the sharer's situa-

tion and allow it to act as a link into our own experiences which take us into our own world.

2. When we stand back and start assessing the situation from our own world.

When we distract ourselves, we also distract the sharer:

1. In processing our own experiences we send unconscious sensory-based information which the sharer receives and so knows that we are not attending to them (session 4: exercise on attending/non-attending). Our sensory-based messages may also link the sharer into their own past experience and so distract them further.
2. We may intrude our own assessment into their situation, either by our sensory-based signals, e.g., frowning, wrinkling our nose; or verbally, by judging, advising, interpreting, etc.

Rapport to Minimize Distractions

Our helping becomes more effective, and both the sharer and we as helpers benefit, when we minimize distractions by directing our awareness outside ourselves to the sharer.

How we direct our awareness to the sharer is by gaining and maintaining rapport. Rapport is the ability to match, to respond symmetrically to the sharer's world (like dancing with a partner), not the ability to be sympathetic or liked. Skill in gaining, maintaining and regaining rapport is essential for us to help the sharer to achieve the growth and changes they want. The sharer is sending messages to us nonverbally as well as verbally. When we match up our words and behavior to their verbal and nonverbal communication, they feel really heard and understood. So rapport, matching, is a gentle way of entering their concept of the world.

Rapport-Building by Nonverbal Matching: Mirroring

Supportive Mirroring

We all mirror unconsciously to some extent; e.g., we sit in the same position as the other person. Mirroring is offering back to the sharer a part of their own nonverbal behavior, like a mirror, without attaching our meaning to it, because we know it carries significant unconscious meaning for them. Mirroring has the same effect as agreeing with the sharer verbally. It helps us to achieve a harmonious relationship, so that while we are mirroring we may even be able to disagree with what the person is saying and yet remain in rapport, remain in step with them.

It is a challenge for us to become more aware of the details of our own and other people's behavior; they indicate our different worlds. Then we may increasingly mirror them—their body postures, gestures, breathing rhythms, facial expressions; their voice tone, tempo and intonation patterns—in order to maintain rapport and help them to understand the meaning of their own messages which neither of us may consciously know.

We may start by discreetly mirroring one aspect and then adding another.

SHARING
Comment in the whole group.

PRACTICE
Mirroring exercises in twos:

(a) Direct mirroring. Having fun and exaggerating.

A leads, making any gestures, faces, postures, etc.

B stands opposite and makes a mirror image of A; i.e., goes in the same direction. Reverse roles.

(b) Cross-over mirroring; i.e., going in the opposite direction; e.g., by going to own left when A goes left. Reverse roles.

(c) Sitting down.

A talks; e.g., how they found the last exercise.

B mirrors as much as possible, developing awareness of mirroring body posture, gesture, facial expression and if possible breathing, voice tone, tempo and intonation patterns. Five minutes each. Reverse roles. Discuss.

SHARING
Discuss in the whole group.

INTRODUCTION

Mirroring Breathing

Noticing breathing may be as important when we are helping others as when we are formally meditating or relaxing. Breathing not only indicates our state of mind and body, it also directly affects it; e.g., we consciously change to deeper slower breathing to become more relaxed.

Just as in formal meditation we may alter our breathing to become more open and aware of reality, so in the helping relationship we may use breathing to become more aware of the other person's reality.

Breathing with the same rhythm is one way we often unconsciously gain rapport with someone.

PRACTICE
In twos, A talks.
B (a) adjusts breathing to A's rhythm.
(b) taps out A's breathing rhythm discreetly with foot or finger.
Reverse roles.

SHARING
Share comments in the whole group.

EXTENSION
Consciously we may use breathing to gain rapport with someone in two ways:

1. By adjusting our breathing to theirs to gain rapport.
   This could be for their benefit, so that we relate better to them, or for our own benefit; e.g., we might copy their deep slow breathing and so automatically become more relaxed.
2. By not adjusting our breathing to theirs and so not getting hooked into their feelings; e.g., if someone is angry or distressed and breathing heavily or fast, we may take a deep breath; we may switch into or maintain a relaxed slower breathing rhythm; we may unconsciously be breathing praying.

We may keep ourselves out and still use their breathing to gain rapport by matching it with our foot or unseen finger.

Some Tips and Traps in Mirroring

The more we practice nonverbal mirroring, the more we become aware of behaviors and rhythms, and whether two people are synchronized or not.

A useful place to look is the eyes, or the left eye. Our peripheral vision enables us to see much of the body and to notice muscle and color changes in the face.

Mirroring needs to be unobtrusive, or it may become mocking. Sometimes it is useful to do the opposite, i.e., cross-over mirroring. For example, if the person is shouting, we may speak very quietly or start at the same level and pitch, and then become quieter, and if we have good rapport, they may copy us and quiet down too. The danger to avoid in mirroring is getting hooked in to the sharer's feelings ourselves.

A good way of finding out whether we have achieved rapport is to change our pace, position, etc., and notice whether the other person follows. If they do not, then we need to do more matching, both nonverbal and verbal, to gain rapport.

D. CONCLUDING

RECOLLECTING
Quietly reflect and journal on the session.

EVALUATION
Briefly share as appropriate.

HOME PRACTICE
Practice breathing praying; being aware of our own and other people's breathing; building rapport by mirroring breathing and actions. Look over all the sessions so far.

LOOKING AHEAD
This session marks the end of the first part of our program: discerning God's Spirit in contemplation and crisis in nonverbal awareness skills. Next session we begin Part Two, discerning God's Spirit in formal and informal meditation and in verbal listening skills.

We shall briefly review Part One, consider what we mean by formal and informal meditation, try some semiformal mini-meditations, then consider how verbal matching may help us to discern God's Spirit by reflecting the actual word.

AFFIRMATION
Close with two verses of the hymn: "Breathe in me, Breath of God." Hold hands to say or sing the grace, making eye contact before breaking up.

PART TWO

Discerning God's Spirit
In Formal and Informal Meditation
In Verbal Listening Skills

Resumé of Part One
Formal, Informal, and Mini-meditations
Verbal Matching (1): Reflecting
the Actual Word

Note extra materials needed: e.g., box of matches and ash tray each; small mirror for each two people.

A. BECOMING AWARE OF WHERE WE ARE

RECOLLECTING
Being still in the presence of God.
Praying silently or aloud.

RECAP

Resumé of Part One

The aim of our whole program is to help us to discern God's Spirit, to become more aware of the ultimately real, to maintain a contemplative psychological approach.

In part one we have been considering what we mean by crisis and contemplation, and the basic nonverbal awareness skills in meditation and counseling. Our sessions have touched on:

Discerning God's presence through being open and gentle and aware;
Asking "Who am I?," and accepting and being true to ourselves;
Considering time and place, personal and inner space, posture, silence, touching, and linking;

Observing and interpreting eye positions and other sensory-based information;
Relaxing, deep breathing, and handling distractions, especially ourselves.

Last session we considered the importance of breathing in praying and in building rapport; and how to cut down on distractions and stay in the sharer's world when helping by matching or mirroring the sharer's nonverbal messages.

SHARING
Share anything important to us arising from Part One.

TODAY'S THEME
Part Two of our program continues aiming to help us to discern God's Spirit, both in formal and informal meditation and in verbal listening skills.

Today we shall practice semiformal silent mini-meditations (including watching a lighted match), and couple sharing and praying. We shall consider how verbal listening skills help us to discern God's Spirit in action, and how we may build rapport by matching words as well as nonverbal messages. We shall practice reflecting the sharer's actual words by reflectors, sub-summaries and summaries, and consider how so many of the words we use indicate our thinking mode—seeing, hearing, feeling, tasting, smelling.

B. BECOMING AWARE IN FORMAL PRAYING

INTRODUCTION

Each person needs a box of matches, ash tray, and hymn book open at the hymn, "O thou who camest from above." If necessary practice the tune, concentrating on the words, and each fitting the words in the way that helps us best to be aware of their meaning.

Formal and Informal Meditation

In each session in our program we set aside time for formal meditation, and then we aim to maintain openness and create links as we turn to informal meditation and the practical aspects of contemplation in crisis.

Informal meditation consists of using what is around and inside us as a link to make us gently aware, to realize the present moment. Formal meditation is using a definite time and place to still our mind and gently become aware (session 3). In the next few sessions we shall consider more systematically the ways we can use an object, image, activity and words in formal meditation, as a base to center our attention to help us become more open, more discerning of God's Spirit.

Semiformal Mini-Meditations

Mini-meditations can be simple fun ways to help us to wake up and be aware in two ways:

1. Making us aware of the immediate NOW in a busy day.
2. As practice for opening ourselves in formal meditation.

The leader will take us into three short semiformal mini-meditations, and then we shall all join in the hymn as another kind of praying.

PRACTICE

Relaxing and sitting quietly.
Mini-meditations:

(a) Now sitting very still. Becoming more aware of your body, quiet and solid like a mountain.

(b) Becoming more aware of your breathing. Being aware without altering or interfering. After being aware of breathing for a while, stopping for a few seconds in between breaths. Hearing the silence it leaves.

(c) Soon, light a match; watching the flame as it burns; slowly blowing it out and savoring being aware. Now lighting the match.

Sing the hymn: e.g., "O thou who camest from above."

Silence and journaling.

SHARING

In twos share anything from our journals, any thanks and needs.

Each in turn have five minutes to share and five minutes to pray and be prayed for.

Sharing in the whole group.

EXTENSION

Mini-meditations

The following semiformal mini-meditations are taken directly from May (1977, 27–28). We can make up our own, too.

1. Light a match. Watch the flame. Just look at it as it burns. Then slowly blow it out and savor your awareness.
2. When you hear some music, let your breathing go with it for a while.
3. Look at your breathing. Just that. No interference. Simply watch. After you've been breathing for a while, stop for a few seconds, in between breaths. Hear the silence.
4. Look at a spot on the wall for a few seconds. Then close your eyes. See the emptiness.
5. Memorize a little child's prayer or song. In the midst of something very adult and important, recite it gently to yourself.
6. Sit very still. See your body quiet and solid, like a mountain.
7. If a breeze blows past you, stop for a moment and feel it.
8. As you walk, breathe in time to your steps.
9. Sit with your eyes closed. Begin counting slowly, silently in your mind. Picture the numbers; imagine what they look like as you count. Then stop! Immediately, be aware of the absolute stillness.

10. As you're driving, sense your hands holding the wheel, your body responding to the traffic.
11. When you pull in to park and turn off the engine, listen to the silence. Or when you turn off the TV or the shower. When any sound stops, just listen to what's left behind it.
12. Each time you breathe out, make a soft humming sound that lasts as long as your breath. Hear this. Then stop making it with your voice and just make it silently in your mind. Then stop that, too, and listen.
13. Rest your eyes for a minute. Check out the back of your eyelids.
14. As you eat, watch your hands.
15. Walk, very slowly, around the room. Pay attention to your body, how it feels. Then sit down and move your hands slowly in front of you. Put them in different positions. Sense the space between and around them. Then let them rest in your lap, close your eyes and sigh. Long, slow, deep.
16. Close your eyes. Watch your thoughts go by like clouds, just passing. Or see yourself as a hollow tube through which your thoughts and senses pass. In one end and out the other. Just watch them going through.
17. Look at the sky now and then.

C. BECOMING AWARE IN COUNSELING SKILLS

INTRODUCTION

Discerning God's Spirit in Verbal Listening Skills

Verbal listening skills are crucial to our helping relationship. Helping the sharer to explore their own words and metaphors is a key to recognizing how God's Spirit may be working. "We discover ourselves with our own words" (Thayer, 1985, 104).

When we come to the verbal part of listening it is essential to remember that we are still listening; that is, we need to stay in the sharer's concept of the world and themselves, stay in their experience and awareness. Our aim is to help them to get or keep in touch with their own inner depths,

the center of their interior castle of awareness, as Saint Teresa puts it (Teresa of Avila, *The Interior Castle*). It is in their own inner depths that they may be helped to resolve their problems, to know what they really want and to experience God, to discern God's Spirit, to realize God's presence, rather than to talk about God.

We shall consider a continuum of verbal listening skills which aim to make both helper and sharer more aware, and to enable the helper to stay in the sharer's experience. The skills are:

Reflectors (mirroring the exact word)
Sub-summaries and summaries (mirroring the key thoughts and feelings)
Using words in the same thinking mode (e.g., matching metaphors)
Open Questions (leaving the answer open)
Outcome Model—open questions helping the person identify what they really want
Specifiers—open questions linking words and experience more closely

SHARING
Any comments.

INTRODUCTION

Verbal Matching (1): Reflecting the Actual Word by Reflectors, Sub-summaries and Summaries

Just as we may gain rapport by matching the other person's nonverbal behavior, i.e., mirroring, so we may also gain rapport by matching their words.

We may match words in two ways:

1. Reflecting (mirroring) back the actual word used.
2. Using words in the same sensory thinking mode, e.g., matching the metaphor.

In this session we shall practice mirroring back the sharer's actual words.

PRACTICE
Reflectors.

In twos. Each couple needs a mirror. A, using sensory-based information only, not interpretation, describes B's mouth (or face). B then looks at their own mouth in the mirror and notes the difference. Reverse roles.

SHARING
Briefly discuss the experience.

EXTENSION
If we try to describe their mouth to our partner in our own words, using sensory-based information without interpreting, it is very difficult for us to convey an accurate factual picture. By holding up a mirror, they can see themselves for themselves. This is what we are doing nonverbally when we mirror back the sensory-based information we receive: holding up a mirror for them to become aware of their nonverbal messages. And this is what we can do verbally when we repeat a key word immediately: hold up a mirror for them to become aware of their verbal messages.

Reflecting the Actual Word

People are often unaware of many of the words they use and of their intensity; but as with nonverbal behavior, their words may carry significant unconscious meanings for them. So we can reflect (mirror back) their own key words to help them become more aware and lead them further into their own inner world where they may meet with God. Many key words express feelings; some in feeling words, e.g., depressed, angry, guilty; some in metaphors using other modes, e.g., disgusted, made me feel sick, everything was black, gloomy, clamoring.

A Reflector

A reflector, a close-up reflection, as in a small mirror, is an immediate repetition of a strong feeling or key thought, using only one word or short phrase; e.g.,
Sharer: "I was thunderstruck when . . ."
Listener: "Thunderstruck."
A reflector needs to be repeated in the same tone and with the same emphasis (which shows we are listening); not as a question (which thrusts the listener into the situation).
Other examples of key feeling words would be flabbergasted, furious, knocked sideways, ecstatic.

PRACTICE
Suggest other feeling words or metaphors which we might reflect.

In twos. A says one sentence with a word in it describing their own feelings. (Remembering that we are interested in the inner world of A, and not what their friend or great-aunt Polly said or did.)
B reflects the feeling word.
A continues and then cuts the sentence.
Reverse roles a couple of times.
It may seem odd at first, but like walking or driving a car, it may become automatic.

SHARING
In the whole group share how we got on.

INTRODUCTION
Sub-summaries and summaries are a development of reflectors. It is often useful for us to make a little summary of the important part of what has been said—not a precis of everything.

A Sub-summary

A sub-summary is often an extended reflector using the sharer's own words; our less immediate response with more perspective. It emphasizes a strong feeling or key thought, and may link this key feeling or thought concisely to relevant outside material: e.g.,

"So when she said that, you were furious."
"So you were stunned when he walked out."

The sharer knows the circumstances (the outside material) so we concentrate on highlighting the thoughts and feelings (the inner material).
Unless some time has passed, we need to avoid repeating a whole sentence (parroting).
Useful phrases are:

"So, you are . . . when . . ."
"So, you felt . . . when . . ."
"So you're telling me . . ."
"You're saying then . . ."
"Let's see if I've got this straight. . . ."

A sub-summary covers what has been said recently.

PRACTICE
In the whole group:
(a) One person shares two or three sentences

—a very brief situation including feeling words, perhaps hassles today before getting here, a minor crisis. We need permission beforehand to cut in and stop them; i.e., we are avoiding being hooked into their story as we are practicing a particular skill.

(b) We each jot down how we might summarize it; then share and discuss the suggestions. If necessary, repeat the exercise to make sure that everyone has the idea.

In threes practice very briefly, taking turns at being observer, listener and sharer. The sharer needs to use feeling words for the listener to practice using in the summary.

SHARING
Comment in the whole group.

EXTENSION
We use a sub-summary:

1. When the sharer is stuck, going round in circles, or going on and on (we can cut in).
2. When we are getting confused or feel we should say something.

A Summary

A summary is similar to a sub-summary. It may cover key words from the beginning, or just highlight the conclusion. It needs to be short, e.g., "So although at first you felt really angry, now you can see it a bit from her point of view too."

"So now you have decided to try, and you feel happy about going ahead."

We use a summary when the sharer has finished or when it's time to stop.

Introduction to Using Words
In The Same Sensory Thinking Mode

INTRODUCTION
Let's consider in more detail the kind of words that the sharer may be using, and what we may learn from them about the way that the sharer is thinking, and how we as helpers need to think and speak in order to gain and maintain rapport with the sharer.

A person's words reveal their sensory thinking modes, just as their eye positions do.

Many ordinary words are actually metaphors,

TABLE 3
COMMON SENSORY AND UNSPECIFIED
THINKING MODE WORDS

Seeing	Hearing	Feeling	Tasting Smelling	Unspecified
see	hear	touch	taste	think
clear	listen	smooth	flavor	know
perspective	talk	handle	relish	understand
picture	loud	grasp	bite	remember
hazy	amplify	firm	aftertaste	believe
focus	sounds	fight	smell	consider
viewpoint	like	rough	scent	change
illustrate	silence	concrete	essence	
show	tone	hurt	whiff	nice
black	quiet	penetrate	savor	trusting
blue	say	absorb	tinge	respectful
obscure	harmony	cutting	tongue	
dim	noisy	creeps	odor	
look	call	warm	pungent	
image	told	hang in	sweet	
		apprehend	bitter	
			stinks	
			sour	

and it helps the sharer if we stay with their metaphor or way of thinking, and avoid mixing it with our own. Mixing the metaphor may confuse the sharer; it may interrupt (F) their own way of thinking.

Next session we shall go further (F) into using words in the same sensory thinking mode. Table 3 gives some common words listed downwards in their thinking mode.

I hope that Table 3 helps you to get the hang of it (F). If it does not sound easy (H), think about it (U). Next session it may be clearer to you (S) and soon you may relish (T) the idea of scenting out (Sm) different metaphors.

PRACTICE
Suggest other common words and their categories.

D. CONCLUDING

RECOLLECTING
Quiet reflecting and journaling on the session.
EVALUATION
Brief evaluation and comment.
HOME PRACTICE
Try out some of the mini-meditations. Practice reflecting key words and feelings with reflectors

and summaries, becoming more aware of how many of our words are metaphors based on our senses of seeing, hearing, feeling, tasting, and smelling.

LOOKING AHEAD

Next session we shall consider centering ourselves using a base to free our awareness. We shall practice with a visual base, think about bases in the helping relationship, and continue our verbal matching by using the same metaphors and thinking mode.

AFFIRMATION

Close with the hymn: "O thou who camest from above," and a group hug as appropriate.

SESSION 9

Centering
Centering with a Visual Base
Bases in the Helping Relationship
Verbal Matching (2) Using the Same Thinking Mode

Note extra materials needed: candle (if not usually in center), matches, small torn corner of paper, Cameron-Bandler's *Solutions.*

A. BECOMING AWARE OF WHERE WE ARE

RECOLLECTING
Being still in the presence of God.
Praying silently and aloud.
Hymn: e.g., "Be thou my vision." Omit v.4.

RECAP
Last session after a review of Part One: discerning God's Spirit in contemplation and crisis and in nonverbal listening skills, we began Part Two: discerning God's Spirit in formal and informal meditation and in verbal listening skills. We practiced building rapport by matching a person's words, through reflecting the actual word used, in a reflector, sub-summary or summary. We also started to identify the thinking mode of different words, i.e., whether they are seeing, hearing, feeling, smelling, tasting, or unspecified.

SHARING
Sharing our reflections, reactions and progress since last session.

TODAY'S THEME
Today's theme is centering and bases: a simple meditation centering sequence with any base; practicing with a visual base; the importance of bases in the helping relationship; and rapport-building by verbal matching, this time using words in the same sensory thinking mode and translating.

B. BECOMING AWARE IN FORMAL PRAYING

INTRODUCTION

Centering

Centering is aiming to become immediately open to what is by using some object, image or activity as a pivot or base to center our attention on. This base is useful to bring our attention back from all the past and future experiences usually going on in our minds. Centering concentrates and calms and deepens our attention so that we may experience God in and through the present moment, may more fully experience the fleeting eternal now. The base we choose gives us something for our wandering minds to return to. As soon as we are aware and open we may forget the base; it is only a stepping-off place for the freedom and openness that may enable us to be aware of God, the reality beyond all images and objects. Attaching too much significance to the base may lead us to identify the base with God, which is idolatry.

Almost anything may be used as a center or base, as in our mini-meditations (session 8). We commonly use bases in all our sensory channels, e.g., S: pictures, images; H: music, sounds; F: breathing, special buildings; Sm: incense; T: bread and wine.

A Simple Meditation Sequence with Any Base (based on May, 1977, 103–04)

1. Selecting my time and place.
2. Finding a comfortable, relaxed position.
3. Stretching and relaxing my body, taking enough time to do this well.
4. Paying attention to my breathing.
5. Starting by centering attention on the object or activity I have chosen, using very little effort. Whatever base I choose, giving myself to it. Deciding how I am going to start, then doing it, and being within it.
6. Letting my mind be. Using no effort and stopping trying to meditate. As I am relaxing into it, letting myself be carried, guided, embraced.
7. Coming back to the base whenever I need to; i.e., when I am aware that I am struggling or that my mind has wandered.
8. Letting go of any part of the meditative process whenever I can while still staying clear-minded and wide awake. Becoming simpler. Returning to the basic practice whenever I need to.
9. When I have finished, stretching, relaxing again and letting my consciousness flow into informal meditation for the rest of the day.

SHARING
Share as appropriate from our own experience.

INTRODUCTION

Centering with a Visual Base

There are two ways of using a visual base for meditation:

1. Looking at any object, image or person
2. Making and keeping a visual image in our minds.

1. Looking at an Object

We may use almost anything as a visual base. Traditional examples are a candle, cross, fish, picture of Jesus or a saint, an icon, a star of David, star, sky, sea, a pebble, clouds, smoke from incense, our hand. Objects of special significance may trap rather than free our awareness. We may start to think about or work on the object in some way, so the simpler the object, the better. Our aim is to attend to the object only until our awareness is free, and we are open to what is happening in and around us at the moment. As we look at the object it may appear to change, and we need to let this happen without getting excited, worried or involved.

SHARING
Share ideas, queries and experience as appropriate.

PRACTICE

Centering with a Visual Base

An object such as a candle may be very rich and useful, but also may have a host of associations, so we shall use a relatively meaningless torn corner of paper.

The leader substitutes a torn corner of paper for whatever may usually be used as a centering object. We meditate, using the relatively meaningless paper as a base for five minutes. Journal as desired.

SHARING
Share in the whole group.
In twos:
(a) share anything from the meditation, or from our journaling since last session
(b) share thanks and needs
Each in turn share briefly and then be prayed with. Divide our time equally.
Share in the group.

EXTENSION

2. Making a Mental Visual Image

One way to make a visual image is to look at an object and then close our eyes and remember it.

Putting our eyes up to our seeing remembered position (to our left if we are right handed), may help us to imagine and visualize the object. Positioning our eyes may also help when we want to make our own mental image without looking at an object, putting our eyes up to the visual creating (constructing) position (to the right for right-handed people), when we want to create a visual image rather than to remember one.

One visual image is a circle of light, like a crown, above our heads, enlightening us and then our surroundings with the light of compassion. Because a visual mental image is more intimate, it is wise to choose one that we want to become part of us. Whatever we choose as a visual base, it is only a base to come home to, a stepping-off place to openness.

C. BECOMING AWARE IN COUNSELING SKILLS

INTRODUCTION

Bases in the Helping Relationship

Any of the meditations may be excellent practice for the openness necessary for us to be effective helpers. In the helping relationship our aim is to use all we receive from the other person, verbally and nonverbally, all we see, hear, feel, smell and taste, as the base or stepping-off point for being aware of what is happening in the person and how God is present in that action. Indeed, in any effective relationship we need to deal with information in this way, as only a base.

We are centering our attention on the sharer's world, and helping them to center their attention on their key verbal and nonverbal messages as a base for them to go beyond their feelings and metaphors, beyond their sensory perceptions, and to discover for themselves the deeper meaning and significance of what is being shared.

As we accompany the sharer on their journey of becoming more aware of the pattern and purpose of their life, we too may become more open to ultimate values, to God at work.

In the helping relationship we center our attention on a particular situation; in our sessions, in order to deepen our awareness we divide our experience into different chunks. But essentially any actions, techniques of meditation, or counseling skills may be thought of as bases, ways to center our attention on our own inner world or on the inner world of the sharer.

SHARING
Comment as appropriate.

PRACTICE

Reflectors

In the whole group share how we got on practicing reflectors and summaries. If needed, have another demonstration in the group, each writing down a summary, and then discussing it in the group.

Verbal Matching (2): Using Words in the Same Sensory Thinking Mode

INTRODUCTION

The Purpose of Matching the Sensory Word

Most people want you to communicate in the language of their internal world, which they indicate by the sensory words they use: seeing, hearing, feeling, tasting, smelling. They usually use one sense category more often and more fully than the others, and so understand the world and represent it mainly in that sense category, e.g., I see it now; I hear what you are saying; I've grasped the idea.

When we match their words by using words in the same sensory thinking mode, we are using a powerful way of building rapport, i.e., of establishing effective communication and understanding. Conversely when we mismatch them, consciously or unconsciously, we are using a powerful tool which may alienate people. Mismatching is a big trap for counselors commonly taught to rephrase the sharer's communication in the counselor's own words.

PRACTICE
Practice in whole group recognising and matching the channel used; e.g., is someone willing to describe for us a recent vivid experience?

What mode are the words used in that last sentence? How can it be put in a different mode or be unspecified? For example, is someone willing to share a recent meaningful experience.

While one member is talking, we pick out the sensory words, and say which thinking mode they are.

An example of a couple speaking in two different modes may be found in Cameron-Bandler, *Solutions*, 41–42, with a further example, 43. If possible, read and discuss it.

In the whole group, A uses one sentence with sensory words, and B replies in the same mode. Practice with different group members until everyone has the idea.

In twos or threes if time permits, with one observer each time. Remember to listen very carefully in all exercises to the instructions and concentrate on the particular area for practicing.

A shares an experience in one or two sentences only, using sensory words.

B replies or continues in the same mode for one or two sentences.

Stop and discuss whether we remained in the same sensory mode. Then reverse roles.

SHARING
Discuss in the whole group.

Translating

INTRODUCTION
The sensory words people use may be a significant factor in whether or not they get on together. They may be using a different language to organize and express their experience without realizing it. Because people relate more effectively when they are using words in the same sensory thinking mode, we as helpers need to be able to represent various experiences in any sensory mode, and to translate experiences from one mode to another. Table 4 gives examples of words which express similar experiences in different sensory modes.

If someone is using unspecified words, e.g., think, remember, we may enable them to get more in touch with their own experience if we ask them how specifically do they think, understand, remember. Their eye positions may give us the answer, but the question helps them as well as us to be more aware of how they organise and

communicate their own experience (session 15: specifiers).

PRACTICE

Practice in Matching and Translating our own Sensory Words

This practice will also indicate which is our favorite (easiest) and which our least used thinking system (the one we find hardest).

First match and then translate into other sensory thinking modes.

Examples:

1. What she said is so vivid in my mind.
   Match: S. Her words are so clear to me.
   Translation: H. I can hear her saying it.
   F. What she said has stuck fast in my mind.
2. John doesn't listen to me.
   Match: H. John goes deaf when I talk.
   Translation: S. John only sees it his way.
   F. John blocks out what I say.
3. Jean gets churned up in a crowd.
   Match: F. Jean gets agitated and nervous in a crowd.
   Translation: S. Jean can't focus in a crowd.
   H. Jean's alarm bells ring in a crowd.
4. My boss walks all over me.
5. I feel no one appreciates me.
6. I can't imagine the future.
7. She's a sweet person.
8. I'm playing this by ear.
9. I ask myself "How did I ever get into this?"
10. Something tells me I'm making a mistake.
11. I need to get hold of what he means.
12. I keep stubbing my toe on obstacles.
13. He paints a clear picture of disaster ahead.
14. It smells fishy to me.

EXTENSION

Using our Nonverbal and Verbal Matching Skills

In the later part of this session we have concentrated on how to build rapport by matching and how to translate our own experience into various sensory thinking modes.

It may surprise us to become aware of how

TABLE 4
EXAMPLES OF TRANSLATING SENSORY WORDS

Seeing	Hearing	Feeling
light	harmony	love
darkness	discord	fear
total darkness	silence	numbness
see red	make a row about	hit the roof
look at it differently	out of tune	head in a different direction
imagine	orchestrate	construct

many common words and phrases are metaphors, expressing ideas and feelings in the various sensory modes. Once we realize the power of communicating in the same sensory mode (mainly matching metaphors), and the effort involved in practicing translating even our own experience into various channels, we may more readily appreciate the simplicity and power of using reflectors, i.e., using the same word immediately or in a summary, when we are listeners (session 8).

When we do use our own words, we need to ensure that we are matching the sharer's thinking mode, and translating our own to theirs. This matching and translating will be especially important when we come to part three of our program—verbal skills for accepting, forgiving and changing ourselves and others—in which we as helpers use our own words.

Building rapport by matching is more than matching nonverbally or verbally, i.e., mirroring actions, intonation, etc. (session 7), and reflecting the actual word and matching our words to their words (sessions 8 and 9). Once we become aware of the sharer's nonverbal and verbal communication, we may match both with either. We may translate our words to match their nonverbal communications; e.g., their eye positions will indicate their thinking mode just as their words do. We may also learn to use our own nonverbal communication of eye position, voice tone, etc, to match the sharer's sensory words, and so perhaps help them to use a certain thinking mode.

Some of this we do naturally. It takes practice to become more aware and proficient; concentrating on one aspect at a time helps us to incorporate it into our own skills.

For a satisfactory relationship we need to be constantly building rapport; we need to gain, maintain and regain rapport throughout. So we need to be using all the sharer's communication as a base for being aware of what is happening and how God is at work.

D. CONCLUDING

RECOLLECTING
Quiet reflecting and journaling.

EVALUATION
Brief evaluation and comment.

HOME PRACTICE
Practice centering with a visual base; matching the sensory mode of the sharer's words, and translating them. Try ourselves out on any of the examples we have not finished in session time.

LOOKING AHEAD
Next session we shall practice centering with sound as a base, and consider open questions.

AFFIRMATION
As we think of centering with objects, ourselves, others or words as only a base, let's sing a hymn such as "Teach me my God and King," vv. 1 and 2 only.

SESSION 10

Centering with Sound as a Base; Questions

Note extra materials needed: something to make a repetitive sound, such as a gong, triangle, or drum.

A. BECOMING AWARE OF WHERE WE ARE

RECOLLECTING
   Being still in the presence of God.
   Praying silently or aloud.
   Hymn if desired; e.g., "At the name of Jesus," or any hymn using name or names for God.

RECAP
   Last session we considered centering with a base, practicing a simple meditation using a visual base. We linked it with using all our senses and skills in the helping relationship as a base to being aware of what is happening in the sharer and of how God is present in them and in their situation. We then explored the importance of matching the sharer's thinking mode and words to keep us in their world.

SHARING
   Brief sharing.

TODAY'S THEME
   Today we shall practice centering with sound as a base, and then go on to consider various kinds of questions we may find useful when we do need to speak, and want to stay in the sharer's world.

B. BECOMING AWARE IN FORMAL PRAYING

INTRODUCTION
   Last session we practiced meditating with a visual base as a method of centering our attention and opening ourselves to the present moment. Now we consider sound as a base, as a pivot for our attention until we are ready for our awareness to be freed, open to reality, to God in the present. As with a visual base, almost any sound may be used as a base for our attention.

   Today let's use a repetitive sound.

PRACTICE
   Silence, sitting relaxing and breathing deeply.
   The leader strikes the instrument regularly every few seconds for about five minutes.
   We use the sound as a base to open ourselves more to God's Spirit.
   When we have finished, journaling as appropriate.

SHARING
   In twos in turn, each share from our journaling, thanks, and needs, and pray, using the sharer's words as appropriate. Remembering to listen, and to share the time equally.
   In the whole group share anything important.

EXTENSION
   There are two ways that sound may be used as a base:

1. Making Sounds

   Making sounds aloud. An example is humming with each outbreath, making it a monotone. The idea is not to make a melody but to pay attention to letting ourselves make the sound.
   Making sounds silently. An example is humming as above, but silently in our mind.
   Chanting. Any repetitive chant.

2. Listening to Sounds

Specific sounds. We may pay attention to listening to a specific sound, either one which we are making (e.g., humming) or one outside ourselves. Music is tricky; it can easily trap our awareness, link us into other associations, or lead us into fantasy. However, a very simple tune may be useful either as a base or as a combination base to keep our breathing or body movements in time.

Sounds in general. We may pay attention to whatever sounds occur, hearing them without labeling them. Using sounds as a base may be helpful in noisy settings so that sounds which might be considered distractions become a focus for meditation.

Mantras

A mantra is a specific sound, word or phrase used for meditation; e.g., the rosary, Hail Mary and Our Father may be used as mantras. Examples of other mantras are word sounds that mean peace; e.g., peace, shalom; the names of God in any language; Kyrie eleison (Lord, have mercy); Maranatha (come); pure root sounds like om, ah, hu; or any sounds or phrases that come to mind.

We choose a mantra to use as a base for a time of contemplative openness, to enable us to be simple, open, present now, taking one word or phrase and repeating it quietly over and over. It is something to center our attention on until we are able to be free and open. When our attention strays, we may bring it gently back to the base.

We need to choose a mantra carefully; one to keep us awake and aware, relaxed without going to sleep. Also, in time it may penetrate so deeply into our unconscious that it becomes part of our being; e.g., the Jesus Prayer, which is known as the prayer of the heart. "Lord Jesus Christ, Son of God, have mercy on me a sinner," or "Lord Jesus Christ have mercy on me," or "Lord have mercy" (session 7). Mantras can be recited aloud or silently. Once again, too much attention to the base will trap rather than free our awareness. The way to tell whether our awareness is being freed or trapped is to stop for a moment and check what we are aware of.

SHARING
Comment as appropriate.

C. BECOMING AWARE IN COUNSELING SKILLS

INTRODUCTION

Questions

Throughout this program we are aiming to increase our awareness, to listen, to center our attention on the sharer's concept of the world and to avoid advising, judging and interpreting. After considering various nonverbal awareness and rapport-building skills, including matching with nonverbal mirroring, we turned to verbal matching by using reflectors and summaries, by matching words in the same sensory thinking mode, and by translating from one mode to another.

In the listening situation, silence, encouragers, reflectors, sub-summaries and summaries are our basic tools. There comes a time in listening, however, when we may need to say something which is not a straight reflector or summary of the sharer's words. One of the most useful ways to speak and still to remain in the sharer's world is through asking open questions.

It is important to realize that when we ask questions we are influencing the direction of the sharing, so we need to be aware of what we are doing and how we are doing it. Our own view of the sharer's world, of our own world and of the helping relationship influences our input.

As Christian helpers, we need to be as open as possible. We are practicing openness in our formal prayer time and ordinary life so that we become more in touch with where the Spirit is moving, so that we can be as open and nondirective as possible with others. We aim to go beyond our own thinking about where the sharer may be going, we aim to avoid intruding our own ideas and judgments, we aim to become aware of the sharer's world, of where the sharer may move, and to enable the sharer to discern whatever way the Spirit is moving in their own situation.

Questions may be open or closed. When we are wording our questions, we may stay in the sharer's world more easily if we mirror their exact words or match the sharer's sensory words.

Closed Questions

Questions are closed questions when they leave the sharer little choice of answer. They may be useful to provide information for the questioner, but they may not help the sharer. With closed questions there tends to be a "right" or "wrong" answer; often the answer is "yes," "no," or one or two words only, with little room for sharing; e.g., "How much did it cost? Where have you been?"

"Why" questions tend to alter the sharer's direction, to lead away from feelings, to interpret. "Why's do not make us wiser."

Open Questions

Open questions are questions which leave the sharer a choice in the way they answer and where they start. "How" and "what" are useful words; "where" and "when" may also be useful; e.g., as door openers: "How're things? How's life? How are you doing? What's on your mind?"

PRACTICE

We may offer various questions, and decide whether they are more open or closed. Later we shall consider various ways that they may be open or closed.

EXTENSION

Open questions leave the sharer free to explore their thoughts and feelings and come to their own conclusions. Open questions may be useful to connect the sharer's outside material with their inner feelings; e.g., "How do you feel about that?" "Where does that leave you?" "What's your reaction to that?" "So . . . ?" "But . . . ?" "And . . . ?"

PRACTICE

Each of us may like to give an example of an open question. Jot it down so that we are free to concentrate on the other questions.

In twos, while still in the main circle, A asks an open question. B answers but stops in mid-flow after not more than one sentence. Both check

TABLE 5
CLOSED AND OPEN QUESTIONS

	Closed	Open
Wording	answer yes, no or limited:	wider scope for answer:
	e.g., Have you heard from Mary?	e.g., What news of Mary?
	Do you . . . ? Are you . . . ? Is it?	
Subject	restricted subject: e.g., What news of Mary?	wide subject: e.g., What's new?
Outer or inner	Seeking outside information:	sharer free to explore inner feelings & thoughts:
	e.g., When did you hear?	e.g., What's your reaction?
	So what did you do then?	So where are you now? How do you feel about it?
	Why? tends to lead away from feelings	How do you feel? What do you want? So . . . ? And . . . ?

whether the question was open. Take turns and repeat the practice two or three times.

In the whole group share how we got on.

Still in the whole group, practice turning closed questions into open ones: e.g.:

(a) Did you enjoy it last night?
    ——How did you enjoy it last night?
(b) Do you like . . . ?
    ——What do you think of . . . ?
(c) Can I help you?
    ——What can I do to help you?
    ——How can I help you?
(d) Did you get angry?
    ——What did you feel like?
    ——What did you do?

EXTENSION

How Open or Closed?

Questions vary from very closed to wide open. They can be open or closed in three main ways: in their form of wording, in their breadth of subject-matter, and in their direction to outside information or to the inner world of the sharer. Table 5 may make these ways clearer.

Inner questions with open wording and a wide subject or no set subject can be very useful in helping the sharer to become aware of their inner reality.

When to Use Open Questions

As well as door openers at the beginning, open questions are useful after a sub-summary and silence. We need awareness and discernment to know which questions to ask.

Practicing Questioning

If we tend to ask lots of questions in ordinary conversation, it may be helpful to practice avoiding all questions again, using only basic listening skills, until we become aware of how open or closed the questions are that come into our mind. Then we may practice using open questions appropriately.

SHARING

Make sure we understand the main points about open questions.

INTRODUCTION

Questions in Problem Solving: In Reaching an Effective Outcome

We as helpers may enable the sharer to reach an effective outcome by only using our basic nonverbal and verbal skills without using any questions. However, our open questions may help the sharer to explore their own thoughts and feelings.

After whatever preliminaries may be needed, open questions on the outcome the sharer wants, such as: "What do you want?" "What are you going to do?," may lead toward solving a problem, i.e., toward an effective outcome. It is usually far more productive to concentrate on the change that the sharer wants rather than on the problem. The sharer may well need us to help them in identifying the changes they want to make.

TABLE 6

AN OUTCOME MODEL: QUESTIONS TO HELP IDENTIFY AND ACHIEVE A GOAL (BASED ON CAMERON-BANDLER, 1985, 85–91)

1. What do you want? i.e., the outcome. (not "What is your problem?") The desired outcome may change.	The outcome wanted must be (a) stated positively (not "I don't want . . ." or "I want to be less . . .") (b) What the sharer may do (not someone else).
2. How will you know when you have it? What will you look, sound, feel like, do, etc?	If sharer can't construct a situation, ask them to remember a time when they had it, or to think of someone who has it and step inside that person (session 26) so that they experience the new internal state and behavior.
3. Where, when, how, do you want this, or will you do this? Always? Immediately?	The desired changes need to be appropriate to the context
4. How will your life be different? How appropriate are the changes for your well-being? How will you keep what you like about what you have now?	The changes need to retain positive features of the present state; otherwise the sharer may become too aggressive and end up alone.
5. What do you need to do to get what you want? What is stopping you?	The sharer may need to realize what is stopping them (i.e., a problem), and then again to ask what they will need (a positive outcome).
6. Do you still want it? Is it worth it?	The sharer may no longer want the original specified outcome, but another.

Process Rather than Content

As helpers we may not need to know anything about the sharer's subject matter (content). In crisis, when time may be limited, it is especially useful to remember to concentrate on the sharer's thinking process rather than on the content. The process is the method, the way the sharer is thinking, the way their mind is working. The content is what they are thinking about.

An Outcome Model

It is important for us all to realize that, much as we may want to, we cannot change other people. But we ourselves may change, and our changing may then enable others to change.

The outcome model in Table 6 provides a useful flexible framework of questions to help the sharer to identify the changes that they want, and what they need to do to achieve them. It may take considerable time to work through the various questions. It is important for the answers to be positive and specified (session 15: specifiers). In Part Three we shall consider further ways of helping the sharer to achieve the desired changes that have been identified.

In other words, what, how, where and when, how different and appropriate, what action, is it what you want?

SHARING

Share any comments and experience.

PRACTICE

If there is time, as a demonstration in the whole group, one person may offer to present a small problem, and the leader or another group member may work through some or all of the questions.

SHARING

Share any comments.

D. CONCLUDING

RECOLLECTING

Quiet reflecting and journaling.

EVALUATION

Brief evaluation and comment on the session.

HOME PRACTICE

Practice using sound as a base to open our awareness. Notice what kind of questions we usually ask, and practice open ones. Go over the outcome model. Revise this term's sessions, including the basic material in session 1.

LOOKING AHEAD

Next time, after further consideration of breathing as a base, we shall briefly review how far we have come this term, and practice recording and evaluating a practice listening session, using what we have learned. We shall end with a group centering on our purpose as Christian servants, in a handwashing ceremony.

Please bring a written evaluation of the program so far, based on the evaluation guide after session 33.

AFFIRMATION

Close with praying, a suitable verse of the hymn chosen, and the grace.

SESSION 11

Centering with Breathing as a Base
Revision and Evaluation of Term 1
Recording and Evaluating a Practice
Verbal Listening Session
Group Centering with Ceremony as a Base

Note extra materials needed: worksheets, cassette recorder, cassette, extension cord; jug, water, basin, towel.

A. BECOMING AWARE OF WHERE WE ARE

RECOLLECTING
  Being still in the presence of God.

RECAP
  Last session we centered with sound as a base, practiced open questions, and considered an outcome model, i.e., a progression of open questions to help the sharer identify, assess, and then act toward achieving a satisfying goal.

SHARING
  Share briefly now, or wait till the evaluation.

TODAY'S THEME
  Today, after centering briefly with our breathing, we shall skim over the ground we have covered this term, and share our comments and evaluations. We'll have a demonstration of how to record a practice listening session and use the evaluation worksheets. To end the term, we'll join in a ceremony of group centering. The one suggested here is a ceremonial handwashing, as a reminder that we are here to serve each other and be hands of God (session 2).

B. and C. BECOMING AWARE IN FORMAL PRAYING AND IN COUNSELING SKILLS

Breathing as a Base

INTRODUCTION
  In the last two sessions we have used sight and sound as a base for meditation. Today we shall first have a little more practice using our breathing as a base.

PRACTICE
  Let's meditate silently with our breathing as a base to bring our attention to the present.
  Being aware of our natural breathing, watching, hearing and feeling it as it continues naturally.
  Attending to our breathing for as long as it takes to free our awareness and bring it back to the here and now.

SHARING
  Sharing in the whole group how we got on, and any other ways we have used breathing as a base.

EXTENSION

Paying attention to our breathing, or using sights and sounds as a base may seem awkward, artificial, or even impossible, but, as in learning to swim or in our helping skills, practicing develops our confidence and ability. So our formal meditation may gradually free us to become more aware and open to the whole of life.

There are three main ways of using breathing as a base:

1. Attending to Our Breathing

(a) Using our natural breathing as our base, being aware of it by seeing, hearing, feeling it without interfering; like watching the rise and fall of a butterfly's wings as it rests on a flower.

(b) Seeing or feeling our stomach or chest rising and falling with each breath, again being aware without altering it.

2. Counting Our Breaths

(a) Silently counting each breath in or out, e.g., counting up to three or up to ten breaths and then starting again, counting the same number.

(b) We can combine our counting with visualizing the numbers, or recalling the sound of them.

3. Regulating Our Breathing

(a) Letting our breath fill first our stomach, then our chest; emptying our chest first, then our stomach, as in yoga.

(b) Timing the breathing to our heartbeat.

(c) Breathing in and out to full capacity, very slowly to avoid hyperventilation.

SHARING

Share as appropriate.

Evaluations

INTRODUCTION

The aim of this Spiritually Aware Pastoral Care program is to enable us as Christian helpers to become more aware of God's Spirit.

In Part One we considered what we mean by contemplative awareness and crisis: we thought of our hands as reminders; asked "Who am I?" "Where am I?," considering time, space, silence, touching and posture in our formal praying and when helping.

We thought about distractions, and how we may minimize our links with our own past distracting us and the sharer, by attending to and accurately reflecting their sensory-based eye and body information and their words in reflectors, summaries and thinking mode, and by using appropriate open questions when we do need to say something.

So far, in formal and mini-meditations we have practiced centering with breathing, a visual object and sound as a base.

The physical bases and our nonverbal and verbal listening skills are all intended to be used only as a starting point to help us to become more aware of God's Spirit at work in our own lives, in the life of the sharer, and in the world around us.

SHARING

In the whole group share our evaluations and where we are in relation to the course:

One way is to share general comments on the course, based on the basic material in session one, such as the aims and covenant.

Then share anything arising from specific sessions, either in formal praying or in counseling skills.

Recording and Evaluating a Practice Listening Session

INTRODUCTION

When we are practicing our listening skills, it is useful to record the session and then play it back, so that we may analyse our own responses. A worksheet each, like the following one, is usually helpful for both listener and sharer, so that we can compare notes afterwards. Sometimes it is helpful to discuss the response together when the tape is stopped in the replay, and then fill in the worksheet. The worksheet is a reminder; we can continue the verbal listening skills comments on plain paper.

AWARENESS SKILLS EVALUATION WORKSHEET

SUBJECT .... SHARER .... DATE ....
1. NONVERBAL AWARENESS (e.g., physical setting; touch; space; body and eye language; mirroring of body postures, gestures, breathing, facial expressions, voice tone, tempo and intonation).

2. VERBAL LISTENING SKILLS USED (e.g., silence, encouragers, reflectors, sub-summaries and summaries, open questions, open questions matching sensory words, specifiers, incongruity).
NB. AVOID telling; e.g., judging, advising, directing, interpreting.

DIAGNOSE	ASSESS		IMPROVE (If needed)
Tape Skill used	Effective	✓	Better type or example
No. (or omitted)	passable	—	
	not effective	✗	

"Tape number" is to record the place on the cassette ribbon. A sample entry might read:

10 (place on tape); closed question (diagnosis of type of response); (passable); open question, e.g., What's on your mind? (possible improvement).

PRACTICE

In the whole group record a short two- or three-minute practice listening session. Whoever shares needs to accept that the sharing is for practice, and is to be interrupted. It needs to be something meaningful, immediate and unresolved, concentrating on their own inside world and feelings. The sharer needs to pause occasionally so that the listener has scope to demonstrate a variety of listening skills in a short time.

SHARING

In evaluating the demonstration:

(a) Nonverbal: discuss how well rapport was built and maintained. Then ask the sharer their opinion.

(b) Replay the cassette, stopping at each significant response. We each diagnose and evaluate it on our own worksheet, and then discuss it in the group.

D. CONCLUDING

HOME PRACTICE

If possible over the term break, link up with another member of the group to practice. The sharer needs to remember to share immediate, meaningful, unresolved, inside material. The listener practices various nonverbal and verbal listening skills, and each fills in an evaluation sheet. The leader may be willing to comment on a 3–4 minute cassette and worksheet brought back on the first session of term 2.

Also practice formal meditation.

LOOKING AHEAD

Next term we shall spend the first few sessions centering in different ways, and improving our nonverbal and verbal listening awareness skills before we get on to part three: discerning God's Spirit in pain, healing and concepts; in our own past and present; and in verbal skills for accepting, forgiving and changing.

The theme of our first session next term is Solomon's prayer "Give me a hearing heart." We shall center with our moving body as a base, and then work on improving our verbal listening skills. For sessions 12–14 please bring cassette recorders (one between two), cassettes, extension cords, two-way adapters if there are not enough wall plugs.

AFFIRMATION

We have been using bases in our individual praying. Today we shall sum up our term's work by centering together as a group.

The handwashing ceremony reminds us of being called to serve others and to be God's hands in the world. It may be a base for us to be more aware that our loving, forgiving God is with us here and now.

After our hands are dried by our neighbor, we keep the towel and dry the next person's hands.

Standing in a circle, all sing the Servant Song: "Brother, sister, let me serve you."

The bowl, jug of water, and towel may be placed in the center.

In silence, two people officiate. B reverently carries the jug of water, (warmed if appropriate), A follows with the bowl and towel.

A gives the towel to C, the next person clockwise in the circle. D, the person next to C in the circle, holds their hands over the bowl held by A, while B pours a little water over them. C then dries D's hands and D receives the towel.

A and B then wash E's hands, D dries them and E receives the towel.

A and B then continue right round the circle. Each person in turn, including A and B, has their hands washed and dried, and receives the towel to dry their neighbor's hands.

When the washing is complete, and the bowl, jug and towel are replaced, all stand in silence.

Then holding hands, quietly sing the first verse of the Servant Song, and if appropriate, the grace.

SESSION 12

Centering with the Body as a Base
The Hearing Heart
Verbal Listening Skills Practice

Note extra material needed: cassette with suitable neutral music; cassettes etc. for participants.

A. BECOMING AWARE OF WHERE WE ARE

RECOLLECTING
Being still in the presence of God.

RECAP
Last term and over the holidays we practiced discerning God's Spirit in nonverbal and verbal awareness skills in contemplation, crisis, and formal meditation, and in the first few sessions of this term we further explore these ways of developing our awareness.

SHARING
Brief comments on our progress during the break.

TODAY'S THEME
Today's theme is effective listening from our center, centering with our body as our base. In session 2 we used our hands as a meditation on openness, and in session 5 we meditated with words and suggested movements. Today we are going to use the free-flowing spontaneous movement of our body as a base for our own meditation.

B. BECOMING AWARE IN FORMAL PRAYING

PRACTICE

Centering with the Body as a Base

Together quietly read aloud the hymn, "Take my life and let it be, consecrated Lord to thee."

The leader reads 1 Kings 3:9: Solomon's prayer for a hearing heart. "Give therefore thy servant an understanding heart (Hebrew: "a hearing heart") to judge thy people, that I may discern between good and bad, for who is able to judge this thy so great people?" (A.V.)

INTRODUCTION
As helpers in crisis we are aiming, like Solomon, to develop "hearing hearts," to listen from our center. "Give therefore thy servant an understanding heart" (in Hebrew: a hearing heart). That is why we are practicing centering. We are aiming to be aware with all our senses, five or six or however many we have. And we use our various senses as a base to center our attention and to link us into the present, so that we may forget the base and open our awareness fully to the present and to God's Spirit.

The leader's suggestions are only a guide, to flow over us and be there if we need them, as we use the movements of our body as a base to become more aware of God's Spirit.

Suitable neutral background music may be played.

Meditation to Music Using Spontaneous Free-flowing Movement of our Body as a Base

Beginning by standing up straight and relaxing; becoming aware of the position and sensations of your own body; breathing deeply and slowly and feeling it.

Slowly beginning to move in whatever way feels comfortable and relaxed. Moving the whole body, as in a spontaneous dance, or moving only your hands or head or trunk. Trying out free, ever-changing movements, as well as repetitive movements. All the time listening and feeling and seeing what is happening in your body.

Letting the movements become small. Being aware. Sensing it all. Keeping it slow. Keeping your awareness sharp and clear.

And when it seems right for you, sitting down comfortably wherever you want to, keeping on attending to how your body feels. Using the body sensations as a base. If you lose "touch" with the body sensations, coming back to the base by making slow easy movements with your hands, or swaying your body a little. Only if you need to. Ideally you will sense the feeling of stillness in your body after the movement, just as you sense the silence after a chant.

When you have finished, stretching and relaxing again, letting your consciousness flow into informal meditation for the rest of the day.

Journaling as desired.

SHARING

In the whole group share briefly.

EXTENSION

Using the body as a base may be especially helpful for those of us who relate to the world primarily through body feelings (F), who need to touch and act rather than to hear or see (session 6).

In session 5, in opening our physical space and in the meditation in movement to music, we experienced the difference of various postures and movements. There are many ways of using our body as a base:

1. Classically Patterned Movement

Tai Chi and Yoga are examples. Our meditation in movement is another stylized form.

2. Spontaneous Free-Flowing Movement

(a) Using our whole body, as we have just done.

(b) Using dancing hands. In session 2 we used our hands as a starting point for our thinking. Now we are using them only as a base for awareness. Sitting comfortably and becoming aware of your hands. Letting them begin to move, slowly, spontaneously. Noticing the way one hand moves in relation to the other. Sensing how they feel. Looking at the space between them. It may be beginning to seem as though it has substance.

Seeing how they move through space. Hearing any sound they make. Feeling them; paying attention to them when you need to. They are the base. Letting them move the whole time or letting them move and then rest, still using their feelings as the base.

3. Walking

Becoming aware of your feet moving, letting all the sensations come into awareness without holding on to any of them.

4. A Specific Part of the Body

Attending to the stillness or spontaneous movement of one part of the body. Choosing one and staying with it; e.g., attending to how your eyes, or eyelids, or tongue or one finger moves or is still during meditation.

5. Massage

Slowly massaging the muscles in your face, neck, shoulders, arms, hands and feet. Attending to the sensations, then resting and being aware of what your body is feeling.

6. The Solar Plexus

Many people feel that their center is their solar plexus. Becoming aware of it and using it as a base to center yourself.

7. The Center of Gravity

The body's center of gravity is said to be about two inches (5cm) below the navel. It has great significance in many spiritual traditions.

PRACTICE

How many of us have a sense of our own center, our center of gravity, our center of equilibrium? If anyone is unsure, let's all try an exercise to locate it.

First, moving round the room and sensing what part of your body seems to be leading, perhaps your head and shoulders. When you have located the leading spot, letting it slip down to the center point, allowing your movements to come from there. Breathing from your center point, centering your attention on the center of gravity.

If this is difficult try another way. Standing upright with your feet slightly apart, knees slightly bent and your weight distributed equally on both feet. Thinking about the spot just below your navel. Then slowly letting your weight shift from your left foot to your right. Doing this as if it 'were heavy sand, running up your leg from your left foot, through the center point and down your right leg into your right foot. Being aware of the center point while this is happening. Then when all the weight is in your right foot, lifting the left foot up lightly and freely and setting it down in front of you. After your left foot is on the ground, letting the weight flow back through the center point and into the left foot. Moving around this way a little. You may feel you look odd doing this, but gently accept it. What is important is that you are centering your body's attention at your center of gravity.

SHARING

In the whole group share as appropriate. Does whether we consider our center high, medium or low relate to our preferred thinking mode?

The body is also useful in informal meditation during the day.

In twos share our experience of this meditation as desired, of meditation over the last few weeks, and any thanks and needs. What is happening in our prayer time at home? Are we keeping up our journals? Take it in turns to pray and be prayed with, remembering to use the sharer's words in our praying. Share as appropriate in the whole group.

C. BECOMING AWARE IN COUNSELING SKILLS

The Hearing Heart: Effective Listening from Our Center

SHARING

Share briefly how we are getting on with practicing listening skills and using our cassettes.

INTRODUCTION

A thorough grounding in listening skills is at the heart of this program on discerning God's Spirit.

Learning to listen effectively is central to being in touch with our own deepest selves and with the inner world of others. It is at the deepest level of ourselves and others that we may become aware of how God is moving in our lives and in the lives of others. God is not only speaking to us but moving, prompting, urging and challenging us on all levels of our being. In other words, being open and listening effectively is the key to discerning the movement, the rhythm, the presence of God in the lives of all of us.

What are we listening to? We are practicing listening to our inner selves in meditation, to our body language and the words we use. And the awareness we gain enables us to listen to the nonverbal and verbal language of others and to enable them in turn to listen to themselves and to the movements of God in them.

So getting a real grip on the basic listening skills is crucial to being an effective helper in the crisis situation.

PRACTICE

Either: Practice listening skills in two groups with one leader in each group.

Or: In twos or threes (with one person as observer), using cassette recorders if possible, practice reflecting and summarizing and, if adding anything, using an open question. Remembering to keep ourselves out of the sharer's world— avoiding judging, advising, directing, interpreting. Staying with the sharer's own words as a clue to their inner world. Making sure that any questions are as open as possible (if necessary refer to session 10, Table 5: closed and open questions).

If we are stuck, remembering that a useful way of summarizing is to say "so you (felt . . .) when . . . ," making the summaries short.

The leaders may go round to the pairs.

SHARING

If there is time, share in the whole group how we are getting on.

D. CONCLUDING

RECOLLECTING

Quiet reflecting and journaling.

EVALUATION

Brief evaluation of the session.

HOME PRACTICE

Practice developing a hearing heart, listening to the Spirit from our center, using our listening skills on ourselves and others, and developing our awareness.

LOOKING AHEAD

Next session we shall practice using touch as a base. Please bring along any small object that you would like to use as a base, such as a stone, a piece of wood, a rosary. An object new to you may have fewer links into your past. Whatever it is, the aim is to touch it in order to free your awareness.

We shall also practice our listening skills. Please keep on practicing them at home and work.

AFFIRMATION

Standing. All sing or one person reads the hymn: "Take my life . . ." Take hands and all say the grace.

SESSION 13

Centering with Touch
Verbal Listening Skills Practice

Note extra material needed: spare objects to touch.

A. BECOMING AWARE OF WHERE WE ARE

RECOLLECTING
Being still in the presence of God.
Praying silently and aloud.

RECAP
Last session we aimed to develop hearing hearts, listening from our center.

SHARING
Brief sharing on progress.

TODAY'S THEME
Today we use touch as a base before working on improving our verbal listening skills.

B. BECOMING AWARE IN FORMAL PRAYING

INTRODUCTION
In the New Testament, touching is often referred to as having power. Jesus touched the dreaded leper and at once the man was healed (Matt 8:3); he touched Simon's mother-in-law's hand, and the fever left her (Matt 8:15); he touched the bier, or stretcher, and the dead young man sat up and began to talk (Luke 7:14). People crowded to touch Jesus. Both Matthew and Mark tell us that in the Gennesaret area all who touched the edge of Jesus's cloak were made well (Mark 6:56; Matt. 14:36).
Today we shall use touch as a base.

PRACTICE
Make sure we each have an object to use later, putting it aside for the moment.
First let's stand in a circle, as we did in session 2, our right hand giving and our left hand receiving. As we stand touching each other's hands, let us become aware of Christ touching us as individuals and through each other.
Then quietly sitting, touching our chosen object, being relaxed and alert, and using it as a base to make us more aware of God's healing presence.
Quietly journaling when ready.

SHARING
In twos take turns to share as appropriate, praying for each other's thanks and concerns, remembering to use our listening skills.

C. BECOMING AWARE IN COUNSELING SKILLS

INTRODUCTION
In session 2 we thought briefly about how powerful touching is, and how sensitive we have to be as to when and what kind of touching is appropriate. As we concentrate on our verbal listening skills, we need to remember also to be aware of the sharer's nonverbal messages.

PRACTICE
Either: first divide into two groups with one leader in each group for a group practice and evaluation before going into small groups;
Or: immediately practice our listening skills in

twos or threes (with an observer who watches, listens, and joins in the evaluating).

SHARING

Comment either in small groups or in the whole group.

D. CONCLUDING

RECOLLECTING

Quiet reflection and journaling.

EVALUATING

Brief comments on the session.

HOME PRACTICE

Notice how touch may make us more aware in everyday life and in formal meditation. Continue practicing verbal awareness skills in practice sessions and informally.

LOOKING AHEAD

Next session we shall be thinking more about using words as a base in formal meditation and in listening skills. It will be the last time that we shall use cassette players and worksheets in a session before going on to develop further verbal skills.

AFFIRMATION

All holding hands sing, "Spirit of the living God, fall afresh on me." The second line might be altered to "Touch me, mould me, fill me, use me."

SESSION 14

Centering with Words: Planting the Seed
Verbal Listening Skills Practice; Choice

Note: Scripture verses to be used as a base may be written up beforehand on a large board.

RECOLLECTING

Being still in the presence of God.
Praying silently or aloud.

RECAP

Last session we used touching as a base to help us to be more aware, and then practiced our listening skills.

SHARING

Comment as desired.

TODAY'S THEME

The theme of today is the seed. In centering with words, whether scripture, koan or prayer, we are planting the seed deep within ourselves, and the seed is the Word, the Logos, of God. We each have some choice of which seeds we cultivate, and that has implications for us as helpers.

B. BECOMING AWARE IN FORMAL PRAYING

Centering with Words: Planting the Seed

PRACTICE

Quietly all read together a hymn such as "Lord, thy word abideth."

As part of the meditation, the leader reads:

"But Mary kept all these things and pondered them in her heart" (Luke 2:19).

Last week our theme was Solomon's prayer, "Give me a hearing heart" (1 Kings 3:9). Today we cultivate Mary's secret: She kept all these things; she pondered them in her heart. She planted them deep within her.

Read Mark 4:26–29. "The kingdom of God is like this. A man sows seed in his field. He sleeps at night, is up and about during the day, and all the while the seeds are sprouting and growing. Yet he does not know how it happens. The soil itself makes the plants grow and bear fruit; first the tender stalk appears, then the ear, and finally the ear full of corn. When the corn is ripe, the man starts cutting it with his sickle, because harvest time has come."

In centering with words, such as scripture or prayer, we are planting the seed deep within ourselves. And the seed is the Word, the Logos, of God.

As we learned in session 9, all the bases that we use in formal meditation are only the pivot for our wandering minds, to bring them back to the fleeting eternal now, so that we may forget the base and open our minds to an awareness of God.

Scripture as a Base

Some suitable verses of scripture could be:

Be still and know.
God is love.
I am the Lord that healeth thee.
Rejoice in the Lord always.

Many scripture verses or passages of poetry are suitable. We are only using the words as a base, not analyzing or thinking about them intentionally.

Each of us may choose one verse to meditate on.

How to Use the Words

We may use the verse or words we choose in several ways:

1. As a visual base; e.g., reading it again and again.
2. As a hearing base; repeating it often very quietly and listening to it.
3. Planting it in our minds by repeating it quietly several times and watching or listening or feeling it there.
4. Reading it once or twice, then sitting back and letting our minds go where they want to with it.

Remember, we are using the words as a base to free our minds, to free us for that open simple present in which we may be aware of God, the Creator, the life-giving Spirit at work within us, enabling us and urging us to allow ourselves to grow.

Time for meditating quietly on our chosen words.

Journal as desired.

SHARING

Share as appropriate.

EXTENSION

Koan as a Base

A koan is a statement, question or problem which we try to understand but which does not have an intellectual answer; for example:

I am what I am.
The first shall be last, and the last first.
The greatest among you, he is the least.

A koan is meant to take us beyond our minds to a level of simplicity and openness in which we are aware with our whole being.

Prayer as a Base

We can use formal prayer, e.g., the Jesus prayer, Our Father, or informal praying, as a base. In informal praying the base can be listening openly to the silence which follows, or watching to see what sort of spontaneous prayer comes up in us. Some people understand this type of spontaneous prayer not as our praying but as God praying through us.

C. BECOMING AWARE IN COUNSELING SKILLS

INTRODUCTION

Choice

Listening Skills Practice: Nurturing the Seed

God is the creator of all, the life-giving Spirit, the gardener and the owner of all the gardens. In Christ each person also is at the same time gardener, garden and the seeds which go to create the garden.

Which seeds will each of us choose to cultivate?

Our purpose as helpers in listening to the sharer is to help the sharer to survey the seedlings and to discern which are vital to them, the seminal thoughts and images of their inner world. We hold up a mirror to help them to see and actively choose which seeds they will encourage and cultivate as having the greatest potential of growth for them. We do not choose for them; we attempt to keep to a minimum our own judgments, interpretation and advice, so that we do not intrude ourselves into their privacy but allow them space to choose and grow. The impulse for growth is already coming from within them; it is the movement and presence of the Holy Creative Spirit.

SHARING

How are we getting on with our listening skills?

EXTENSION

Choice

We shall shortly go into more detail about how to enable people to realize that they have choice:

choice of seeds;
choice of how they cultivate the seeds they have chosen as vital to their growth;
choice of being willing rather than willful before God;
choice of how they live with the paradoxes of life and the promises of the gospel;
choice of learning how to dig in their unwanted seedlings, deal with their unwanted feelings and thoughts, so that the nutrients from these seedlings can be broken down and drawn up into the chosen

plants, their energy and life transformed into creative possibilities for growth.

PRACTICE

Practice verbal and nonverbal listening skills in twos with cassette and worksheets.

SHARING

Comment in the whole group.

D. CONCLUSION

RECOLLECTING

Quiet reflecting and journaling.

EVALUATING

Any further brief evaluation and comment.

HOME PRACTICE

Practice planting one word or phrase in our hearts and using it as a base. As we practice our listening skills, continuing to think of the sharer's world as their garden with their own seeds.

LOOKING AHEAD

The theme next session will be centering in the here and now with all our senses and our mind process. We shall consider forming, specifying and changing our concepts.

AFFIRMATION

Holding hands in the group, each say quietly the verse we took as our base in the meditation.

Say the grace together.

Centering in the Here and Now
Processing our Sense Experiences:
Forming, Specifying and Changing
our Concepts
Congruity and Incongruity

A. BECOMING AWARE OF WHERE WE ARE

Note optional extra material: soft music, scented flowers or incense, objects to touch, etc.

RECOLLECTING
   Being still in the presence of God.
   Praying silently or aloud.

RECAP
   Last session we thought about planting and nurturing the seed in our inner garden, and practiced listening to help the sharer cultivate their own inner garden.

SHARING
   Share anything appropriate.

TODAY'S THEME
   Today we shall practice centering in the here and now with all our senses and our mind which organizes and processes our sensations. We shall consider in some detail how our mind processes this sense information, i.e., how we form our concepts, and how we may specify and change our concepts, and help the sharer to do the same. We shall also briefly explore mixed messages, i.e., where words and nonverbal messages disagree.

B. BECOMING AWARE IN FORMAL PRAYING

Centering in the Here and Now with All Our Senses and Our Mind Process

INTRODUCTION
   Today we are centering with here and now as a base. This entails using all our senses and our mind process as a practice for informal meditation.
   Sing together a hymn: e.g., "For the beauty of the earth."

To see a world in a grain of sand,
And a heaven in a wild flower,
Hold infinity in the palm of your hand,
And eternity in an hour.
   (Blake, *Auguries of Innocence*, 1.1–4)

In our program, in considering opening ourselves to God's presence through the day and in crisis, we have practiced discerning God's presence through nonverbal awareness in such areas as who and where we are, inner space, handling distractions, effort and relaxing, and breathing. Following some semiformal mini-meditations, we have been practicing centering with various senses as a base: sight and images (seeing), sound (hearing), breathing, the body, touching (feeling), words (hearing or seeing).

The senses of smell and taste may equally be used. We may use incense, flowers, pine trees, burning wood, whatever smells are around us. Some suggestions for tasting as a base are savoring a drink, sucking a mint, remembering a special taste.

The Mind

The mind may also be used as a base.

When we use remembered or imagined pictures, sounds, feeling, smells and tastes, we are using our minds as a base.

However, we use the mind more directly as a base when we sit back, relax and become aware of how our mind is processing all the material it is receiving from our senses, either at the present moment or from the past; i.e., when we become aware of how and what we are thinking, without interfering. We are letting the mind be; we are being aware of the stream of consciousness, like watching the clouds roll by (session 8: mini-meditation 16). If a thought captures our attention and we drift away with it, the thought becomes a distraction (session 6).

PRACTICE
Meditation:

As we are sitting here relaxing, keeping our eyes still,
becoming aware of what we are seeing;
becoming aware of what we are hearing;
becoming aware of what we are feeling;
becoming aware of what we are smelling;
becoming aware of what we are tasting;
becoming aware from the outside of what is going on
    in our minds;
using everything that we are conscious of here and
    now as a base to become more open and aware to
    the eternal Now, to receive the poured-out grace
    of God, which is everywhere.
Silence.

Journal as desired.

SHARING
In twos share our thanks and concerns, and pray.

In the whole group discuss how we are getting on with meditation and journaling.

EXTENSION
Formal meditation is using a special time and place to become open to what is, often using an object, image or activity to center our attention. Informal meditation is becoming gently aware of the here and now, the immediate moment, the I AM; and just being, in the midst of our daily living (session 3).

The purpose of being more awake, present, sensitive to now, whether through formal or informal meditation, is to become aware, sensitive, open to being affected by the Almighty, the eternal Now; more open to grace, to the givenness of each situation.

C. BECOMING AWARE IN COUNSELING SKILLS

INTRODUCTION
In using our mind or any of our senses as a base, we are letting go of the urge to interfere, to hold, control and interpret. And this is exactly what we are also aiming for in the listening situation; we are aiming to be aware of the sharer's world, without interfering or wanting to control, without introducing the distractions of our own feelings and thoughts, our own advice and interpretations.

Processing our Sense Experiences; Forming our Concepts

Just as we helpers aim to become more aware, more open ourselves to reality through our formal and informal meditation, so we are aiming to help the sharer to become more open.

Becoming more open includes making effective links between their own present and past experience and the contemporary and past experience of others, especially their spiritual experience (session 1: aim). It also includes associating more closely the actual experience with their concept of that experience, i.e., the way they choose and process the sensory information they receive. A simple example is whether they remember a particular gesture as an attack or as a sign of friendship.

All of us choose from our countless sensory experiences how we represent to ourselves a specific experience or event; we select and choose what become our concepts, our inner world. For example, two people present at an accident will receive different sense impressions, they will also process the sensory information differently.

To understand our experience of reality, i.e., to form our concepts, we use three main ways: deleting, generalizing, and altering (or distorting) our sensory experience.

1. We delete or choose to be aware of certain parts of our experience; e.g., we may not usually notice a ticking clock or how our feet are moving as we walk.
2. We generalize from our experiences; e.g., once bitten by a dog, we mistrust all dogs.
3. We alter or distort reality; as when we plan for the future, listen to a story, draw pictures, look through a telescope or at a nature film.

These ways of processing our experience are essential to effective living. They allow us to survive, grow, understand and experience the richness of the world. As we get some order into our sense impressions and relate them to our previous experience, we each develop a unique and changing concept of our own world. But often our concepts are too restricting. We may have deleted, generalized or distorted a particular experience to the point where it does not tally (or connect) with our wider experience. Our concepts may limit us and deny us flexibility; they may diminish our ability to make effective choices and change. We need to realize how wide our choices are, and how much wider reality is, how much wider God is, than our concepts.

In all our helping, we are aiming to work with the sharer's own concepts of the situation.

SHARING
Discuss anything arising.

INTRODUCTION
Lately, while remembering our nonverbal awareness skills we have been practicing a continuum of verbal listening skills to help us to be more aware and to enable us to stay in the sharer's experience. These are reflectors, sub-summaries and summaries, matching the sensory thinking mode, and open questions, including the outcome model (which leads the person to consider specifically what they want to change.)

From now on we shall consider a number of specific ways in which the listener may intervene to help effect actual change in the sharer's perception of reality. Intervening is different from interfering; we still stay in the sharer's world, not our own.

Specifiers (simplified from Cameron-Bandler, 1985, 223–232)

What Are Specifiers?

Specifiers are a useful type of intervening open question. They usually ask who, what, how about specific words that the sharer uses. Their purpose is to encourage the sharer to expand their concept of their world, by associating or reconnecting more closely the words they choose to use about their experience with the actual sensory experience that the words represent:

S. "I'm hopeless."
L. "Hopeless at what?"
"How specifically do you know you are hopeless?"
"What lets you know you are hopeless?"

Specifiers differ from ordinary open questions: ordinary open questions accept the sharer's concept of their inside world and invite the sharer to explore it. Specifiers encourage the sharer to expand their concept of the world.

With this kind of who, what, how, question we are no longer simply mirroring the experience the sharer chooses to share, we are actively intervening to help the sharer clarify their use of words and their concepts. Our aim in intervening is to help them to understand how the way they are using their words indicates and affects the way they are able to understand their experience.

Our questions, specifiers, lead them to question their own representation of reality, and to explore areas of their own experience that they may have been denying, generalizing from or distorting, to their own detriment. Often these areas of experience have been closed off because they were painful.

At the moment of pain or crisis, the person

may not have the ability to assess the experience in broad perspective; e.g., if they are punched on the nose. But the sharer may generalize from this one experience, denying and distorting other experiences, and use it to represent the whole of their experience. Our purpose is not to deny the hurtful experience but, when the sharer is ready, to help them to explore how they can widen and change their representation of the experience so that they are freer and more open in the present.

When to Use Specifiers

There are three main uses for specifiers:

1. When the sharer leaves out, i.e., deletes or denies, information: to gather information.
2. When the sharer is limiting their world by excessive generalization: to widen the limits.
3. When the sharer is distorting or making faulty links: to identify the distortions.

PRACTICE

In the following examples, after the leader has read out the type of specifier and the suggested type of response, take it in turns round the circle to read what the sharer says, with the person on our left reading the listener's response.

1. To gather information
(a) *When something is missed out,* ask "About whom, about what?":

S. "I just don't know."
L. "You don't know what?" or "What don't you know?"

S. "I'm worried."
L. "Worried about what?"
S. "I hate it."
L. "What do you hate about it?"
S. "She's the worst."
L. "She's the worst what?" or "Worst out of whom?"

(b) Asking *"How, specifically, do you know?"* may give us information about how the sharer represents the experience:

S. "We don't think the same way about it."
L. "How specifically do you know that you don't think the same way?"
S. "I see it quite differently." (Seeing).

(c) *With limiting generalizations,* ask "Who/what, specifically, exactly?"

S. "It's not fair."
L. "What exactly isn't fair?"
   or "What exactly isn't fair for you?"
S. "No one agrees with me."
L. "Who exactly doesn't agree with you?"
S. "They say . . ."
L. "Who (exactly) says . . .?"

(d) *With vague verbs,* asking "How, specifically?":

S. "He hurt/understood/ignored/made me . . ."
L. "How did he hurt/understand/ignore/make you. . . ?"

(e) *To change abstract nouns back into verbs,* ask "How, what, who?" When we turn an abstract noun back into a verb we are able to understand it not as an event beyond our control but as a continuing process which can be changed:

S. "My prayers seem empty?"
L. "How is your praying empty?"
S. "I want a bit of praise/thanks/admiration/relaxation."
L. "Who do you want to praise/thank/admire you?"
   "How do you want to be praised/to be admired/to relax?"
S. "It was a bad move."
L. "Does anything stop you from making another move?"
   "What stops you making another move?"

2. To widen the limits
(a) *With extreme generalizations* such as "all, every, always, never, every, nobody", exaggerate the generalization by voice tone and by adding more of the extreme words, or ask whether the sharer has had an experience that contradicts their own generalization:

S. "She's always late;/never on time."
L. "Always late;/never ever on time?"
S. "She can't ever be polite."
L. "Has she ever been polite?"
S. "He never says anything kind."
L. "He absolutely never ever says anything kind?"

"Has he ever said anything kind?"

(b) *When the sharer indicates no choice*, e.g., "have to, must, can't," ask, "What stops you?" (referring to past experience) or "What would happen if you did?" (future consequences):

S. "I'll have to/must go back."
L. "What will happen if you don't go back?"
S. "I can't let her do it."
L. "What will happen if you do let her?"
  "What's stopping you from letting her do it?"

3. *To identify the distortions*

(a) *With cause and effect*, ask "How does A cause B?"

S. "She makes me mad."
L. "How does she make you mad?"
S. "His grin annoys me."
L. "How does his grin make you feel annoyed/annoy you?"
  "How is it possible for his grin to *make* you annoyed?"

(b) *With mind-reading*, ask "How, specifically, do you know?" or "What lets you know?":

S. "Everyone thinks she will win."
L. "How exactly do you know that everyone thinks she will win?"
  "What lets you know that everyone thinks she will win?"
S. "I'm sure you can see it my way."
L. "How can you be sure that I can see it your way?"
S. "I know what you're thinking."
L. "How do you know what I'm thinking?"

(c) *With judging and making rules for other people*, ask "For whom?":

S. "It's easy enough to do."
L. "Easy for whom to do?"
S. "It's wrong/stupid to stay home all day."
L. "It's wrong/stupid for whom to stay home all day?"

It is essential to maintain rapport while using specifiers (as with all these skills). A judging or clever tone of voice may easily alienate the sharer and delay the changes they want.
  Discuss in the whole group.
  In twos go through the three uses, making up at least one example of each of the different uses.

Congruity and Incongruity

INTRODUCTION

Concepts that Tally

By using specifiers in the three ways outlined above (i.e., to gather information, to widen the limits and to identify distortions in the words the sharer uses to communicate their model of their world), we are helping the sharer to make links (session 5: associating). We are helping them to make their personal representation of experience, their concepts, tally with their own wider experience and with the experience of other people. When they realize which of these areas do not tally, they have already started to change.

Mixed Messages
Words and Nonverbal Messages
that Do Not Tally

When the sharer is saying one thing with words, but sending us a different message nonverbally, this may give us an important clue about their concept of their world; e.g., if the sharer is saying, "I'm not angry," but their voice is loud, face flushed, their teeth clenched and body tense, they are hardly communicating peaceful acceptance nonverbally.

It is important to detect such incongruity so that we may help the sharer to discover the source of their conflicting messages and then help them to change their perception of their experience so that their words and nonverbal messages agree. Our nonverbal awareness skills are the ones to develop to help us to detect mixed messages; e.g., watching the person's body posture, gestures, and facial expression, their face, hands, feet and breathing; listening to their voice tone, volume, tempo, intonation, etc., and noticing what is incongruent for the sharer.

We need to beware of deciding for ourselves, without checking, which parts of the sharer's messages are real, and what the messages mean.

Some Ways of Checking What
is Causing a Mixed Message
(Based on Cameron-Bandler 1985, 81)

1. Saying, "But. . . ." For example:

S. "I really want to tell him how I feel."
L. "But . . ."

S. "But I'm afraid that he'll take advantage of it."

2. Asking, "Do you entirely agree with what you said? Feel, listen or look for any part of you that may disagree as you say it again to yourself."
3. Noticing which thinking position their eyes were in, leading their eyes back to that position, and asking, e.g., "What were you seeing/hearing/feeling/saying to yourself as you said that?"
4. Using specifiers to challenge the sharer's perceived lack of choice, for example:

   "What stops you?"
   "What would happen if you did?"

5. Mirroring, even exaggerating, the sharer's words and incongruent behavior, but only if we have built enough trust and rapport.
6. With two people, asking the listener what they heard and saw, and what it meant to them; then asking the sharer what they meant; and then helping the sharer to express what they mean so that it gets the response they want.

The important thing with mixed messages is to recognize that they point to what needs to be changed in order for the sharer to become more at one, more in harmony with themselves, more aware and open.

SHARING
Discuss.

PRACTICE
In twos watch each other's nonverbal messages as the leader asks the group to recall as fully as possible the following experiences: a time when—

1. Someone you cared for gave you a present and you opened it in front of them only to discover the gift was something you disliked, found hideous, or already had at least one of and no use for. Remember what you said to them and how it felt.

2. You accepted an invitation from someone you didn't like.
3. You told someone you would do something you not only didn't want to do, but resented being put in the position of being asked to do it.
4. You told someone that you were completely sure of something that you were actually unsure of.

Contrast those experiences with memories of—

1. Telling someone about an activity you were absolutely and positively determined to carry out.
2. Complimenting a friend on some significant accomplishment he or she had achieved.
3. A situation in which you were operating at the height of your own competency and confidence.
4. Saying, "I've missed you" to someone you dearly love after a seemingly long separation. (Cameron-Bandler, 1985, 78)

Comment on the experience in twos and then discuss it in the whole group.

D. CONCLUDING

RECOLLECTING
Quietly reflecting and journaling.

EVALUATION
Brief comments on today's session.

HOME PRACTICE
Practice centering in the here and now, using specifiers, and becoming more aware of mixed messages.

LOOKING AHEAD
Next session we start Part Three of our program by considering pain, crisis and impasse, and identifying and owning our feelings.

AFFIRMATION
As we prepare to leave, let us center ourselves again in the here and now, becoming more open and aware, receiving the poured-out grace of God which is everywhere. Amen.

PART THREE

Discerning God's Spirit
In Pain, Healing, Words and Concepts
In Our Own Past and Present
In Verbal Skills for Accepting,
Forgiving and Changing

SESSION 16

Centering with Pain as a Base
Crisis, Pain, and Impasse
Identifying and Owning our Feelings

Note extra materials needed: flip-sheets of Figures 4 and 5, i.e., development of crisis, and accepting our powerlessness in impasse and crisis.

A. BECOMING AWARE OF WHERE WE ARE

RECOLLECTING
Silently centering in the here and now.

RECAP
Last session we practiced centering in the here and now, with all our senses and our mind processes. We considered how we process the experiences we receive through our senses, i.e., how we form our concepts. Two helpful ways to clarify our concepts are by using specifiers and by noticing whether our words and actions are congruent.

SHARING
Sharing our reflections, reactions and progress since last session.

TODAY'S THEME
Today we start on Part Three of our program: discerning God's Spirit in pain, healing, words and concepts, in our own past and present, and through verbal skills for accepting, forgiving and changing. This session we are concerned with pain; pain as a base in crisis, how crisis arises, the intense crisis of impasse, the importance of identifying and owning our own painful and pleasurable feelings, and expressing them in I-messages.

B. BECOMING AWARE IN FORMAL PRAYING

INTRODUCTION
After a few moments of centering in the here and now, we shall each recall a painful experience, which we may then use as a base for centering our awareness.

PRACTICE
Each now remembering a situation which still has physical or emotional pain attached to it. Being sure to experience it, not from the outside looking on, but from the inside as though you are actually experiencing it now.

Seeing what there is to see.
Hearing the sounds.
Feeling what is around you and how you are feeling inside.
Smelling and tasting the smells and tastes that are in the situation.
Sensing it fully.
Feeling it fully.

When you are in touch with these feelings, and have identified them, bringing them back into the room and writing them down.
Now each of us silently using our present painful feelings as a base for centering our awareness, as we open ourselves and become aware of the here and now.
Journaling as desired.

SHARING

In the whole group as we are willing and as it seems appropriate:

(a) Name the painful feelings and list them on the board.

(b) Identify how we feel now about our original experience.

(c) What is the difference between how we felt originally and how we feel now?

(d) What has made the difference? (i.e., we perceive it differently).

C. BECOMING AWARE IN COUNSELING SKILLS

INTRODUCTION

Today we are considering our reaction to pain in crisis. The meditation was to help us be more aware of how pain may be used in contemplation to open us up to God in crisis.

SHARING

In the whole group read together the following notes on crisis, pain and impasse in sections, referring to the diagrams and to the group flip-sheet. Let's discuss and respond to it, relating it to our own experience.

How Crisis Arises

Perceiving the Situation

In our last session we saw that we make the world manageable and understandable for ourselves by a continuous process of deleting, generalizing and altering the information that flows into us through our senses. By reducing it in this way, we arrive at our perceptions, our concepts of reality, our inner world.

This process is essential to effective living, but if we take it too far we may break any effective link between reality and how we perceive it. We delete, generalize and distort not only our information about the world outside but also our information about ourselves and our resources. All this has a direct bearing on our handling of crisis (session 2).

If we reduce our perception of ourselves and our resources to the stage where we exclude significant resources (including God), we severely limit our ability to cope.

Assessing and Reacting to the Situation

In reducing each event to what we perceive it to be, we assess how it relates to us, so that we may be able to control or cope with it. Our assessment will usually evoke in us some emotion, which may range from intense love to intense fear. If we judge the event to be positive for us, i.e., pleasant and creative, we may open up and feel a degree of love and positive experience. If, on the other hand, we judge the event to be negative for us, i.e., threatening, painful and dangerous, we may close up, withdraw and feel some degree of fear and negative response.

In assessing the whole situation, we assess whether the event seems positive or negative for us, and also how adequate we consider ourselves and our resources are for us to function comfortably, to retain or regain our control, to maintain our power to survive or succeed, to grow and realize our full potential.

It is when we feel that we are losing power or are powerless and our resources seem inadequate that a crisis arises (Fig. 4). A crisis is an internal reaction to an external hazard (session 2).

Pain and Impasse

Pain

Pain is the name we give to any sensation that we perceive as negative and threatening, i.e., painful and dangerous. How much we are afraid or suffer in response to pain depends on our assessment of how negative and dangerous it is and how adequate our resources seem.

If we assess our coping resources as adequate, our initial negative reaction may change to a positive one of pleasure, e.g., biting into an acid fruit which we then enjoy; plunging into a cold sea for a swim.

Dealing with Pain

Our aim when experiencing pain is to get rid of it, to make ourselves comfortable again, to regain control. We may do this by:

1. Perceiving it differently (as with the fruit or sea), i.e., altering our concept (session 25).

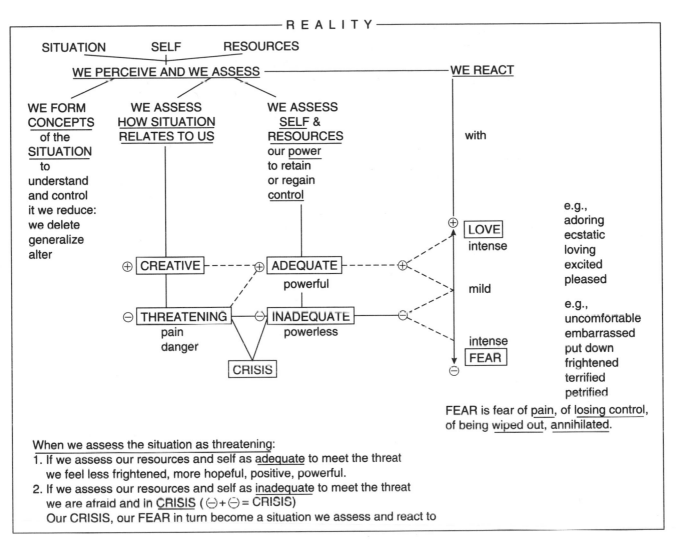

Fig. 4. Development of crisis

2. Accepting it.
3. Removing the source of the pain.
4. Withdrawing from it.
5. Numbing our senses so that we do not feel it.

In crisis we are responding to our negative assessment of two factors in the situation:

1. We perceive the precipitating event as threatening or painful.
2. We perceive ourselves as lacking in power, and our resources as inadequate.

In this double negative situation of crisis we assess our resources as inadequate to remove, accept or perceive the pain differently (3, 2 and 1 above). Many of us initially experience some de-

gree of shock, i.e., we withdraw, our senses are numbed (4 and 5). The shock usually passes as we marshal or increase our resources and work towards a resolution of our pain.

Impasse

In extreme crisis we may feel that neither we ourselves nor any of our resources or possible solutions is adequate. Even God may seem to have deserted us. "My God, my God, why hast Thou forsaken me" (Mark 15:34). Now that our resources seem so inadequate, the precipitating event seems even more threatening. We see ourselves as completely powerless to deal with the pain. Our fear compounds our fear.

We withdraw, we close ourselves up tightly,

we numb our senses so that we do not suffer our pain and fear, our growing fear of being wiped out, of annihilation. Our numbness paralyses us. This is impasse—impotence, utter powerlessness.

Resolving Impasse and Crisis

Yet even in impasse we still have a choice; impasse is full of paradox. We may choose either:

1. To despair in the face of a seemingly all-powerful situation or,
2. Accept our own powerlessness and turn to other resources, other people, to the source of all resources, God.

As we accept our own powerlessness, as we let go of our own need to be in control, we may begin to trust in the power of the all-powerful, the Almighty, the God who is Love. We begin to let go of our numbness and allow ourselves to feel; we start to open up our tightly-closed withdrawn selves; we identify and acknowledge our situation, including our pain. We muster our resources. We may muster enough new resources to remove part or all of the pain or its source; if not, we may now be able to accept the situation; we may perceive it differently. In this second way, paradoxically, our situation of no potential may become one of possibility for creative change and transformation.

In a genuine impasse one's accustomed way of acting and living is brought to a standstill. The left side of the brain, with its usual application of linear, analytical, conventional thinking is ground to a halt. The impasse forces us to start all over again, driving us to contemplation. On the other hand, the impasse provides a challenge and a concrete focus for contemplation. . . . It forces the right side of the brain into gear, seeking intuitive, symbolic, unconventional answers, so that action can be renewed eventually with greater purpose (Lane, 1981).

Pain as a Base

One way to perceive pain differently is to use it as a base. As we open ourselves up more, instead of treating pain as a distraction or an obstacle to our awareness of the present, we may use it. We may use it as a base, as a stepping off point to free us to be more fully aware of what is happening to us now on all levels of our being, to open us to an awareness that everything is a gift given to us by the Almighty.

Using pain as a base, stripped of the need to be in control, we may become aware of all sorts of possibilities that our minds were closed to before. We may experience a new freedom to accept the restraints of our situation without struggle. We may learn to open ourselves more to God, to trust God, and to open ourselves to God in other people. When we know that God is with us, is in us, and loves us, our resources increase and we may have new power to face crisis.

"God is Love. . . . Perfect love drives out fear" (1 John 4:16,18).

Love and Acceptance Driving Out Fear

As we become more open and trusting, we reassess our situation, and we find that one of the two negative factors in the crisis, the perceived lack of power, the inadequacy of our self and our resources, is reduced. It may even have disappeared. It may no longer frighten us. The power of God's love is driving out our fear. So we look again at the other negative factor in the crisis, our assessment of the precipitating event. We are back to square one. We reassess the event. And we assess it differently. We may even perceive it more fully, with less deletion, generalization and distortion.

If we assess it as less intense but still threatening, and if our resources still seem inadequate, we are still in crisis, but less crisis. So we need more resources. As we trust in God, as we give up the struggle to be on top, to fight or resign ourselves to the situation, paradoxically we are given resources and power to cope, to transcend the situation.

In the concentration camps in World War II, Victor Frankl describes two types of people:

1. Those who could not see beyond what was happening to them tended to die; they were victims.
2. Those whose view transcended the situation lived; they were the survivors (Frankl, 1964, 74).

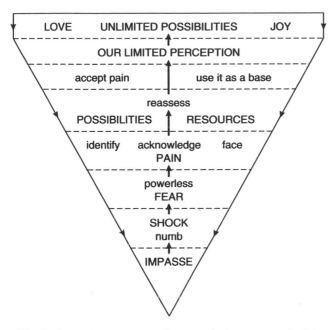

Fig. 5. Accepting our powerlessness in impasse and crisis

When we have worked through the pain, when we accept the situation, as we perceive it more fully, we may even start to assess the precipitating event as positive, as creative, however negative, painful and threatening we judged it previously. We now accept the crisis situation as a turning point, a learning time, a growing time. It becomes one of life's treasures.

One man terminally ill in the hospital, used to the cutthroat business world, suddenly found himself on the receiving end of care and love. His whole perception of hospital and other people altered. He found new values in life. He could then say with conviction, "I wouldn't have missed this experience." Similar comments are often made in a hospital.

Our reaction of fear and suffering is turning into joy. Perfect love is driving out fear (Fig. 5).

In impasse and in crisis:

We admit our powerlessness.
We emerge from our impasse or shock.
We identify and face the fear and pain.
We reassess our selves and our resources, and how we relate to the event.
We widen our perception of the event, ourselves and our resources.
We open ourselves to love, to God, in all areas.

When we accept our powerlessness, stop struggling for control, we are given the power we need.

Identifying and Owning our Feelings: I-Messages

INTRODUCTION

The Sharer's Words

When we reflect and summarize we accept the sharer's own key words and hold them up as a mirror to the sharer's inner world (session 7).

When we use specifiers we intervene to encourage the sharer to be more precise about the words they have used, so that they may realize what their assumptions are, and how much they have limited their concept of the world by their particular use of the universal processes of deleting, generalizing and distorting (session 15).

When we ask the sharer to use I-messages, we are asking them to go a step further back, to choose different words, so that their words express what the sharer is actually feeling.

I-Messages

I-messages express from the inside the sharer's own feelings; e.g., "He makes me cross," becomes, "I feel cross."

To express feelings, the sharer needs to know what they are feeling, i.e., needs to identify the feeling so that they can acknowledge it.

I-messages, then, have a double benefit:

1. They encourage the sharer to discover and put into words what they are feeling, and so understand themselves better.
2. They enable us as hearers to get a more direct, accurate concept of the sharer's world in a way that is relatively unthreatening and noncontroversial.

As listeners we aim to avoid judging, interpreting and advising. With I-messages, we are encouraging the sharer to do the same. We are helping them honestly to explore, identify and to own their real feelings, and to send their message in such a way that it has maximum benefit to themselves as well as to the receiver (especially if the

TABLE 7
THREE PARTS OF AN I-MESSAGE
(based on Gordon 1978, 127)

How I Feel	Description of The Situation	Tangible Effect on Me Consequences for Me
I panic	when he shouts at me	because I think he's going to hit me
I worry	when you come in late	because I'm afraid you have had an accident

cf. He mustn't shout at me. You're not to come in so late.

receiver is the person directly involved), e.g., "You upset me . . ." becomes "I feel upset. . . ."

PRACTICE

Practice several I-messages like, "I'm cross," (instead of, "You make me cross").

EXTENSION

Effective I-Messages—Owning My Feelings

To be most effective, an I-message needs three parts, as shown in Table 7.

A You-message judges, advises, orders, interprets, often in an unacceptable form which may well lead to confrontation and possible crisis.

An I-message leaves the receiver free to choose to respond appropriately. The greater the rapport, trust and love, the more likely the sender is to evoke a favorable response. If the I-message does not evoke the hoped-for response, the sharer may need to become a listener, and then embark on mutual problem solving and the outcome model (session 10).

Remember:

1. We cannot change others. We may be able to change some environmental factors. We ourselves may change and hope that our change will enable others to change.
2. Concentrate on the positives, the changes we want, rather than on the problem; i.e., look beyond the pain to the possibilities.

D. CONCLUDING

RECOLLECTING

Quiet reflection and journaling.

EVALUATION

Brief evaluation and comment.

HOME PRACTICE

Becoming more aware of how our concepts affect our reaction to pain, crisis and impasse; using I-messages to identify, own and express our feelings of joy and sorrow, pleasure and pain.

LOOKING AHEAD

Next time we shall work on accepting pain; opening ourselves to love; and identifying our basic emotions and our basic resources.

AFFIRMATION

Holding hands and centering in the here and now.

Saying the grace together.

SESSION 17

Accepting Pain
Opening Ourselves to Love
Basic Emotions and Resources

Note extra material needed: sheets of paper, colored pens or pencils, flat surfaces for drawing on.

A. BECOMING AWARE OF WHERE WE ARE

RECOLLECTING
Being still in the presence of God.

RECAP
Last session we recalled a painful experience and used that experience as a base for becoming open to the here and now, to the God of the here and now. We considered how accepting pain and using it as a resource is one way of dealing with a crisis positively rather than negatively. We may identify and face our pain and negativity, our shadow, rather than deny it. Rather than fighting, we may come to accept and make friends with the tiger within us, the anger arising from our basic fear of annihilation that is behind our own sense of inadequacy and powerlessness.

Even in impasse, the extremity of crisis and impotence, by accepting our powerlessness we may choose to open ourselves to new, creative possibilities for change and transformation previously unimagined. Every death holds potential for new life, for resurrection. The choice of realizing the potential lies with us.

Accepting and embracing the crisis, the impasse, the pain and anger, and realizing its potential for growth and change requires deep trusting in a loving, ever-present God who is continually active in and through ourselves, others and our total situation. Through this deep trusting we are affirmed.

We also considered the value of using I-messages to help us to recognize and express our feelings.

SHARING
Any comments.

TODAY'S THEME
Today's theme holds the key to unlocking impasse—meditating on opening ourselves to love. We shall also consider our basic emotions, and think about anger, guilt and grief, ending up by reviewing our basic resources.

B. BECOMING AWARE IN FORMAL PRAYING

INTRODUCTION
In today's meditation we open ourselves to God's loving Holy Spirit (based on Ferrucci, 1982, 237–38).

PRACTICE
The leader reads 1 John 4:7–12, 18a, and then the meditation.
Gently relaxing our breathing and our bodies.
Resting our feelings and opening them to serenity and calm.
Stilling our thoughts and becoming aware of our center.

Letting our self open and return towards its origin, its source of life. Imagining ourselves becoming truly ourselves. Becoming aware of God in our depths; radiant, loving, timeless, free.

Experiencing God as love, as loving; wonderful, nourishing, creative, positive loving. Experiencing loving we have known and felt ourselves, loving we have heard about or can imagine.

Thinking, too, of how we may distort loving in our lives at present. What is hindering and blocking love in our life? What are we are afraid of?

What are our needs? What values and benefits may loving bring in our life.

Becoming aware again of God's love surrounding us, pervading us, all through us. Opening ourselves to the flowing in of loving energy, to the essence of God's love, to intuitions and imaginings of love.

And as we are ready, still keeping ourselves open to God's loving energy, becoming aware of our own bodies, aware of our physical environment, aware of the here and now, realizing that we may communicate to others the inner riches we have become aware of.

Journal as desired.

SHARING

In twos share and pray about anything arising from the meditation.

C. BECOMING AWARE IN COUNSELING SKILLS

Basic Emotions

INTRODUCTION

Our basic emotions have been categorized in many ways; e.g., love; hate; anger; guilt; fear; grief; envy. In assessing our situation (session 16: Fig. 4) we thought of our range of feelings as on a continuum between love and fear. It may well be helpful (and accurate) to consider love and fear as the two primary emotions.

Fear seems to underlie all our negative feelings.

Anger may seem to be a basic emotion, but underlying the anger is nearly always some type of fear; e.g., we feel embarrassed, put down, hurt, terrified, etc., and anger is one of the re-

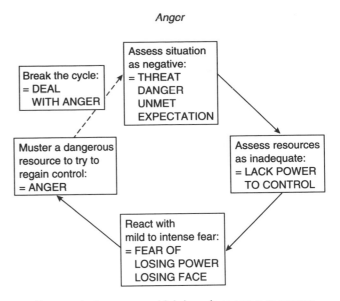

Fear underlies anger which is a dangerous resource to gain control.

Fig. 6. An anger cycle

sources we muster to gain our control. But we sense that the anger itself may be a danger to us. We are in the anger cycle (Figure 6).

SHARING

Discuss.

EXTENSION

Dealing with Our Anger

To break free of the anger cycle we draw on other resources, some more effective than others. Some ways of dealing with our anger:

1. Directing it at someone.
2. Displacing it onto someone else, generalizing it; i.e., "they. . . ."
3. Repressing it (Figure 7).
4. Owning the anger, with I-messages; e.g., "I feel cross. . . ."
5. Diagnosing the underlying feeling and owning it; e.g., "I feel hurt . . . embarrassed . . . let down. . . ."
6. Expressing it alone; e.g., by beating it out, and affirming our value, the threat which led to our being afraid, and so triggered our anger (Figure 6: Anger Cycle, and session 22).

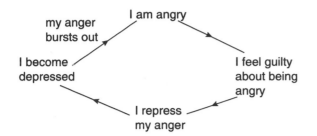

Fig. 7. Repressed anger, guilt and depression

Directing, displacing or repressing our anger may be effective as a short-term coping mechanism. But long term it may prove to be inadequate or even precipitate another threatening situation and heighten the crisis. Owning the anger, expressing it alone, diagnosing and owning the underlying feeling and value, and affirming the value may be effective short term and long term.

When we feel guilty about being angry, and repress our anger, we may become depressed. If our anger finally bursts out, we may be caught into a cycle of repressing our anger and becoming depressed (Figure 7).

There are more useful ways of dealing with anger than repressing it; e.g., breaking this cycle by owning the anger, and identifying and owning the feeling, and affirming the value behind the anger.

SHARING

Discuss.

A Grief Model

INTRODUCTION

The anger cycle (Figure 6) depicts anger arising as a resource when we feel that we cannot cope, that our other coping methods are failing us. So we are in crisis.

In crisis, the failure of our usual coping methods and resources is a loss, a source of grief.

PRACTICE

Each of us have a large sheet of paper and colored pen or pencil. Each reexperience from the inside a grief experience, starting from just before the experience began, reliving the experience as it happened, and after we have fully experienced it, reliving a later time when we were starting to come to terms with our grief. Thinking of any milestones or significant moments when there was a change in how we were coming to terms with the situation. Coming right up to the present moment. And when we are ready, making simple drawings from the beginning of how we have progressed in accepting and dealing with our grief.

Decide beforehand approximately how much time to allocate.

SHARING

Discuss in either small groups or the whole group as appropriate.

EXTENSION

When we are in crisis and grieving, the Kübler-Ross grief model may apply (Table 8). Table 8, a grief model, is similar to Figure 5, session 16: Accepting our powerlessness in impasse and crisis. It enumerates the various stages that we move back and forth, in and out of, in our loss and fear.

We may react first with withdrawal and shock, even be in impasse.

TABLE 8
KÜBLER-ROSS GRIEF MODEL
(adapted from Kübler-Ross, 1978, 34–138)

	In Grief		In Rejection
Shock	Numbness	Hurt	
Denial	"Not me"	⎫	Pretend it's not there. "I don't care."
		Bitter	
Anger	"Why me?"	⎭	"They've no right to."
Bargaining	"Me but"	⎫	"If I flatter, they may like me."
		Defeated	
Depression	"Poor me"	⎭	"No one likes me."
Acceptance	"Me and"	Facing reality ⎫	"Not everyone likes me, but many do."
Rebuilding		⎭	"I'm in command of me."
			"I will accept rejection. So what!"
			"I will stop feeling rejected."
			"I will use it to show greater understanding of others."

We move back and forth, in and out of these stages.

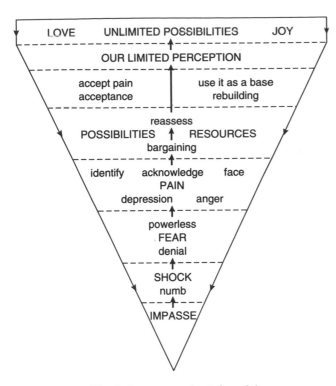

Fig. 8. Impasse and grief model

perception there is God's sustaining love, which is an all-important resource.

One way of considering resources is to think of having a fund of resources to draw on, a fund of four Fs: facts, i.e., the situation; feelings, i.e., assessing and reacting to the situation; faith, i.e., discerning God in the situation; and freedom (of choice), i.e., being aware of possibilities.

Figure 9 depicts these four Fs leading to decision and action.

As we become more aware on all levels: understanding and dealing with our feelings, opening ourselves in faith and realizing our freedom of choice and the possibilities we may have, we perceive the situation differently; we alter our concept of the facts. We learn, we grow, we become more open to love, the loving which drives out fear.

SHARING

Link up any new insights from the opening meditation on love with our basic emotions and our resource fund of four Fs.

It is important to realize that we move back and forth, in and out of these stages. The stages of acceptance and rebuilding are positive outcomes; acceptance is different from resignation, which may be a negative armed truce, repressed anger. The hoped-for outcome is for us to assess our resources and to accept all the choices that we do have in the situation.

The Kübler-Ross grief model may be integrated into an impasse model as in Figure 8.

SHARING

Discuss as appropriate.

The Sharer's Resource Fund; Four Fs

INTRODUCTION

In crisis the sharer assesses their resources as inadequate. As helpers we aim to enable the sharer to recognize and to develop their resources and to use them creatively. As the impasse and grief model, Figure 8, indicates, and as our beginning meditation reminded us, beyond our limited

D. CONCLUDING

RECOLLECTING

Let's use this time to reflect particularly on our resource fund.

EVALUATION

Brief comments on the session.

HOME PRACTICE

Practice becoming more aware of God's sustaining love, our most important resource; con-

Fig. 9. Our resource fund: four Fs

sidering what lies behind our anger, and how we deal with our anger and grief at our loss of power in crisis.

LOOKING AHEAD

Next session we shall practice discerning God's presence in crisis through one of our peak faith experiences, and then start on some ways we may change our own perception of the facts in our past, and help others to do the same.

AFFIRMATION

A hymn, quiet, the grace and a group hug as appropriate.

Discerning God's Presence in Crisis through Reliving a Peak Faith Experience Some Ways of Changing Reassessing and Changing our Reactions to Our Past and Our Future

Note: The leader may write up on the board beforehand the questions to follow the meditation.

A. BECOMING AWARE OF WHERE WE ARE

RECOLLECTING
Let us be still in the presence of God.

RECAP
Last session we experienced something of God's love, and our faith in discerning this love as part of our 4F resource fund. We thought of love and fear as perhaps our basic emotions, of anger as arising from threat and our lack of power, of grief in loss, and of loss or lack of power as an essential element in crisis.

SHARING
Brief sharing as appropriate.

TODAY'S THEME
Today we shall consider how linking into one of our own past peak faith experiences may help us to become more aware of God's presence in crisis, i.e., drawing on the faith in our resource fund. We shall also try out some ways of using our freedom to choose how we assess the facts

and our feelings, in the present, in remembering the past, and in the future.

B. BECOMING AWARE IN FORMAL PRAYING

Discerning God's Presence in Crisis Through Reliving a Peak Faith Experience

INTRODUCTION

How Do We Know that God is Loving, Working and Active in our Lives?

Recollecting a deeply meaningful experience and awareness of God at work guiding us at an important moment of life is a foundation for discerning God's loving presence and guidance in times of uncertainty, deep disturbance and pain; e.g., when someone close to us dies.

Remembering and sharing such experiences is important. It re-roots us individually and corporately. It reconnects us with each other as well as with the tradition that makes up our own and other people's background. In the resulting wider perspective of our own and others' pilgrimage, we realize our unity and diversity of faith and experience.

So for a peak experience to be most effective in crisis, it needs to be recognized, remembered and shared with others before the crisis occurs.

When we relive such an experience it is important for us to experience it fully from the inside; i.e., to see, hear, feel, taste and smell it for ourselves now, so that its full potential for growth and development may be resurfaced at a time of confusion and indecision and brought into dynamic interplay with our present situation of pain, disturbance and questioning.

To recall it more easily, we may recognize and use specific links that already exist, and also systematically associate a specific link with our remembered experience (session 5).

Today for our meditation let's recall a peak faith experience, linking it at its intensest point by touch, gesture, breathing, or whatever is our usual link, and using the experience as a base to center ourselves in our meditation.

PRACTICE

Taking time now to recall an intense or peak experience on your spiritual journey.

Scanning the past for a turning point in your life when God seemed very real to you; when you were very aware of his presence. Putting yourself right inside the experience, seeing and hearing and feeling and smelling and tasting all that is in this situation for you. Remembering to link in the experience at its height. And using this experience as a base for openness and awareness. And when you are ready, using these questions to write down your reactions:

(a) How did you think and feel in the original experience?

(b) How did the experience originally affect your immediate situation?

(c) How do you think and feel about the experience now?

(d) What to you are the features of a faith experience?

SHARING

Share and pray in twos. Activate our link and note the effect.

In the whole group, on the board draw up a list of the main features of a peak faith experience.

EXTENSION

What is a Peak Faith Experience?

Here are some common characteristics of a peak faith experience:
A sense of —

God's presence, of mystery, of awe
The unexpected
Inclusiveness—being part of the universe; being in touch with a reality far wider than ourselves
Being loved and affirmed, urged on and encouraged because we are ourselves
Being willing to trust this love, finding God trustworthy and so having our trust deepened
Being led
Being protected and provided for, having circumstances falling into place
Being open to ourselves and others
Being helped to let go, to shed our burdens
Having peace about the outcome
All these intangibles are gifts to us, given by God.

*Some Questions for Reflecting
on our Awareness and Experience of God*

Recognizing what God is to us and having a real desire for God and commitment to God and to others is basic for discerning God in ourselves and in other people.

We need to ask ourselves, "What is God for me?"

The more we become aware, i.e., the more we discern, experience, know God's Spirit moving in our own lives, urging us on to greater possibilities, the more we recognize God in the people and world around us. In our lives there are high peaks and lower peaks.

It may be useful to ask ourselves: "What has been an experience of God in my life this week? Recently?" "What is one of the high peaks, a turning point, a pivotal, basic faith experience in my life?"

**Reflecting on Our Own Experience
(Based on Shalem Institute
for Spiritual Formation 1986)**

Here are some suggestions to help us reflect on our own experience so that we may be more aware, may discern more clearly what is happening and what it means.

Ask yourself:

1. A favorite name I have for God is . . .
2. The name by which God calls me is . . .
3. Something in my life more important than God's will for me is . . .
4. How it feels when my will is in harmony with God's will . . .
5. How it feels when my will is not in harmony with God's will . . .
6. Where I often experience God's presence . . .
7. What helps me to be sensitive to God's presence . . .
8. What dulls my sensitivity to God's presence . . .
9. A sacred place on my journey where I experienced some clarity about my special path to holiness . . .
10. How I came to recognize my call to my present state of life . . .
11. How I see my present occupation as a response to God's will . . .
12. Something that helps me in making such choices . . .
13. A sign that I have made choices in response to God's will . . .
14. A significant decision I am now facing . . .
15. Something that might impair my freedom to make this decision in accord with God's will . . .
16. A discipline that might help me be more free in making this decision according to God's will . . .
17. How my faith community has been a help/hindrance to the significant choices in my life . . .
18. How the Bible illumines my path . . .
19. I forget myself when . . .
20. When I see a sunset . . .

C. BECOMING AWARE IN COUNSELING SKILLS

Some Ways of Changing: Direct Thanking Prayer, Affirmations, Associating

INTRODUCTION

Last session we considered how crisis may develop from our own perception and assessment, of whether the event is creative or threatening for us, and of our resources for coping. We may react on a continuum from love to fear, and if we assess both the event and our resources negatively we are in crisis.

We also saw the importance of identifying and owning the feelings aroused in a negative situation and expressing them as I-messages; considering anger as an often ineffective resource that we substitute for identifying and dealing with the underlying feeling. We related the Kubler-Ross grief model and impasse model.

In this last section of our program we shall be concentrating more directly on how we can identify and use the positive resources we have, and how we can open ourselves more, how we can change and grow.

Direct Thanking Prayer

When we have a negative attitude we want to change, we may pray directly and successfully for the opposite attitude. The most successful praying may be to accept that we already have it and to thank God for giving it to us. This is one kind of affirmation. We may also use more structured approaches to help us accomplish the changes we want and may pray for.

Affirmations

Affirmations are one way of owning our feelings and altering them. Each of us is encouraged by being affirmed by other people, appreciated for ourselves. But how often do we accept our own or someone else's negative judgment of ourselves and plant that inside ourselves and let it bear fruit?

If we identify a negative feeling or attitude we hold toward ourselves, and we want to change it and replace it with a positive one, we may have to work on it in a concentrated way to replace all the previous messages we have sent. One way of doing this is to identify the positive feeling or attribute and imagine ourselves as having it in the future. And remember, the future starts now. We lock it firmly into ourselves by saying or writing it.

It is important to:

    make it positive (not negative positive).

put it in the present tense.
put in our own name.

One way is to divide the page into two columns, headed affirmations and response. Under affirmation we write "I . . . (own name) am/ feel . . . ," and opposite, under response, write our immediate reaction. We do this ten times, probably with a different response each time. We repeat it a further ten times, using the form "You . . . (own name) are . . . ," and again ten times using "S/he . . . (own name) is. . . ." Then we read them over and discover in what way our immediate reaction is changing. It may be useful to repeat the affirmations often; e.g., on waking or going to sleep; saying them aloud; writing them or speaking them to ourselves in a mirror.

PRACTICE

Each write an affirmation and response as described.

SHARING

Share results as appropriate.

EXTENSION

Some people use touch in a different way to link in affirmations as a positive resource. They tap between the cheek bones and the eyes saying "I . . . (own name) accept myself, as I am, with all my faults and with all my great potential. I can and I will. . . . This program is accepted. Negative out. Positive in." They repeat the words while tapping with three fingers on the side of each hand below the little finger. A follow-up affirmation that may be repeated during the day is "I . . . (own name) am very happy with. . . ."

Another way is imaginatively to put one hemisphere of our brain in one hand and the other in the other hand, stretch our arms sideways and bring out hands slowly together, repeating the affirmation till our hands are together. We may then bring our hands to our center to incorporate the affirmation more fully. This way is known as visual squash.

Systematic Associating

In session 5 we realized that we are continually associating experiences seemingly at random. We are continually using established links; we are acting in our usual way and continuing to link ourselves into our past and present experience in positive and negative ways; e.g., our body posture, tone of voice.

As we considered in session 5, associating does not have to be random; it is a resource that we may use systematically.

Touch is a useful link to use systematically as it is with us in crisis to help us to draw on our positive resources. To be effective it needs to be repeated in the same place with the same intensity.

In our program we are concerned with the way we may use systematic associating to center our attention, and to effect permanent changes that we want to achieve; to establish useful associations and ways of associating our past and present experience; to expand our vision and widen our range of choices in a way that has a satisfying outcome for us, and that makes us aware of God and of resources beyond our own.

SHARING

Comment as appropriate.

Reassessing and Changing
Our Reactions to Our Past and Our Future

INTRODUCTION

Process and Content

When we are helping someone to change, just as when we are using our verbal listening skills, attending to the content may be interesting, even exciting, but may be a distraction.

Attending to the sharer's processing, rather than to the content, frees the sharer from our reactions. Our job as helpers is to gain and maintain rapport and enable the sharer to explore their own world and open themselves more fully to their own choice of possibilities and resources, including God's Holy Spirit.

Reasons for Changing our Past Associations

Because our own past is made up of how we ourselves perceive, assess and react to past events, we may alter our perceptions, our concepts, to reassess the event, and to react more positively now. Our past perceptions and reactions affect us continually in the present; we also use our memories to anticipate and choose our future.

One way of changing how we perceive and

react to our past, of linking it more satisfyingly to our present, is by breaking some of the links, and making more useful associations.

The following exercise suggests one systematic way to set about reassessing our past and changing our reaction to it, and then testing the changes.

PRACTICE

Reassessing and Changing
Our Reactions to Our Past

The idea is first of all to identify the feeling and behavior you want to change; then to relive three or four experiences, starting with a recent example and going back to one of the earliest that you can remember, of the feeling which you want to change; at the height of each experience to link it with a different specific stimulus, and to identify it by your name or by your age at the time. Then after a break to identify the resources you needed in order to feel and behave in a more satisfying way; to relive real or imaginary strong experiences of feeling and behaving in this satisfying way, and to associate each of them with different systematic links.

When you introduce your strongly satisfying feelings and behavior, by using all the satisfying links, into your memory of each past event, they become integrated into it, and modify your present assessment and reactions to your memory of your past.

An easily accessible stimulus is to press a different finger of your right hand on your right thigh for each unwanted experience and use your left hand and thigh for your satisfying experiences.

The leader may give a demonstration with one person or practice with the whole group, using the following wording.

Then if there is time, practice in twos.

Practice Wording for Changing Our
Reactions to Our Past

Note: Be as aware as possible of the sharer's reactions and timing.

Let's practice using a systematic link by associating one now with a satisfying fairly intense experience, e.g., pressing your thumb on your wrist and then testing it. In the exercise we will use our thighs.

Giving a signal, e.g., a nod each time you are ready to go on.

First of all, identifying the feeling and behavior that you want to change.

And when you are ready, reliving a recent experience of the feeling you want to change, and at its height associating a link by pressing with one finger on your right thigh. Experiencing it fully from the inside, becoming aware of what you are seeing and hearing and touching and feeling and smelling and tasting. Giving it a name or your age. Indicating when you have finished.

And when you are ready, still associating the first link; e.g., pressing your finger, going back through time to find another significant experience when you felt the same way. Experiencing it fully, and at its height linking it by pressing your next finger. Then naming it.

And now perhaps going back to the earliest time you can remember feeling that feeling, experiencing it fully, and at its height associating it with another finger. Then naming it.

Now remembering exactly where they were, releasing the links and coming back to the present. Perhaps taking a deep breath, or moving in some way.

Now taking your time to identify the resource you needed for the past experiences to have been satisfying, preferably almost the opposite of the unwanted feeling and behavior you identified and made links with before. It needs to be a resource or feeling which influences your own behavior, not someone else's.

Soon, when you relive experiences of using these satisfying resources, you will need to associate them with different links in a different place; e.g., with your left fingers on your left thigh. Three or four may be enough. Or you may like five. Your experiences may be real or imaginary; you may like to imagine what you would like to be or do in your wildest dreams, or imagine excitement or danger.

So now, remembering to link it in at its intensest, reliving a situation when you experienced this satisfying feeling fully. Experiencing it now fully from the inside. Being aware of what you are seeing and hearing and touching and feeling and tasting and smelling.

And now finding another time when you intensely experienced this feeling that you want to have, and associating it with the next link.

Reliving or imagining from the inside one or two more deeply satisfying experiences, and linking them with other fingers. Three or four may be enough. Or you may like another. If at any time you need more, you may come back and associate more.

Now, holding all the links to your satisfying resources, press the finger that is the one link to the most recent unwanted experience, and go through that experience using your satisfying resources, feeling and behaving the way you want to.

When you are satisfied, still holding all the positive links, move on to the next unwanted experience by pressing the next finger. If necessary you can get more or different satisfying resources.

Still holding the satisfying resource links, going through each unwanted experience fully, back to the earliest, till you are satisfied.

Now without holding any of the links, recalling the past unwanted experiences one by one, noticing the changes (however slight) in your memory, i.e., your perception of the event. If you do not notice the change, you may need to repeat the exercise with stronger satisfying experiences, real or imagined.

When you have noticed the change, imagining the next time you are likely to be in a similar situation, reliving it using your satisfying resources but no systematic links. Do you think, are you sure that you will be more comfortable in the future? (If necessary, project a color slide up on a screen in front of you to see. When you have projected a slide of the situation, step into it with your wonderful resources, pressing no systematic links).

Now associating your satisfying experiences and resources with your usual systematic link, to have them readily available; e.g., by pressing on your left thigh with the fingers which were satisfying links, and pressing your left wrist at the same time.

SHARING
Comment in the whole group as appropriate.

EXTENSION
Some of the exercises that we have used today may seem strange, but they are all ways that may help us to do our part in feeling and behaving the way we prefer to and pray to be able to. They are practical ways to break or dissolve the automatic negative links from the past which imprison us, by linking in positive and deeply satisfying feelings and behavior which may then more easily arise in similar situations. When we repeat the last exercise with different situations, drawing on our own peak faith experiences, reliving other real or imaginary satisfying ones, and introducing these satisfying resources into our own negative memories at their intensest point, we may be using a practical way of opening that part of our experience to God's Spirit and to the gifts which God wants for us.

As Hart puts it, "When we come in touch with our own deepest orientation and desire, . . . we have also found God's direction for our lives. This is the fundamental principle around which the discernment principle pivots" (Hart, 1980, 75).

D. CONCLUDING

RECOLLECTING
Quietly reflect and journal.

EVALUATION
Briefly comment on the session.

HOME PRACTICE
Practice direct thanking prayer formally and at various times during the day. Practice affirmations, and at least once practice substituting deeply satisfying links for the unwanted behavior that we still associate with one or more past experiences, remembering to introduce them at the intensest point. If possible, practice the exercise in twos, taking turns.

LOOKING AHEAD
Next session we consider how we may become more aware of God's presence on our inward and outward journey, through surrendering our own wills. We also practice overlapping our awareness of various senses, and separating negative feelings from a memory.

AFFIRMATION
Close with the grace, holding hands.

Discerning God's Presence: The Journey Inward and Outward; Surrender: Overlapping to Increase Our Discerning Separating Negative Feelings from a Memory

A. BECOMING AWARE OF WHERE WE ARE

RECOLLECTING
Being still in the presence of God.

RECAP
Last time we considered how recollecting a deeply meaningful experience, and our awareness of God at work guiding us through it, is foundational for discerning God's loving presence and guidance in times of uncertainty, deep disturbance and pain; and that remembering and sharing such peak faith experiences beforehand makes them more effective in crisis.

We considered the power of using other past satisfying experiences systematically to counteract the unsatisfactory effects of past experiences on our present and future. Some suggested ways were direct thanking prayer, affirmations, and reassessing and changing our associations with our past.

SHARING
Brief sharing.

TODAY'S THEME
Today we consider the two-way nature of the journey to knowing God, and the place of surrender, conversion, and prayer in discerning how God is guiding our lives.

We use overlapping to increase our awareness, and practice one way of separating negative feelings from a memory.

B. BECOMING AWARE IN FORMAL PRAYING

Discerning God's Presence: The Journey Inward and Outward

INTRODUCTION
Decide on twos for later sharing and praying together.

In the group sit quietly and slowly sing two verses of the hymn "Be still and know"; i.e., "Be still and know that I am God. I am the Lord that healeth thee."

Silently open ourselves to God in whatever way is appropriate for us. Taking all the time we need to appreciate God's presence.

SHARING
In twos aim to stay or to get in touch with a deeper level of awareness, i.e., God in the situation, taking it in turns to share. The listener starts with an open question about a recent experience. As appropriate, the listener then may introduce open questions such as:

(a) How do you sense God (Jesus, the Spirit) in this?

(b) How do you sense yourself/others in it at the deeper level of your/their awareness?

(c) How is this situation affected by/affecting your praying?

The listener uses their verbal listening skills and concludes with a summary as a formal prayer.

Brief journaling as desired.

Share in the whole group as appropriate.

EXTENSION

Basic Assumptions about Discerning God's Presence

To discern is to sort out, sift through. This is the root meaning of discernment. In Greek the word is *diakrisis*; through or because of a crisis, verdict or negative judgment; the ability to distinguish good and evil.

A basic assumption of the discernment process of this program is that God is present and active as a loving, personal, integrative force at work in the world, in the universe and in the lives of all of us, whether we recognize God or not (session 1: aims and assumptions).

A further assumption, originating from the first, is that discerning this presence and activity involves a movement, a change, a journey toward knowing God both in toward self and out toward others.

The Journey Inward

Discerning God's loving presence and activity, in our own and other people's lives in the world which God is creating, begins with Jeremiah's understanding that God's law is written in our hearts, deep within us: "Deep within them I will plant my Law, writing it on their hearts" (Jer. 31:33. *The Jerusalem Bible*). Luke expresses it this way: "The Kingdom of God is within you" (Lk. 17:21).

Both writers express a similar idea: that deep within us, at the point of our deepest desire and orientation, God speaks to us, God touches us, God's purpose is made known to us. When we are in touch with that desire, when we are open

to that touch in the deepest recesses of self, we may know God's direction and guidance for our lives. (Compare Jung's process of individuation and Ignatius Loyola's approach to discernment, referred to in Hart, 1980, 76–83).

So freeing the gift of God's word and presence in us, for us and for others, involves a movement inward.

The Journey Outward

But discovering God, being discovered by God, i.e., being impressed by God, involves a movement not only inward but also outward toward knowing God as found in others, in the world, in the universe. The journey out to others involves serving them and recognizing God working in them. A test of the validity of our own self-discoveries is how far we are willing to be led by God both inward and outward, and a test as we move either way is whether we are adaptable, whether we are willing to be led in the opposite direction.

So the two-way journey that the discernment process addresses leads both to the universe within ourselves where God may be experienced and heard, and to the universe beyond ourselves where God may likewise be encountered and speak to us and to others. When these journeys together issue in appropriate choices and action, they balance and validate each other.

Surrender, Conversion

The processes of surrendering, being converted and praying are fundamental to the discerning journey toward knowing God.

Discerning God's call on our journeying, being open to God, involves a willingness to surrender, to be converted from willfulness to willingness. It involves sifting through the options and sensing where they lead; e.g., "Do the choices that I see lead toward God in willingness or away from God in willfulness?" "Am I listening to myself on all levels of my being, the rational as well as the feeling, the conscious as well as the unconscious?" "Is my mind telling me one thing and my heart another?"

A basic principle of discerning guidance is whether heart and mind and soul, the inner self, are in agreement. In discerning God's desire for us we feel a basic sense of integrity, we recognize the best choice for our whole self. In other words, our choices as we understand them, what we propose to do in relation to what we are, need to be in agreement with our deepest desire. Discerning God's guidance is a matter of "getting head and heart and faith together" (Doherty, 1986).

Discernment in Praying

Praying is learning to be open to God in the depths of ourselves. Much of what we have already said about opening ourselves to God and helping others to open themselves to God has been about the need to listen to ourselves and be aware on all levels, especially at our deepest level where God speaks and touches us most, and the need to listen and be aware in a way that helps others to do the same. Basic listening and awareness then, which leads us inward and outward in openness to God, to others, to God's world, is praying. It is the essence of communion with God.

Praying, understood as opening ourselves, surrendering our willfulness to God's willingness, and encouraging in others this open prayerful approach to life, is basic to our discerning God's presence and guidance in ourselves and others. So it is basic to the helping relationship which we are aiming to develop in this program.

Many people in crisis, for example, while in the hospital, may not understand prayer in this sense, and they may not label what we are doing through nonverbal awareness and effective listening as an attempt to help them to grow in praying. But in fact they may already be engaging in this kind of praying and living, and the crisis of coming to hospital heightens their awareness and their need to develop this approach further. One basic supposition of spiritual guidance is that people need to pray in the sense of opening themselves to more of God, more of reality in themselves and others. We need to encourage them in this process without labeling what they are doing in terms which may put them off by linking them into past unhelpful perceptions of what praying means.

However, open questions such as those we used in our praying in twos may be useful in en-

abling the sharer to come to a deeper appreciation of their situation.

SHARING
Any comments and questions.

C. BECOMING AWARE IN COUNSELING SKILLS

Overlapping to Increase Our Discerning

INTRODUCTION
Last session we considered several related ways of changing our perception of ourselves: through direct prayer, accepting that we are different, and thanking God that we are receiving or have already received what we desire; through written or verbal repeated affirmations and visual squash; through systematic associating to change our present reactions to past events. When we were changing our associations with our past, we experienced the unsatisfactory events as fully as possible and then brought resources from our fully experienced satisfying situations to replace our negative reactions in the present.

One way of opening ourselves, of increasing our awareness on all levels, expanding our awareness of the here and now, and of God relating to us through all our senses, is through overlapping. Overlapping is a process of helping the sharer to make links between their various sensory ways of processing material (i.e., their seeing, hearing, feeling, smelling, tasting), so that their own inner resources are more readily available to enrich and deepen their lives.

In our daily lives we continually overlap, but if an event is too painful we may block part of it from our memory. In conscious overlapping we as helpers may begin by helping the sharer to remember an event in the way they usually do, perhaps by feeling, perhaps visually, and then at the most natural point, introduce a second way of experiencing, e.g., move from feeling to seeing.

PRACTICE
As the leader goes slowly through the following example of overlapping, we may each imagine ourselves to be the sharer:
For example, the sharer may choose to remember being barefoot on grass; the sharer may

tell us that they are in touch with the situation and know how it feels. So we know that their main thinking mode is probably feeling, we know that they can think in the feeling mode.

We may say something like this: "And as you are there on the grass, feeling the air against your skin, feeling the air being drawn into your lungs and out again, just seeing your chest rising and falling. And as you are feeling the grass against your feet and feeling your feet moving against the grass, seeing the grass moving as you move. Seeing the color of the grass. And as you see the color of the grass and see your chest rising and falling in the rhythm of your breathing, hearing your breath going in and out of your body making its own sound and own rhythm. And as you are feeling your breath and hearing it going in and out rhythmically, becoming conscious of the other sounds that you hear around you."

EXTENSION

The idea is to keep away from inserting any of our own ideas, staying only with what must be there in the given situation, i.e., process not content. Using participles, e.g., "feeling," "seeing," is a gentle noncontroversial way of overlapping, in comparison with an order "see, look at," or a phrase like "you can"—perhaps at this stage they cannot.

Overlapping may be a useful, pleasant and versatile way of enabling us to enter more fully into a wide range of experiences, present and past, as well as reassociating in our conscious minds parts of an experience which was so painful that we have buried some parts.

SHARING

Share comments.

PRACTICE

If there is time, practice briefly in twos.

SHARING

Share in the whole group.

Separating Negative Feelings from a Memory

INTRODUCTION

*Reasons for Separating
Negative Feelings From a Memory*

In this session we shall consider a way of enabling change in ourselves when the feeling associated with the memory of a past event is very strong. Indeed our feelings may be so intense as the result of a severely traumatic experience in our past that when anything associated with the trauma occurs in the present or we imagine it in the future we are overwhelmed by our past feeling, and are precipitated into crisis; i.e., we have a phobia or phobic response, such as a terror of the dark or of being closed in. Often a person is not conscious of the actual past event, and may need help to recover it by going back in time, as in changing our reaction to our past or by using overlapping.

Once the sharer has identified the past or the imagined future experience associated with the intense present feelings, our aim as helpers is to help them to have a choice of feelings. The response is then no longer automatic; they may choose whether to respond in their old way or in a different way that is more satisfying and creative.

So far in our sessions when recalling an experience we have put ourselves inside the experience. This is the intense way to reexperience the event directly, and is the way we normally recall our pleasant experiences, especially when visualizing them (seeing remembered).

But the natural way to see our past unpleasant experiences is to construct a picture of ourselves that we are looking at from outside the event so that we have feelings about the situation rather than in the situation. When we dissociate ourselves in this way from our unpleasant feelings, we may learn from an event without reexperiencing it.

So when the sharer has a strong negative response that they want to change and they have identified the traumatic experience, if they can look at and hear the experience from the outside and separate their feelings from the picture and the sound, their negative response will no longer be automatic: they will have a choice of how they will react.

*An Example of Separating
Our Negative Feelings from a Memory
When?*

This way is useful:

1. With a strong emotional response or phobia.

2. To prepare for something in the future.
3. To improve something we already do well and would like to do better.

How?

As in all these techniques and helping relationships, we need to gain and maintain rapport by being aware of and matching the sharer's nonverbal messages. We may also establish an agreed signal, such as a nod or finger movement. We also need to explain the procedure clearly, and ensure that the sharer understands how to associate satisfying experiences systematically, wants to change, and has identified an unwanted experience.

PRACTICE

The leader may choose to demonstrate this way with one person. We may either learn by watching or by being the sharer ourselves, even though the timing may not be fine-tuned for us. So join in as the leader goes through the preliminaries with one sharer.

When we are using this way with a sharer, we first establish the above framework. We may then use the following suggested words in quotation marks; the brackets enclose notes for us as helpers.

"Now imagining that we are both sitting in the middle of an empty movie theater, (for plenty of distance)" and you are bringing with you all your positive resources. You may like now to link in one by one a whole lot more positive resources, taking all the time you need and getting as many as you want. Getting plenty and if you need more, you may always come back and get some.

"And when you are ready, looking at the empty screen in front of you and putting on to it a slide of the younger self that was you just before the event occurred; only looking at it, from a distance."

(This is the first dissociation. If they cannot visualize the situation, we may return to overlapping or ask them to go inside themselves and ask the part of them that knows).

"And as you see that younger self over there on the screen as you sit here safely with me, now floating outside yourself and standing directly behind yourself here." (To link in this second dis-

sociation we put our hand on their shoulder, and keep it there. If they find it difficult to float out, we may get them to imagine putting a life-size doll of themselves where they are sitting).

(This double dissociation makes it easier for the sharer to keep the feelings separate from the picture of the event. If at any time the sharer does start to reexperience the original feelings, we need to bring them back completely to the present and establish more satisfying links. We need to distinguish between a response to what happened, i.e., tears now, and a reexperiencing of the past).

"And now you have floated out, moving further back, to the back of the theater, into the projectionist's booth, watching us sitting here comfortably in the middle of the theater, as we watch that younger self over there on the screen.

"And when you are ready in the projectionist's booth, changing the slide into a movie of the event, taking all the time you need to watch that younger self over there going through that experience. Seeing it as slowly as you need to, and using as many of your resources and links as you need.

"And when the film is over, scanning the film again to check whether there is any part of the film that has been left out or needs replaying, perhaps making some picture smaller or turning down the sound. Taking all the time you need to learn what that younger self needs from you and making sure that you are satisfied. And indicating when you have finished.

"And now you have finished watching the film, coming back from the projectionist's booth and floating back here into your body, indicating when you are back here. And now you are comfortably back, I'm going to take my hand off your shoulder so that you can go with all your resources to comfort that younger self over there, knowing that God's Spirit is in you, providing the resources you need."

(If the sharer is not back comfortably, and needs reassuring, we may keep our hand on their shoulder until they have linked in more satisfying resources. Once they have reintegrated those two parts of themselves, we no longer need our hand there to mark that dissociation).

(If this first reintegration is difficult, the sharer may separate out again to a distance, and reintegrate the younger self first, as in the following sections, and then join the self from a distance with the other two).

"You have just been watching that younger self going through a terrible experience and you're the only person in the world who knows exactly what s/he needs to feel comforted and reassured. That younger self did the best s/he could at the time with the resources s/he had. But you, the older you, are coming to him/her from the future, with more resources, coming with God's healing love.

"So now going forward to comfort that younger you, perhaps taking him/her in your arms, and telling him/her that what has happened will never happen again, and being sure to tell him/her that s/he did the best s/he could at the time with the resources that s/he had. Taking all the time you need until you know that s/he feels comforted and reassured and safe. And letting him/her know that s/he can stop worrying about it now because you are older and you will take care of everything now.

"And when s/he is comforted and reassured and safe enough, bringing the younger you back into your body."

(We watch for a deep breath as a sign of integration. If integration is difficult, the sharer may need to use visual squash, with arms stretched sideways and one self in each hand; bringing the two selves together until the two hands touch, and then pressing them to their center. It is preferable for the sharer to integrate at the time, but it may have to be deferred till a bit later).

"And now you are back together sitting here safely, without pressing any systematic links, but making use of your good resources, thinking of a similar event in the future, or picking one from the past and imagining it is future, or imagining yourself watching a similar situation on T.V.; then stepping into the picture to experience it."

"And when you are ready, indicating how that was for you." (We need to check whether anything more is needed, e.g. the event may need to be divided into more manageable chunks. Even when further work is needed, there is almost certain to have been some change).

SHARING
Comments and questions.
If there is time, practice in twos.

EXTENSION
People have been dissociating themselves from destructive, negative or socially unacceptable past behavior from time immemorial. As we have learned, it seems a natural reaction to dissociate ourselves from unpleasant memories by visualizing them from the outside rather than from inside ourselves, so that we have feelings about the situation, rather than in it. Dissociation is not an end in itself. What is important is that it results in healthier, more freeing integration. Like the other ways of changing that we are learning about in this program, this way of separating feelings from a negative event may often produce effective and lasting change by opening the sharer to a greater choice of reacting in the way that they really want and the Holy Spirit within them wants.

D. CONCLUDING

RECOLLECTING
Quiet reflecting and journaling.

EVALUATION
Brief comments and evaluation.

HOME PRACTICE
Practice asking ourselves the discernment questions, becoming aware of overlapping, and if possible practice with someone else separating negative feelings from a memory so that we each have a turn as listener and sharer.

LOOKING AHEAD
Next session we shall practice discerning God's presence in the last twenty-four hours; consider our role as spiritual guide-friend; relate the A.B.C. crisis method to three areas of creative change; and practice discerning God's love for us through loving ourselves as someone else loves us.

AFFIRMATION
Holding hands sing one verse of the hymn: "Be still and know that I am God."

Practicing Discerning
The Role of Spiritual Guide-friend
An A.B.C. Crisis Method
Discerning God's Love for Us

A. BECOMING AWARE OF WHERE WE ARE

RECOLLECTING
Being still in the presence of God.
Praying silently or aloud.

RECAP

Practicing Discerning:
The Two-Way Movement

Last time we considered discerning God's presence as a two-way movement: an inward opening of ourselves to God as experienced in our own depths, and an outward opening of ourselves to God as encountered in the depths of others, in the world and in the universe, including all God-given structures.

This prayerful opening of ourselves and growing trust in reality, in God, is indispensable to discerning God's call. This two-way movement, issuing in appropriate action, is the self-validating test of whether our awareness comes from willing surrender or willful resistance to God. In other words, if our search either inward or outward leads to the exclusion of one side of the movement, then we may doubt whether we are discerning God's call aright. Each movement is a complementary aspect of the other.

We used overlapping to increase our aware-

ness, and practiced separating negative feelings from a memory.

SHARING
Brief comments.

TODAY'S THEME
In this session we consider further practical implications of discerning God's call, and of our role as Christian helper and spiritual friend to others. We relate an A.B.C. crisis method to three areas of creative change, and practice loving ourselves as someone else loves us.

B. BECOMING AWARE IN FORMAL PRAYING

Meditation on Discerning God's Presence in the Last Twenty-four Hours

PRACTICE
First of all today, let's be still again.
1. When you are ready, starting from here and now, looking backward over the last twenty-four hours; letting those hours roll back, perhaps hour by hour from now to this time yesterday.

What is emerging?
Are you noticing things you often take for granted?
How do you feel?

2. Looking backward again, from now back over the last twenty-four hours, asking God to show you how God has been present in your life; in you, in others, in the many events of the day.

a. How did you meet God in the last twenty-four hours?

In fears, misunderstanding, weariness, suffering, joys, work, freedom? In a friend, an event, a book, nature, music?

b. When did you and God seem to be cooperating, working well together? In which areas did you not respond, not cooperate with God?

c. In which area of your life do you sense God calling you to a change of heart?

d. How are you sensing the poverty in your life? What are you sensing that you can be grateful for? Just allowing gratitude to take hold of you. Expressing your gratitude and thanks to God, speaking or moving in whatever way is appropriate for you.

Journaling now, asking ourselves such questions as:

In this experience of the last twenty-four hours, when I was first considering my life, how much was I considering my life in relation to God?

What have I learned about myself and about how God is working in my life?

Which learning has any particular significance? What do I need to stay with, to pray about?

SHARING

Share and pray for each other in twos or in small groups, remembering to use rapport and listening skills.

Share in the whole group as appropriate.

C. BECOMING AWARE IN COUNSELING SKILLS

INTRODUCTION

Our Concepts of God May Need to Change

Prayerful opening of ourselves to more of reality may mean letting go of God as we at present conceive God, and embracing a more inclusive concept. Such openness to an expanding view of God, of reality, may be scary but indispensable to following Jesus. Concepts of reality, of God, are essential for effective living, but they have no ultimate significance (session 15: forming our concepts; session 9: centering). God is within and beyond all attempts to categorize God, to categorize reality, including our own reality.

The Role of Spiritual Guide-friend in Discerning God's Call

Being Aware

In discerning God's call, as with listening generally, effective guidance involves being aware: being aware of the nonverbal behavior and the sensory words which are the clue to the sharer's deepest inside response to what is happening to them.

> The quality of listening is decisive in the discernment process. . . . As spiritual guide-friend, it is not our role to impose our discernment on others. The locus of discernment is in the other person. And one of the greatest gifts that we can offer others is to allow them, to encourage them, to be where they are, to be with them, in compassion. Then the word of God may reach, may touch them where they are (Doherty, 1986).

So being a spiritual guide-friend to another person involves all that has been said about effective listening. It involves establishing and maintaining rapport and trust. It involves attending to the inside world of the sharer, to their thoughts, feelings and assessment of satisfying resources, by reflecting the sharer's words and images, summarizing, and using open questions and specifiers.

Because our specific role as spiritual guide-friend is to enable the discerning process in ourselves and others, it also involves asking open questions that encourage the sharer to explore the meaning of what is happening to them, and how this affects their basic values, concepts and response to reality. It involves asking open questions about how God may be present and moving in the situation, in the people and the relationships involved (session 19).

In short, the discernment process involves listening to and being aware of our deepest self, where God's Spirit may be most clearly discerned, and it involves listening to and being aware of others in a way that enables them to listen to and be aware of their deepest self, and make discoveries about what they really desire at their deepest level.

SHARING

Discuss how this relates to our own role as helpers.

Options and Decisions

INTRODUCTION

Opening ourselves prayerfully to God, as experienced in our deepest selves and in the deep recesses of others, lays the foundation for realizing what options we have, and for making decisions. Without opening ourselves, it may be difficult for us to experience God, to be impressed by God. In times of confusion and crisis, when we are at the crossroad and are being pressured to make choices and decisions, it may only be possible for us to discern God's presence and guidance by prayerful openness and attention to the direction in which our life is heading.

Many people may deny this need or be unwilling to label their search for meaning, purpose and direction in conventional religious language, until they are in dire straits, but in desperation they may well open themselves enough to call out. It is at this point that we may help them to listen for the answer; not an answer valid for us that we may impose on them, but the answer being given to them which they may discover for themselves if they listen. We may help them to dissolve the barriers which limit their choices, decisions and awareness of greater possibilities for openness and movement.

This opening in desperation is what makes crisis a unique opportunity and responsibility (session 2; crisis).

SHARING

Discuss briefly.

An A.B.C. Crisis Method
(based on Stone, 1976, 32–48)

INTRODUCTION

The basic assumption of crisis theory as outlined by Stone is that we perceive a gap between the situation we are facing and our perception of the resources that we have to cope with it (session 2).

An A.B.C. crisis method for Christian helpers is:

A. Attuning and achieving rapport with God, self and sharer.

B. Basic listening to extract the essentials.

C. Creative change to cope with crisis.

Undergirding this method is the understanding that God is the one who initiates, guides and fulfills our search for meaning, purpose, values and direction.

As we have seen, when we are attuned and are achieving and maintaining rapport with God, ourselves and the sharer, A, then basic listening, B, may be enough to enable the sharer to listen to their inner depths, the God within, and to raise questions of meaning, purpose and values, whether or not the term God is used (sessions 8–15,18). When the sharer is moving toward identifying the desired change or the problem to be solved, the outcome model provides a sequence of useful open questions (session 10).

Sometimes the helper needs to take a more active share in creating change, C, while still using A and B, and while still staying with the sharer's concept of their world. In this last part of our program we are considering some ways in which we may share actively in enabling change, i.e., the C part of the A.B.C. crisis method.

The Three Areas of Creative Change

There are three interrelated areas in which creative change may occur in order to cope with crisis: outer (environment), inner (emotions), and ultimate (meaning).

1. Outer (Environment) Area of Change

When the change is in the outer area of environment and action, listing the pros and cons or using the following R.I.P.A.L.C.A.R.T. framework may be useful in helping the sharer to clarify the issues intellectually, to realize the extent of choice and to make decisions which lead to action.

Pro and Con

If the choice has been identified as a yes-no decision it may be helpful to suggest that the sharer divide a page into two columns, and write down all the pros and cons (all the things for and against the proposal); or divide it into four columns and also write the pros and cons for the opposite, and then weigh up the possibilities.

R.I.P.A.L.C.A.R.T.

R.I.P.A.L.C.A.R.T. is a simple adaptable framework for change and decision which presupposes in the sharer a prayerful openness to possibilities for spiritual, emotional and physical change.

1. *Rapport:* build and maintain rapport with God, self and sharer, i.e., open and center self, and maintain openness (all sessions).
   Use nonverbal awareness skills throughout (sessions 2–7).
2. *Identify* the difficulty and the desired outcome.
   The outcome needs to be consistent with the sharer's values and able to be initiated and maintained by the sharer.
   Use verbal listening skills throughout (sessions 8–15).
   Use the outcome model to make the difficulty and outcome specific and stated positively (session 10).
3. *Perceive* and *assess positive resources* and *assets.*
   Consider the sharer's values, feelings, personality, abilities, previous experience, etc. (sessions 16,17).
4. *List* all possibilities, at least three, however wild.
   Include the option of doing nothing.
5. *Choose* a plan of action.
   Sift the possibilities (pros and cons may be useful).
   Remember rapport, listening skills, values, and the desired goal.
   Decide on one plan, work out details and possible blocks.
   Set time for review.
6. *Act.*
7. *Review.*
   If necessary, repeat.
8. *Thank.*
   "In everything give thanks" (Eph. 5:12).

Steps 1–3 of R.I.P.A.L.C.A.R.T. (Rapport-build, Identify, Perceive and Assess), are the A and B of the A.B.C. method of coping with crisis; i.e., attuning and achieving rapport with God, self and sharer; basic listening to extract the essentials.
Steps 4–7 (List, Choose, Act, Review) are directed toward deciding and acting, i.e., C: creative change to cope with crisis.
Step 8 (Thanking), like steps 1–3, is basic to the Christian helper's attitude, whether or not it is expressed aloud with the sharer.

2. Inner (Emotional) Area of Change

When the desired change concerns the sharer's emotions, relationships and values, or when at R.I.P.A.L.C.A.R.T. 3 the sharer assesses resources as inadequate, the helper may enable the sharer to change by using the ways of accepting and forgiving ourselves and enabling change which we are currently practicing; i.e., systematic associating, affirmations, changing our reaction to our past, overlapping, separating negative feelings from a memory (session 5, 18, 19), and others which we shall learn in later sessions.

3. Ultimate (Meaning) Area of Change

Questions of ultimate meaning, purpose, direction and values permeate the inner and outer areas of our lives.
In crisis many people who may not be overtly religious recognize that their value system is inadequate, and that if they had a clearer sense of direction in their lives they would be able to cope more creatively and effectively with the ongoing tensions of life.
As we have seen earlier in this session, it is our role and specific responsibility as spiritual guide-friend to attend to these questions in ourselves and to help others to discover their own God-given answers, and the resources to live with questions that are unanswered or unanswerable.
As the sharer experiences our basic rapport and listening, they, too, may be enabled to listen, and as they explore their inner depths, their awareness develops and changes. When the sharer has explored some of their ultimate questions, it may then be appropriate to help the

sharer to relate their new perceptions of reality back to the present situation and to their assessment of it; e.g., by using the ways of change for the inner emotional area, 2, or the outer environment area, 1, which we have just been considering.

It is essential for us as helpers to be maintaining our openness throughout, so that we may discern where the Spirit is leading us. There may be a place for sharing overtly our own perceptions of reality, meaning, and our experience of what we have found valuable, but we need to be wary of providing our own answers instead of allowing the sharer the joy of discovering for themselves God-given answers, promises and assurance.

SHARING
Discuss in the whole group.

Discerning God's Love for Us

INTRODUCTION
The whole Christian discernment process turns on the understanding and recognition that God loves us and accepts us as we are, forgiving us as we in turn forgive others, and calling us to be with Christ and like Christ in serving others.

How may we accept that God really does love us, and so accept ourselves as God does?

As with all grace, this love and acceptance is something that is given, even when it comes as a realization within ourselves. But more often it comes through our experiencing the love of another person. So loving ourselves as someone else loves us is one way of realizing the love that surrounds us, that we may open ourselves to. Because God loves us we may love ourselves, and so love others more.

Loving Ourselves as Someone Else Loves Us

Last session we thought about enabling openness and change through overlapping and by separating negative feelings from the remembered event. Now we shall practice a specific kind of dissociation which aims to take us outside ourselves, and so may enable us to change our perceptions of ourselves to more satisfying ones. Loving ourselves as someone else loves us may

help us to feel more lovable, and so open ourselves more to giving and receiving love.

In the helping relationship the sharer may be saying that God loves them while at the same time feeling that they are unlovable. They may feel worthless, depressed and lonely. The good news which Jesus brings us is that God knows everything about us and still loves us. We are precious to God.

If the sharer's concept of God or Jesus is forbidding, in the following exercise they may prefer to take someone real or imaginary whom they know loves them, perhaps the father in the story.

PRACTICE
As the leader goes through the following exercise we may each use it for ourselves.

*An Example of Loving Ourselves as
Someone Else Loves Us
(based on Cameron-Bandler, 1985, 185–7)*

First, gain and maintain rapport with the sharer, and ensure that the sharer's body and breathing is relaxed, probably with their eyes closed.

Read the story of the lost son and the loving father (Luke 15: 11–32).

Silently meditate on the story.

Then using such words as:

"And now taking time to experience someone who knows all about you and loves you. You may choose to take the father in the story as loving you in the same way that he loved the lost son; you may choose to think of God or Jesus; you may prefer to take someone real or imaginary whom you know loves you; whoever seems most appropriate.

"Starting by imagining yourself in a definite time in a definite place, and then imagining them also.

"Perhaps putting into words some of what makes this person so special for you; what you admire and respect and respond to; what you see in them; what you hear them saying to you, or have heard them say; how you feel toward them; how your smelling and tasting respond. Enjoying any satisfying feelings as you respond to their loving feelings towards you.

"And now, still in your definite place, leaving yourself there, and taking up the position of this person who loves you, becoming this person who loves you. You may want to move or turn your chair to help you to become this special person.

"Going inside and feeling all the loving qualities inside this person who loves you. Becoming aware of how this person who loves you feels and thinks about you, this person who loves and forgives and accepts you as you are. Sensing as they sense, feeling all the love that this person who loves you feels for you. Seeing through loving eyes what there is to love and admire and appreciate about you. Hearing through loving ears the sounds you make, telling yourself what it is that makes the everyday you so special and unique. Feeling the love that rises in you as you see and hear and feel and experience the everyday you whom you know so well and love so much.

"Taking all the time you need to explore and sense in your loving way qualities and memories, failures and successes, savoring them lovingly. Seeing and hearing and feeling them as you enjoy and appreciate and forgive and accept. Enjoying the everyday you who are lovable and loved, who are special and cherished because you are uniquely you.

"And now, still loving and cherishing the everyday you, and holding on to your loving admiration for your unique qualities, coming back inside yourself in your definite place and time, still feeling and remembering how precious you are to someone who really loves you. Taking all the time you need to enjoy being loved and lovable, and loving and cherishing yourself.

"Taking time, too, to respond to someone who loves you, showing them your love and gratitude, and thanking them in whatever way seems appropriate for you.

"And now moving ahead, perhaps to a particular situation, and experiencing now from the inside how lovable you are growing, how you are free to develop the unique qualities which you appreciate and love, and which make you you.

"When you are ready, returning to this room, and noting down whatever is appropriate. You may like to note down the qualities which you cherish in yourself when you experience yourself in the same way as someone who really loves you.

"Remembering that whenever you need to, you may again experience yourself in the same way as someone who really loves you."

Taking whatever time you need to come back to the group.

SHARING
Share in the whole group.

D. CONCLUDING

RECOLLECTING
Quiet reflecting and journaling.

EVALUATION
Brief evaluation of the session.

HOME PRACTICE
Practice discerning God in our everyday situations and loving ourselves as God loves us. Think about our role as guide-friends, and about how we may use an A.B.C. crisis method in three areas of creative change.

LOOKING AHEAD
Next time we shall think about healing, and practice a way of healing early relationships and memories with Jesus.

AFFIRMATION
Saying the grace in a group hug.

What Is Healing?
A Way of Healing Early Relationships and Memories with Jesus

A. BECOMING AWARE OF WHERE WE ARE

RECOLLECTING
Being still in the presence of God.
Praying aloud or silently.

RECAP
Last session we practiced discerning God in the last twenty-four hours and in loving ourselves as someone else loves us. We considered our role as guide-friend, and how we may incorporate an A.B.C. crisis method into three areas of creative change.

SHARING
Brief sharing.

TODAY'S THEME
Today we shall consider what we mean by healing, think about healing in our helping relationships, and experience a way of healing our early relationships and memories with Jesus.

B. AND C. BECOMING AWARE IN FORMAL PRAYING AND IN COUNSELING

PRACTICE
In the whole group sharing briefly and praying about our needs and celebrations.
Silently meditating, using our experience of God's love as a base.
Journal as desired.

What Is Healing?

INTRODUCTION
Healing, like discernment, takes us back to the beginning of this program and all that we have learned since then about prayer and the helping relationship. Healing is basically a process of growing together, of becoming integrated, unified, whole. "Healed" means made whole. The Latin word for well, safe, *salvus*, gives us our word "salvation." In healing we are becoming open and aware, becoming at-one with ourselves and others and God. Healing happens when we connect with the basic energy of the universe, which is love, when we get into step with the basic rhythm of the world, a rhythm whose main features are change, decay and renewal. So connecting with this rhythm often means that healing does not happen as we want it to happen.

Healing takes place on many different levels. And connecting with the basic rhythm of life may mean paradoxically connecting on some levels with disconnectedness. It may mean letting go of life, easing present attachments so that we may connect with and experience life in greater fullness; cf. the merchant who sold all that he had to buy the pearl of great price (Matt. 13:46). The process of discovering and being discovered by God, experiencing greater meaning in life, may literally mean dying. This may not be a denial of the process of healing; rather, it is healing being experienced on a different level from physical healing.

All healing is God's gift to us. What we, with God's help, may do is to remove some of the blocks, to create a positive environment in which God's healing may occur. Healing happens when we surrender ourselves as we are, with all our imperfections, to God's love, when we realize who we really are and that God's love is already present and active in and through everything.

As with discernment, and as with the Christian way generally, conversion (prayerful surrender of our willfulness to the willing love of God) is the prerequisite for the deep healing which we term fullness of life and which is promised to us when we turn to God in faith, in deepening trust.

SHARING
Discuss.

Healing in Counseling

INTRODUCTION

As helpers, our role is to encourage people in this process of simple prayerful openness and trusting, which helps them to discover who they are and the reality which is God's love for them now. What enables them to make this discovery is partly our use of our skills but also largely how much we have discovered for ourselves who we are and how much God loves us. The more we are in touch with our own reality, the more God can touch others through us.

Last session we considered discerning God's Spirit through the A.B.C. crisis method; i.e., by attuning ourselves to God, self and others, and by basic listening in three areas of creative change to cope with crisis. The three areas we thought about were:

1. The outer intellectual area of decision and choice (pros and cons, R.I.P.A.L.C.A.R.T.).
2. The inner area of emotional choice and reaction.
3. The ultimate area of choice of meaning, purpose and direction. We saw that when change or greater clarity is achieved in this ultimate area through basic listening and open questions, the choices in the outer and inner area are seen in a different perspective.

So far, in enabling change in the inner area of emotional choice, by associating, affirmations, changing history and separating negative feelings from a memory, we have used any satisfying resources, especially those which are the opposite qualities to the negative feeling. In sessions 16 and 17 we considered negative feelings as being on a continuum from fear to the positive feelings of love. Last session we used a special form of separating ourselves, i.e., loving ourselves as someone else loves us, to help us to become more open, loving and accepting of ourselves. This session we shall work with a way of opening ourselves and allowing all our early relationships and memories to be permeated by healing love, not only human love but perfect love, God's healing love.

In later sessions we shall consider first how we may deal with negative aspects of specific emotions; then by opening ourselves in specific past memories to all the positive qualities that we associate with God's love, how we may change and open ourselves more to accepting and forgiving others and ourselves.

When we consider our emotions as negative, we are considering them as inappropriate and having an effect which we consider undesirable and negative in the context. All our emotions may have positive effects in certain situations, and may be inappropriate in others.

A Way of Healing Early Relationships and Memories With Jesus

PRACTICE

Because the leader cannot adjust the timing to each member of the group as might be possible in an individual situation, we need to treat the words as a guide only, and to use them as appropriate.

In the helping relationship, after we have achieved rapport and the sharer is relaxed, we may introduce the healing of memories in some such way as the following:

"We know that many things in the present link us back into past negative reactions, that there are many situations in our past that we have not dealt with. Elisabeth Kübler-Ross (1978) calls them our "unfinished business." When these areas are opened, like a wound, they may be healed and may become beauty-spots or pearls. So it may be important to relate differently to significant people in our childhood in order to relate to people differently now.

"Jesus is the great healer, our Savior who loves us unconditionally. So now as we are letting the Holy Spirit of Jesus come into those areas of our past, we may trust Jesus to understand and keep on loving us. We may not feel different, but we may expect results. It is important for us to be inside the situation now, seeing, hearing, feeling, smelling, tasting, now from inside ourselves."

We then gently lead the sharer through the following steps, elaborating as appropriate. It may involve the sharer more deeply if we give them actual words, e.g., "Saying to Jesus . . . ; hearing Jesus saying to you . . . ."

1. Affirming Jesus' loving presence, thanking him, trusting him and asking him to return with you to your childhood.
2. Remembering a particular place when you were about four or five. Sensing Jesus coming in and taking you on his lap and holding you in his arms; knowing all the hurts, guilt, failings; drawing them out of you; healing and freeing you deep down by filling you with his perfect love.
3. Letting yourself be filled with gratitude, thanking Jesus and accepting that you are healed and will experience new freedom and openness.
4. Jesus calling in your mother or mother-substitute. You sensing her own fears and hurts, appreciating what she did for you, telling her you forgive her for her failures and asking her to forgive you. Then with Jesus' healing love dissolving the barriers, embracing each other. Your mother leaving in peace and you letting yourself feel gratitude and thanking Jesus for the healing and for being released from failure, guilt and hurt to new openness.
5. Repeating this situation with your father or father-substitute, and then with any other

family members, close friends or your children.

Inner healing is an ongoing process, like peeling off the layers of an onion. We especially need to repeat this way of healing if we find ourselves blocked in some way while doing it. It may be useful to repeat the core often:

"I forgive you . . . (name) for every hurt.
Forgive me for every way I hurt you.
Thank you Jesus for healing me and making me free and open."

It may also be useful after this blanket forgiveness in a relationship to chunk it, i.e., to take one specific event at a time, still using the same framework.

In later sessions we shall work with other frameworks.

Journal as desired.

SHARING
Share as appropriate.

D. CONCLUSION

RECOLLECTING
Quiet reflection and journaling.

EVALUATION
Brief evaluation and comments.

HOME PRACTICE
Thinking about healing. Take a past situation and use this way of healing it with Jesus.
Looking over all the sessions so far.

LOOKING AHEAD
Next session we shall practice healing through discerning some of our unconscious messages, releasing and transforming some of our fear, grief, anger and guilt.

AFFIRMATION
Closing prayer and grace.

Healing through Awareness of Our Unconscious Messages and Touch Releasing and Transforming Fear, Grief, Anger and Guilt

Note extra materials needed: newspaper and short hose, approx. 30" (.7 m) long for each person.

A. BECOMING AWARE OF WHERE WE ARE

RECOLLECTING
Being still in the presence of God.
Praying aloud or silently.

RECAP
Last time we discussed healing, and practiced a way of healing early memories with Jesus.

SHARING
Share as appropriate on anything arising from last session, and then briefly evaluate the course so far.

TODAY'S THEME
Today we shall consider healing through our unconscious messages and touching, and practice releasing and transforming some of our fear, grief, anger, and guilt.

B. BECOMING AWARE IN FORMAL PRAYING

Healing through Awareness of Our Unconscious Messages

PRACTICE
Relaxing and silently becoming more open and aware in the here and now.

Checking our awareness through our different senses; e.g., being aware of, without interfering with, what we are hearing, feeling, tasting and smelling. Allowing these things to flow past.

Taking time to become more aware.

Becoming Aware of Physical Messages from Inside Ourselves.

A healing gift leading toward integration is to become aware of physical messages from inside ourselves; as we are comfortably relaxed being aware that God may often want to use the unconscious part of our mind to communicate with us in consciousness. But we may be too preoccupied to sense this communication. God may be sending us messages which we do not hear; in our hearts we may know something which we are blocking from our conscious mind.

So now, being aware that God uses the situation we are in, the senses that God has given us, to communicate with us, letting our unconscious mind know that we are ready and willing to attend to its communication.

Asking your unconscious mind if it is willing to communicate directly with you and if it will, please will it give you a physical sign for yes. And then attending very carefully and gently to any physical changes. It may be a change in your breathing, a tightening of your muscles in your face, hands, legs or body, a twitching or movement. Any change, whatever it is for you. If you are uncertain what the yes signal is, asking your unconscious to give you time to get more used to attending to it and asking if it would please intensify the signal so that you can be sure; explaining that it is fun, like playing a new game.

When you have identified a yes signal, thanking your unconscious and then gently asking for a no signal, and once again attending to any changes. The no signal may be the absence of the yes signal, or a separate signal. Again, asking gently for the no signal to be intensified so that you are sure of it. Then thanking God for these signals. And taking time over the next week or two to practice gently becoming aware of your yes and no signals in this way, and noticing them when seeking guidance in some decision.

Journal as desired.

SHARING
Sharing as appropriate.

C. BECOMING AWARE IN COUNSELING SKILLS

Touch in Healing

INTRODUCTION
Last session we experienced one way in which we Christians may open ourselves to healing our early relationships and memories by using our understanding and experience of Jesus, our loving healer, as our great satisfying resource. In our inner selves we experienced Jesus' comforting unconditional love through his touch as he held us in his arms and enabled us to reach out in loving forgiveness to touch those closely related to us. We realized that the more we are in touch with God and our own inner reality, the more God may touch others through us.

Touch is a universal and powerful way of communicating togetherness, at-oneness, wholeness, health. Jesus knew and used the healing power of physical touch; we know it ourselves from our earliest infancy; the laying on of hands for healing is widely used and is once again becoming a recognized part of Christian experience.

The modern emphasis on holistic health reminds us of the possibilities of physical healing through touch, and also of the necessity of spiritual awareness in unblocking and balancing the life energies and restoring the flow of energy from the source of energy; e.g., in such disciplines as therapeutic touch, touch for health, polarity, reflexology, acupressure and psychosynthesis.

SHARING
Either in the whole group or in smaller groups first, discuss the healing power of touch in our own lives.

Attending to Fear, Grief, Anger and Guilt

INTRODUCTION
Last time we saw that the foundation of healing, like discernment, is a prayerful opening of ourselves, in which we become more at one with ourselves, others and God. In other words, healing happens as we open ourselves to reality, to life, to the world, to God.

Fear, anger, grief and all our other responses are part of the real world in which we live. The way we deal with them may lead us to health and integration or to sickness and disintegration, to guilt and to a breakdown in ourselves and our various relationships (session 17).

These emotions demand attention and expression. For a while we may postpone dealing with them; e.g., nature has a way of helping us to do this in crisis when we become numb, our feelings go into neutral, in order to give us time to rally our resources to cope with the crisis. But eventually we need to attend to such emotions as grief, anger, and fear in order to produce a healthy outcome and avoid destructive repercussions.

As we considered last session, healing may be experienced on different levels. For healing to occur, such emotions as grief, anger, and fear may also be dealt with on different levels. In a mild form, we may treat our negative emotions and response to pain as a base for prayerful contemplative opening to God in the here and now (session 16). This opening, the opposite of being heavily and exclusively attached to one or more features in the situation, may defuse our anger and ease our grief and fear without denying our attachment.

But for most of us, our attachment is so intense and our emotions so distracting that we need to release them in other ways, e.g., physically, before we may use them as a base for contemplation.

Releasing Repressed Emotions

The physical act of being touched by another may galvanize our healing processes. However, sometimes we ourselves need to act physically and appropriately (apart from ensuring that we get enough physical exercise). This is especially true of negative aspects of our emotions which we have distorted and repressed and which we need to let out harmlessly. Otherwise they may fester inside us and lead to ill health, guilt and unhappiness on many different levels.

SHARING

Briefly discuss what has been raised, and as appropriate also comment on the following emotions as we consider them.

Fear

Fear itself is built in for our safety and survival. But repressed, it may lead to anxiety, pain, obsessional thinking and compulsive behavior. Because in fear we assess the world as frightening and terrible, we tend to see ourselves as victims, and in doing so, attract more experiences that frighten us and confirm our belief.

To release repressed fear we may need to scream. Usually screaming is socially unacceptable and a suitable place is not available, though a screaming room, a windy hillside or beside a noisy sea may be possibilities. Some forms of singing may be a possible partial substitute.

Grief

Grief may lead to understanding and compassion for others. But repressed it may lead to prolonged bad moods, a "poor me" attitude, or to depression, which may be crushed tears from long ago, a mourning for the unconditional love we never received. Releasing the grief through tears, wailing and sharing the loss with another may be the start of real healing.

Anger

Anger may lead to our making positive loving changes. But as we have seen (session 17) anger may be considered as usually secondary to some feeling of powerlessness, some degree of fear.

Repressed anger may lead to a sulking, critical, judging, depressed or revengeful attitude; resentment may become hate, a person may alternate between being sweetly negative and exploding in anger. The physical action to release anger without harm to self or others may be to beat it out; e.g., in the air, on cushions, an old telephone book or a punch bag, or to tense our jaws and clench our fists and then let go, preferably using words as well in all these actions.

Guilt

All our repressed emotions refuse to be denied or go away. They demand to be acknowledged and released. Otherwise they assert themselves in the present in many inappropriate forms of health and behavior, and may drag us down into guilt, self-hate and self-destruction.

One proven way of dealing with guilt as the church has taught since early times, is to face it and to confess it, preferably with someone we feel is loving and trustworthy. And the great hope of the Christian message is that God loves us and forgives us our sins completely when we in turn have a forgiving attitude to others.

Once the repressed emotion has been released and dealt with, the energy formerly used to keep it repressed may be released for more creative, loving, forgiving, fulfilling purposes and so the whole person may become more open, aware and at one with themselves and God.

PRACTICE

Our aggressive energy is a natural drive to assert and affirm ourselves, but it may be misused, distorted or repressed as anger.

Each of us needs a piece of hose, a newspaper, and space to swing the hose.

One Way of Releasing Anger Harmlessly: Beating it Out

1. Review of Anger.
   Write down:
   (a) What are my usual ways of expressing anger?
   (b) What are my usual ways of showing repressed anger?

(c) What is my attitude to the anger I feel: do I fear it, despise it, enjoy it, save it up, etc.?

(d) What are the specific situations, people and patterns that tend to arouse it?

(e) What are my childhood experiences with anger?

(f) What is one situation or relationship that I want to work on now?

2. Releasing the anger physically and harmlessly by beating.

You can use such items as a short hose and newspaper or the floor, or a tennis racquet and bed or cushion. Imagine that the objects of your anger or frustration are in front of you and that you are breaking them down, smashing the blocks. Allowing your rage to surface and continuing to hit out. Also speaking out aloud, verbalizing, even shouting, what was unsaid and needs to be said. At first you may need to pretend to be angry and make an effort to speak to get into your "unfinished business."

Continuing this vigorously for fifteen to twenty minutes until you get your second wind; i.e., a sense of release, freeing of muscles, lightening of the body and perhaps tears, laughter and/or screaming (after fear).

3. Connecting with the value you stand for.

At the end it is essential to affirm the positive value you stand for; i.e., to say aloud "I stand for . . . ; e.g., confidentiality, being myself."

Journal as desired.

SHARING

Share as appropriate.

EXTENSION

This physical release of an emotion may surprise us by its intensity and make us realize why we keep it in check. It is a way of diagnosing what is wrong, and harmlessly using up the adrenalin in our bodies which would have been appropriate in a primitive fight-flight situation.

This way may deal with large blocks quickly and so clear the way for the gentler approach to forgiving others that we shall use next session. The beating-out process may need to be repeated, even daily for a while, to empty out all the stored anger.

Transforming Aggressive Energy from Destructive to Constructive Use

PRACTICE

As we resolve the anger, we may direct our natural aggressive drives into more creative and healthy uses. The following sequence may be useful:

1. Choosing a project I want to give more energy to. Temporarily putting it to one side.

2. Arousing my aggressive feelings. Becoming aware of their strength and the effect they have on my body. Observing them without labeling or judging or trying to influence them.

3. Realizing that this energy is at my service and can do things: it may be used to hurt or to be the motive power behind my chosen project.

4. Imagining myself inside myself involved in my chosen project, harnessing all this energy and vitality. Seeing, hearing, feeling, smelling, tasting from inside myself all the variety of details affected by my new-found vitality.

Journaling.

SHARING

Sharing as appropriate.

EXTENSION

Our health is not merely a personal matter. Our wholeness is incomplete to the extent that others' wholeness is incomplete and vice versa. Health is concerned not only with physical well-being but with the whole of society. While others are displaced, disadvantaged and oppressed in a fractured world, our health is incomplete. Just as the searching for and opening of ourselves to meaning in our own depths commits us to deep caring for others in their depth search, so the search for an opening of ourselves to health, healing and wholeness similarly commits us to action on many levels.

Contemplation in a world of action commits us to deep caring and to prophetic action against injustice wherever it is found: in ourselves, in others, in the world that God has made. Caring and criticism must be held in creative tension. And it is in the name of justice that we need to pay attention to pain, grief, anger and fear.

SHARING
Comment briefly.

D. CONCLUDING

RECOLLECTING
Quiet reflecting and journaling.

EVALUATION
Brief evaluation of the session.

HOME PRACTICE
Practice attending to our physical messages from inside, and to touching; take another situation to release our emotions: beating out anger again, screaming out fear, wailing out grief, confessing guilt, being sure to end by linking up with the positive value that we are affirming. Notice whether we are channeling the energy we released this session into the creative project we chose today.

Write an evaluation of our progress and reactions this term, referring to our journals.

LOOKING AHEAD
Next session we start on the final area of our helping skills: contributing ideas and words, and we shall practice a way of forgiving other people.

AFFIRMATION
Close with silence and the grace.

SESSION 23

Contributing Words and Ideas
Praying in Our Own Words and in Tongues
Forgiving Others

A. BECOMING AWARE OF WHERE WE ARE

RECOLLECTING

Being still in the presence of God.
Praying silently or aloud.

RECAP

Last session we considered becoming aware of our physical messages from inside ourselves; healing through touch; releasing and transforming our repressed emotions, e.g., getting rid of anger by beating it out, and affirming the value that we stand for that was being denied.

SHARING

Share from last session and our term evaluations.

TODAY'S THEME

This session we start on the last term of our program. We finally consider our own contribution of ideas and words in the helping relationship. Today our theme is praying in our own words and in tongues. We shall also practice a way of forgiving others.

B. BECOMING AWARE IN FORMAL PRAYING

PRACTICE

Sing one verse of the hymn "Be still and know that I am God."

Repeat last week's practice of becoming aware of our physical messages from inside ourselves.
Sing; "I am the Lord that healeth thee."
Extemporary praying. The leader may suggest a particular theme to begin with, e.g., one-sentence thanking prayers. We need to give gentle opportunity for all who want to pray aloud, especially the more hesitant.

SHARING

Share anything arising from the praying, as appropriate.

EXTENSION

Contributing Words and Ideas

In dealing with the three closely interrelated areas of change we need to achieve rapport and use our listening skills to help people surface their thoughts and feelings. Then if necessary we may help them in the outer area to reach decisions and in the inner area to change their reactions (session 20).

In the same way, in the ultimate area we first use our listening skills to help them to surface and work with questions of meaning, purpose, direction and values. We may use verbal skills for accepting, forgiving and changing. After that we ourselves may contribute words and ideas to help them to form appropriate concepts and continue their own exploration.

Praying in words, Bible reading and sharing

our own experience briefly as appropriate are the helper's verbal input that we shall consider in the remainder of this program.

Praying in Our Own Words and in Tongues

God, knowing all there is to know about us, loves, forgives and accepts us as we are. When we, deep within, accept ourselves as God accepts us, then we discover a new freedom to be ourselves, to be who we really are. As we accept ourselves and others, energy that was tied up in our negativity is released for us to be outgoing and expressive in a way that was not possible when we were bound up in our own hurt, fear and guilt.

One way of expressing ourselves is in words, though in the presence of great beauty and mystery, words, even music, may be inappropriate. A silence which expresses the disposition of creature to creator may be far more effective than many words. Sounds or a tongue given to us which we do not understand consciously may enable us to communicate at a deeper level.

But words, too, have their place.

We may formerly have found it difficult to pray aloud with others, but when we accept ourselves and God's forgiveness, we may find we can pray with greater ease. So we do not need a book with someone else's words. We can use our own words, or sounds if we are speaking in tongues, to express our sense of awe, worship, need, failure, gratitude.

When we feel the need to be explicit in our praying (praying in the narrower sense), we need to recognize that we are falling back on using concepts, none of which can ever embrace the total reality to which they point, neither in nor beyond ourselves (session 20). Even the word "God" falls into this category. Some interpretations of God are very narrow. So we need to lean very gently on any of our concepts of God, of reality, of what we are doing by praying.

Being flexible, willing to allow our concepts to change and develop, is the key. In later sessions we shall consider how as Christians we may develop concepts from the Bible and from our own experience appropriate to our stage of development.

Nothing we may do can have any appreciable effect on who God is. Prayer in the last analysis is not "doing" at all, it is a quality of "being," an inner disposition in relation to the reality which is ourselves and to the reality beyond us, in which we open ourselves to be impressed. Prayer dissolves the obstacles to that mysterious coming together.

As awareness grows, so may the sense of being separate. The paradox is that as we become more aware, we need to let go the sense of being separate, self-sufficient, autonomous. Knowing dissolves into unknowing (cf. *The Cloud of Unknowing*).

So using words in prayer to express a sense of oneness, longing, or need, at best has to be as simple, open and direct as possible, and needs to avoid any sense of manipulating or twisting the arm of either God or the person we are praying with. Our words may need to have a certain tentativeness in expressing what we feel about ourselves, others and God, and we need to remember that silence may be more appropriate.

Nevertheless, just as when we say we love or forgive someone and communicate it congruently, our feelings may become better known to ourselves as well as to the other person because we have expressed them in words and may have heard the words (i.e., we have reinforced them by feeling movement and hearing) so praying in words which express the rhythm, the flow, of what is happening to us, to others, and to the world, may serve to open up communication and set the seal on the relationship.

SHARING
Discuss briefly.

C. BECOMING AWARE IN COUNSELING SKILLS

Forgiving Others

SHARING
Share what we do when we find it difficult to forgive someone else.

INTRODUCTION
Healing through physically releasing our repressed negative emotions in a harmless way,

and redirecting the energy so freed was a theme of our last session. This drastic catharsis or purging may be a necessary preliminary to more specific forgiving.

We have probably all had the experience of intending to forgive and forget but then finding that we have not forgiven and forgotten. How may we forgive more effectively?

One way is to take steps to convince the unconscious part of our mind, which may be thought of as not responding to reason but responding to what we perceive through our senses of seeing, feeling, hearing, etc. The action of speaking, hearing ourselves and moving to different positions may enable us to integrate our intention into our inner selves.

The gospel tells us "Whoever is angry with his brother will be brought to trial. . . . So if you are about to offer your gift to God at the altar and there remember that your brother has something against you, leave your gift there in front of the altar, go at once and make peace with your brother and then come back and offer your gift to God. . . . Settle the dispute . . . while there is time" (Matt. 5:22–24,25).

We may offer forgiveness to another person directly or in their absence.

A Way of Forgiving Others in Their Absence and Opening Ourselves to Healing

PRACTICE

The leader may briefly go over the following exercise. Then we may use it in twos, taking it in turn to forgive another person in their absence and to open ourselves for healing, while the helper uses the sharer's nonverbal and verbal indications to help them with the next step.

A person alone may use this way, but it may be easier if we as helpers have previously guided them through it. The helper needs to achieve rapport with the sharer.

1. Centering yourself; opening yourself to the highest you know, i.e., God: love, peace, harmony, wisdom, understanding, mercy, forgiveness, etc.

2. Identifying and choosing one specific situation and person.
   Remembering the outcome model and aiming for change in yourself, not in someone else.
   It may be helpful to stand.
   Saying aloud, or writing, "I choose and I will to stop punishing myself and holding back my own growth, health and wholeness—physically, emotionally or spiritually—for what . . . (name the person) did or is doing . . . (name the situation)."

3. From inside yourself, imagining that the person you need to forgive is in front of you, becoming aware of them with all your senses. Perhaps closing your eyes, positioning them to the constructing side (usually your right). Saying to the person, ". . . (name), I would rather you had . . . (said or done)." This needs to be specific, identifiable, acceptable behavior stated positively (no negatives).
   (Note: If at this point you are too emotionally charged, you may need to release the pent-up emotion; e.g., through crying out the grief, beating out the anger, screaming out the fear, or confessing the guilt (session 22). After doing this, stating the value that you stand for that was ignored by the other person; e.g., "I stand for . . . and I seek to express it in my life." Then start again at step 3).

4. Saying "But you didn't do that, and I now will to be healed of the effects of this incident. I choose to be free of the pain it causes me. I am tired of being uncomfortable. I choose to be free and to be healed."

5. Saying "I accept now that you did not come up to my expectations of you, that what happened was different from the way I would have chosen.
   I now cancel those expectations and demands that you . . . (say, do or be what I should have preferred). I cancel my demands that you be any particular way. I accept you as a human being. You are responsible for your own life and actions and I release you to your own highest good."

6. Now closing your eyes and opening yourself to the highest that you know. Perhaps holding up your arms. Becoming aware of God's love

and warmth and light flowing into you, God's compassion filling you and dissolving all the expectations and conditions that caused the hurt and pain. Becoming aware that God is in you and you are in God. Opening yourself to such loving, compassionate qualities as understanding, wisdom, patience, forgiveness.

Becoming aware of the God within you protecting, nurturing and loving you all your life. Allowing the warmth and light and fragrance of love to flow into all the parts of your body where tension, pain and disease were felt and sensing those parts whole. Allowing love and compassion to flow into your whole body; then into the hurting part of your emotions; and into your mind to heal the hurtful thoughts. Receiving love into the deepest parts of you, flowing through you and filling you completely.

7. With eyes still closed, continuing to be aware of this powerful love and saying to the person (the demands on whom you have just cancelled) "I send this love which is filling me, out from myself and from God within me to you, just as you are or have been. I send my love unconditionally."

Taking time to experience fully this love overflowing through you to the other person and giving the other person time and space to change.

8. Now checking your body, feelings and thoughts. If you still have some expectation or demand that the other person should be different, repeating the process as often as required for each separate action and incident.

(Note: If you do not get the expected release, then examining your willingness to be free, becoming aware of any small leads which may show you where the blockages lie. You may need more release of negative emotions or the exercise on forgiving self in the next session before repeating this one).

9. Making affirmations to maintain the change; e.g., saying "I will to keep this change in me intact," claiming God's help, and thanking God for the forgiveness and healing. (It is important to avoid going over an event forward again in your memory and reinfecting it. But going over it in this new forgiving way allows the forgiveness to root and grow, and healing to take place).

Journal as desired.

SHARING
Share as appropriate.

EXTENSION
Repeating this act of forgiving and releasing often, especially with those we are close to, may help us to be more aware of God's all-pervading love and understanding, and so help us to turn our intention to forgive someone into the reality of forgiving them.

A Way of Praying in Five Stages of Grief and Forgiveness

Hurts are bitter attitudes kept alive by our unwillingness to forgive. When we are hurt, instead of dealing adequately with our feelings, we may suppress them and then repress them. Repressed unforgiving feelings may undermine our health, our wholeness. They may produce mental or physical symptoms, binding us in bitterness to the person who hurt us, and blocking our openness to God.

Another way to help us to forgive may be to use as a framework for our praying the five-attitude model for grief, loss and rejection (session 17).

1. *Denial:* pretending the experience did not happen; denying or minimizing the hurt.
   New Attitude: Acknowledging and confessing the hurt, symptom, resentment.
   Beginning to face the hurt, supported by the love of Jesus or another trusted friend.
   Getting in touch with the feelings and asking God to show us where we have been hurt and what is at the root of our symptoms.
   Allowing the pain to surface, releasing it in words and tears as they want to flow.

2. *Anger:* blaming the other person.
   New Attitude: Emptying out our hearts to God about our feelings towards the other person.

Imagining the other person is there and telling them aloud everything that we needed to but were not able to.

Asking God to help us to understand the hurt behind the other person's behavior, to see them through God's eyes.

3. *Bargaining:* demanding that the other person change before we will forgive them.

New Attitude: Getting in touch with and verbalizing some of the conditions we may have stored up before we will forgive; e.g., what we might want that person never to do or say again; what they might do to make it easier for us to forgive them. Asking Jesus to give us his power to pray his prayer from the Cross, "Father, forgive them, they know not what they do." God's forgiveness is unconditional.

While saying the words of forgiveness, breathing out all the conditions we set before we will forgive.

Perhaps saying, "Jesus, help me to forgive this person, not because they deserve it, but because they need it too."

By a choice of will, forgiving the person specifically for each attitude or action that caused the hurt, speaking aloud to them as if they were there; ". . . (name) I forgive you for . . . ."

Asking God to forgive them specifically for each of the hurts that resulted.

4. *Depression:* blaming ourselves. "I should have; if only; etc."

New Attitude: Asking God to forgive us for the bitterness, unforgiveness, resentment, hatred, revenge, etc.

Hearing forgiveness spoken to us in God's name, if someone else is present, and thanking God that we are forgiven.

Renouncing and breaking the judgments we made against that person.

Inviting God's Spirit to fill and heal the areas of our hearts and memories which have been harboring hurt and unforgiveness. Asking for help to depend on God to meet the needs which only God can meet.

Asking God to make us aware of what God wants to change in us.

Spending time breathing in God's love and transforming power and breathing out that habit or behavior.

5. *Acceptance:* beginning to see light and goodness from the hurtful experience.

New Attitude: Asking God to make us aware of some of the growth and goodness that has come out of the hurtful experience, perhaps writing a list.

Thanking God for this growth and goodness. Asking God fully to bless the other person and to bless us too.

Asking God if there is a loving way to reach out to the other person.

SHARING
Discuss as desired.

D. CONCLUDING

RECOLLECTING
Quiet reflection and journaling.

EVALUATING
Brief evaluation and comment.

HOME PRACTICE
Notice how and when we are contributing ideas and words. Practice forgiving another person with the way we have been using today.

LOOKING FORWARD
Next time we shall continue praying aloud; consider concepts, including our self-concept and sin; and then practice forgiving ourselves. Come prepared with one or two situations to work on in which we need to forgive ourselves.

AFFIRMATION
Closing prayer and thanksgiving.

SESSION 24

Praying Aloud
Our Self-concept and Sin
Forgiving Ourselves

A. BECOMING AWARE OF WHERE WE ARE

RECOLLECTING
Being still in the presence of God.
Praying silently or aloud.

RECAP
Last session we thought about praying in our own words and in tongues, practiced a way of forgiving others, and considered a way of praying in five stages of grief and forgiveness.

SHARING
Share anything arising from last session.

TODAY'S THEME
Today we shall again pray aloud, consider concepts, sin, and some ways of accepting God's forgiveness and forgiving ourselves.

B. and C. BECOMING AWARE IN FORMAL PRAYING AND IN COUNSELING SKILLS

Praying Aloud

PRACTICE
Praying aloud. The leader may suggest a theme to start with, e.g., anything arising from the previous discussion, remembering to stay with the sharer's words.
Silent prayer.

SHARING
Share as desired.

Holding Lightly to Our Concepts

INTRODUCTION
Last session we were reminded that concepts of God, people and tradition have no ultimate reality but they are essential for effective living (sessions 23,16). The process of reducing reality to concepts helps us to make living understandable and purposeful. It gives us a sense of direction, without which we may well experience a sense of being lost and directionless.

Yet there is an inherent danger in the need for concepts: if we become too attached to our concepts then reality, i.e., what the concepts represent, may elude us and we may be left in a state of delusion and confusion. As with feelings (session 22), concepts are part of life but they are not life itself, life in all its fullness. So there is a continual need for us to ease our attachment to them. We need to be open and ready to reach beyond concepts and feelings, beyond the confusion which they generate, open and ready to be touched by reality itself.

When we are open, we have the freedom to lean less heavily on our concepts, to let go of concepts that may have been appropriate and helpful in the past and to replace them with ones more appropriate for the present. This may be particularly true of our concepts of ourselves and of sin.

Our Self-concept and Sin

Last session we practiced a possible way of achieving the forgiving attitude that we desire to have towards another person.

Many of us judge ourselves even more harshly than we judge others; we consider ourselves failures or worse and do not in fact extend to ourselves the forgiveness that we know in theory God freely offers us. This may be inverted pride, a pride complex. But who are we to think we know better than God?

Our culture and church teaching in the past may have emphasized not only our sins but ourselves as miserable sinners doomed to failure. However, from the beginning, Hebrew writers saw God's creation as good. As part of God's creation we are good in God's eyes, made in God's image. Are we undervaluing this image?

We cannot change our ultimate self, that is given to us by God. But we can change our concept, our perception of ourselves, i.e., our ego. When we attach too much significance to our own image or concept of ourselves (ego) and lose touch with our real self (God's image) then we are missing the mark. When we realize that there is a distinction between our real selves, our concept of ourselves, and our actions, then it becomes easier for us to accept God's forgiveness.

How do we change our perception of ourselves, ease our attachment to our concept of self and so allow our real self to develop? We are intrinsically good, loved and forgiven, capable of developing and growing, and also capable of sinning.

SHARING
    Discuss briefly.

What is Sin?

INTRODUCTION
    Sin has long been defined as missing the mark or not achieving the goal, a term derived from archery. Sin has also been defined as anything that holds us back from our potential, whatever causes us to miss what God intends for us.

The procedure to adopt when we have missed the mark, whether in archery, in learning any other skill, or with ourselves, is:

1. Discover what has caused us to miss.
2. Make the appropriate adjustments.
3. Try again.
4. Repeat these three steps to improve our performance.

As in any skill, a performance that might be considered poor from a top-grade participant may be excellent from a beginner. To change the metaphor: once we have set out in a certain direction, we can bewail the fact that we have not arrived at our destination, or we can chunk our journey and rejoice and be thankful as we reach each milestone or each lamp-post.

This chunking and rejoicing is a far cry from setting ourselves an imaginary perfection or unattainable goal, failing, feeling guilty, thinking of the self made by God as inherently evil, thinking of our failure or sin as a deformity or stain in ourselves for which we deserve punishment, finding the guilt and hurt too painful and so repressing it. When we repress our sense of failure and guilt, we may still continue to punish ourselves unconsciously, closing ourselves off from relationships with others and the enjoyment of God's world and perhaps developing physical or emotional dis-ease.

The Bible has pointed us to the way of dealing with our sins: "If we confess our sins, God is faithful and just and will forgive us our sins and cleanse us from all unrighteousness" (1 John 1:9).

We openly need to admit that we have missed the mark, say that we are sorry and open ourselves to God's forgiveness. Then it is important for us to accept that forgiveness. Our part is not to wallow in our sins, sorrow and regrets but to learn from the mistake, to make amends and to move on; to accept that God has cleansed us and refreshed us for the next stage on our journey, and to continue on our way rejoicing.

SHARING
    Comment briefly.

Some Ways of Accepting God's Forgiveness and Forgiving Ourselves

INTRODUCTION
    Earlier this session we were praying aloud. As we found last session when forgiving others (ses-

sion 23), praying and affirming out loud where we stand may be important in re-forming our concepts, especially in creating more appropriate images of ourselves and in helping us to accept and reinforce our new position. This may be particularly necessary in the following suggested ways of accepting forgiveness for ourselves. The physical act of praying aloud, of mouthing (feeling) and hearing the words may contribute powerfully to forming and reinforcing our concepts and positive attitudes.

SHARING

Comment as appropriate while the leader goes briefly over some ways we may accept that we are forgiven.

Church Liturgy

We may already be familiar with some of the set forms of confession and absolution found in many Christian traditions.

Informal Confession and Acceptance R.I.C.A.T.

It is important for us to use words that are acceptable and meaningful. If we are asking for forgiveness ourselves, we may prefer to use our Christian concepts. But in helping a sharer who finds Christian words an obstacle, it may be more appropriate when using much of this material to substitute such words as the Source of life, Creating Spirit, Life Energy, Spirit of Love. Our listening skills can direct us in adapting the following simple framework:

1. Rapport building and relaxing.
   Just relaxing, breathing slowly and deeply, tensing any tight muscles and letting them go loose, relaxing your facial muscles, your jaw, your hands and feet, your stomach, your mind.
2. Identifying the situation that needs forgiveness.
   As you are relaxing, allowing a situation to surface in your mind in which you need to forgive yourself. Indicating, perhaps by holding up a finger, or nodding, when you have identified the situation that you wish to confess and to receive forgiveness for.

3. Confessing.
   Confessing aloud in your own words, in some such way as—
   (a) "Spirit of love, I have sinned against your law and myself. I have missed the mark."
   (b) "I am sorry that I . . . (did what I did or did not do)."
   (c) "I will to learn the lesson I need to learn from this experience and to lead my life now with greater wisdom, love (etc)."
4. Accepting.
   "I am opening myself now to your healing, accepting, forgiving love. I am allowing your spirit to flow into me and to release me from this stress" (or "Forgive me and let your love flow through me, cleansing me and healing me from this missed opportunity"). In the silence, breathing in this healing forgiving love, letting it fill you and penetrate deeply inside you. Then saying aloud, "I accept your forgiveness with all my heart and mind and soul and strength. From now I am beginning to lead a new life."
5. Thanking.
   Now in your own words aloud thanking the Spirit of love in some such way as, "Thank you spirit of love, source of all life, for taking away my guilt and stress. Thank you for forgiving me, for releasing me, for making me free. Thank you for opening me to your healing. Thank you for restoring my mind, my body, my emotions, my soul."

   Taking all the time you need to feel how grateful and thankful you are and to express it aloud in words. Allowing yourself to express whatever feelings may need to be expressed, in tears, laughing, whatever.

Forgiving Ourselves When Younger

Separating negative feelings from an event (visual-kinesthetic dissociation) may be useful (session 19).

Loving Ourselves as Someone Else Loves Us

Loving ourselves as someone else loves us may also help us to alter our self-concept and to accept forgiveness (session 20).

I in Christ and Christ in Me or Identifying
with the Source of Forgiveness
(based on Assagioli, 1975)

PRACTICE

If we find it hard to forgive ourselves and to accept forgiveness, we may find it helpful to use this special way of dissociating ourselves from our negative feelings, of associating ourselves with the highest and the best that we can conceive, and then reassociating ourselves and including forgiveness in our new concept of ourselves.

The following outline is again worded for us to use with a sharer.

The leader may go over it briefly, then we divide into twos, and each in turn be the helper and the one accepting forgiveness and healing.

1. Rapport building and relaxing.
2. Identifying the actions, etc., to be forgiven, the events and experiences in your concept of your past that are blocking a fuller flow of love through you. Perhaps writing a list.
3. Kneeling or sitting and from inside yourself looking up (e.g., to above a chair), to whatever power you conceive as higher and better than yourself; e.g., Jesus, God the loving Father or Mother.
   Confessing specific actions or thoughts and asking for forgiveness separately for each one; e.g., "On . . . day I did . . . and because of this . . . (I feel angry, hurt, ill, etc.).
   I am truly sorry.
   I intend, choose and will to learn from this mistake and choose and will to be healed from . . . (this experience).
   I ask for your forgiveness. Please forgive me."
4. Putting an object such as a cushion or book where you were kneeling, to represent your personal self, now moving to stand in the position where you previously imagined Jesus or a higher power. (This physical move may be important in helping you to relate to a higher power.)
   Breathing deeply and identifying yourself with all the highest and best qualities that you can conceive. From inside yourself sensing yourself being filled with understanding and unconditional love, with patience and wisdom, with beauty and truth and goodness, with the peace that passes all understanding, with glowing warmth and light. Being filled with all the highest and best qualities you know and beyond what you know. Sensing the living energy of loving forgiveness, and compassion without limit.
   Now looking down from inside yourself with compassion and true understanding and love to cancel and forgive all the expectations and demands and failures that the personal self down there put on him/herself. Sending your unconditional love and forgiveness. (If you feel blocked by sadness or emotion, stand on something to go up higher, and then once again identifying with the ultimate qualities of unconditional love and forgiveness.)
   And as you are sending down your unconditional love and forgiveness and cancelling the personal self's demands and expectations, saying something like:
   "I should have preferred you to . . . but you didn't."
   "I now cancel all the demands, expectations and conditions that you put on yourself at that time. I forgive you for. . . ."
   "I give you my love and forgiveness. I fill you with my unconditional love."
   "I accept you and love you the way you were then and the way you are now."
   "I again give you responsibility for the way you lead your new life."
   "I will be with you. My unconditional love and forgiveness will surround and uphold you."
5. Kneeling or sitting in your former place, becoming the personal self again, looking up and receiving this gift of forgiveness. Realizing that you are receiving this higher power into yourself, appreciating and thanking the higher power that the power is in you and is part of your deepest self. Being thankful that Christ is in you and that you are in Christ, that God's forgiveness is part of you and can flow out through you to others.
6. Taking time to experience and enjoy your wholeness.
7. Stating aloud your will to accept and keep the

change in you. This will help to confirm and establish it; e.g., "I will to accept forgiveness for. . . .

"I will to keep this change in me.

"I will to learn from this experience and to go forward from now, maintaining the flow of God's loving forgiveness and acceptance through me to myself and to others."

Note. If you find yourself unable to identify adequately with the source of life, Christ, etc., even when you have gone as high as possible, the situation may need chunking.

Chunking to help identify with the source of forgiveness:

1. Separating several parts of yourself; e.g., putting on the floor one book or one cushion for trial and error (personal experience), another for your critical self, another for your self trying to identify with the source. Then going higher and forgiving each one.
2. If you still cannot forgive, coming down into the personal self space again. Using lots of cushions or books for your sub-personalities, e.g., critic, playful child, protector, adventurer, etc.; appreciating in turn what each part is doing for you. Thanking each part and receiving its gift to you.
   Taking time to appreciate your wholeness and variety.
   Then going higher and forgiving.
3. If you still cannot forgive, remaining in your personal self. Asking yourself, how did I get the idea of being perfect, of failing, of sinning, of not being able to be forgiven? (i.e., examining your beliefs and where and who they came from). Use one cushion or book for each person you specify. Go through the forgiving others exercise to each person (session 23), e.g., "I choose and I will to stop punishing myself for what you . . . (name) taught me. I

would have preferred you to . . . (appreciate me, etc.). But . . . , etc."

After completing the forgiving others exercise, continue the forgiving self exercise.
Journal as desired.

SHARING
Share as appropriate.

EXTENSION
The healing and openness resulting from our accepting God's forgiveness and so being able to forgive ourselves may occur on many different levels. It may be helpful to record our experiences in our journals; writing down the lessons learned, our feelings of gratitude and release, etc., so that when we reread them we may reexperience our sense of perspective and renewed energy.

D. CONCLUDING

RECOLLECTING
Quietly reflecting and journaling.

EVALUATION
Brief evaluation and comment.

HOME PRACTICE
Examine further our own concepts of ourselves, sin and forgiveness. Practice forgiving ourselves with a different situation.

LOOKING AHEAD
Next time we shall be praying and singing from the written word. Each of us please bring a favorite prayer and be prepared to say what makes it especially meaningful for us. Also bring or list any favorite prayers or anthologies of prayers or hymns. We shall also be practicing a way of separating the purpose from our behavior.

AFFIRMATION
Close with praying and the grace.

Praying and Singing from the Written Word Beyond the Written Word Changing by Separating the Purpose from Our Behavior

A. BECOMING AWARE OF WHERE WE ARE

RECOLLECTING

Being still in the presence of God.
Praying aloud or silently.

RECAP

Last session we considered praying aloud; holding lightly to our concepts, including our concepts of ourselves and sin; and various ways of helping us to accept forgiveness.

TODAY'S THEME

Today our theme is praying and singing from the written word; beyond the written word; and a way of changing our behavior by separating the purpose from the behavior.

B. BECOMING AWARE IN FORMAL PRAYING

PRACTICE

Hymn: e.g., "Fill thou my life, O Lord my God."
Silence.
Written prayers: each in turn sharing what is meaningful for us about the written prayer we have brought and then all joining in praying it.
End with the Lord's Prayer in whatever version we feel comfortable with.

EXTENSION

Praying and Singing from the Written Word

As a Link with our Past

Today we have shared written prayers and what their special meaning is for us. The appropriate use of prayers and hymns learned from others, from the church's liturgy, from the written word, may be a powerful way of linking ourselves with our tradition (session 5). In the helping relationship such prayers and hymns may be an equally powerful way of helping others to make the link between their tradition, their earlier development and what is happening to them in the present.

This link may, of course, be productive or counterproductive. If the words of the prayers, hymns and readings introduced to us during our earlier development, e.g., in our childhood and adolescence, helped us to build positive concepts of ourselves and our relationship to God and to others, then the benefits in a crisis of recalling these concepts and any associated positive feelings and reactions may be inestimable (cf. General Thanksgiving, *Book of Common Prayer*). But the reverse may be the case if these concepts or the situation evoked were unhealthy and negative.

Once again, our openness as helpers and the sensitive use of listening skills are our best guide in discerning whether written prayers of a particular kind may or may not be helpful.

To Help Develop Appropriate Concepts and Behavior

Praying and singing from print and using the words of others may also be a powerful way of developing concepts of reality and behavior more appropriate to our present stage of growth.

Jesus inherited a rich cultural tradition of singing and praying aloud, praying from the written and learned words of scripture. The dynamic interplay of this written and oral tradition with his relationship to his immediate family, friends and contemporaries was deeply formative of his spiritual understanding, his concepts of reality and his relationship to God and others. We know that to express some of his deepest needs Jesus drew on the psalms.

In the same way our own concepts and relationship to God, to other people and to tradition may develop and be enriched through singing and praying that arises from the written word. This prayer may arise in two ways: first, through the written word generally, and secondly, through scripture and other people's prayers and hymns written down or learned by heart.

First we turn to the written word in general. Writing of all kinds, novels, non-fiction, poetry, the newspaper, advertisements, may all widen our experience and awareness and provide the base for contemplative openness.

Secondly, we may use other people's prayers and hymns, as well as scripture. Jesus' prayer is the great pattern for us. But other people's prayers may also be models for our own praying. They may express in words our own deepest needs, and give meaning and direction to our own desires and yearnings. In this way they may serve as a map or a track to save us from getting lost or going round in circles. We all probably have some favorite prayers and hymns that we find meaningful. As well as using anthologies drawn up by others, it may be helpful to write prayers in our journal or our own prayer anthology, especially if we need to bring the language up to date.

SHARING
Share any prayers or anthologies with special meaning for us.

Beyond the Written Word

Written words in general and specific prayers may be the base for the same freedom that may come from expressing our needs and longings in our own words. Both formal and spontaneous words may be a base for opening ourselves to God and developing our concepts (session 14: centering with words). Both may lead to a freeing of our imagination that expands us beyond the written word, beyond our own words, and leads us in silence and awe to an awareness of God; to the mystery that lies beyond all concepts and words, written, spoken or imagined.

A Caution

A caution needs to be sounded here. There is a subtle temptation to use words in praying as magic formulae which can manipulate unseen forces and bend them to our purposes; e.g., to repeat prayers, the liturgy or rosary as though the mere doing without being holds some magic power, or will give us our own way. The mystery of God is on a far different level, far above manipulation, requiring repentance, forgiveness, commitment to change in ourselves, and calling forth the devotion and gratitude of our heart, mind and soul together.

Where healthy, positive feelings and reactions are evoked by the use of written words, there may be no difficulty. But we need to be alert to written words, prayers and hymns which may have been and still may be a powerful source of inculcating unhealthy negative concepts and reactions.

SHARING
Discuss briefly.

C. BECOMING AWARE IN COUNSELING SKILLS

Reorganizing Our Concepts

INTRODUCTION
We considered last session and earlier in this session that as we develop through life, our concepts of reality need to change to embrace our

enlarged experience. Because they are our concepts, not reality itself, because they are our own perception and assessment of reality, we have the opportunity to change them in useful and beneficial ways.

A way of changing our concepts is to reorganize them and make wider associations, to perceive them in a different context or perspective. When we change the context or alter the focus with which we perceive a situation, we inevitably alter our concept of it in some way; we change its meaning, and our responses and behavior change. This is especially useful if we are responding to some outdated need or inappropriate concept. When our unwanted behavior changes into behavior that we find more acceptable, we may become more open, and our energy may be freer for more creative purposes.

Two useful ways to deal with our inappropriate and unwanted behavior are:

1. Keep our present behavior and change its context to one more appropriate or socially acceptable.
2. Change to more acceptable behavior which fulfills the underlying purpose as well or better than our present behavior.

SHARING
Discuss briefly.

A Way of Changing Our Behavior By Separating It from Its Purpose (Based on Bandler and Grinder, 1979, 137–160)

INTRODUCTION
In this session we are concentrating on changing behavior which we want to change but have not been able to. When we have tried everything we can think of to change a certain behavior pattern, when we have little or no idea of what is going on, and when we want to change the way we are reacting to messages from our past in the present, then we may find it helpful to reorganize our concepts systematically by using our unconscious resources.

The assumptions behind separating our behavior from its purpose are that we know far more unconsciously than we know consciously; that basically we have available to us all the resources that we need to make the changes that we want; and that every behavior, symptom and communication is meaningful in some way, and has some useful purpose.

The essence of this way of reorganizing our concepts is to distinguish between its purpose and our behavior, in order to find new more acceptable behavior to fulfill the same purpose.

One way of getting in touch with our unconscious resources is by calling on the part of us that knows or the Holy Spirit within us to provide us with guidance and different behavior patterns that may dissolve the automatic links with past unhelpful behavior, and so may enlarge our range of choices in responding to the present with satisfying feelings and behavior.

We may interpret our unconscious resources as the part of us that knows, our creative part, or for Christians perhaps as Jesus, the Holy Spirit, God within—whatever is most helpful for us (sessions 22, 23). However, when first using the exercise, it may have fewer associations with past concepts and feelings if we simply refer to our resources as the part of us that knows.

PRACTICE
The leader may go over the following exercise briefly. Then we may practice it in turn in twos, matching our wording with the sharer's own timing.

When we use this exercise as helpers, we need to pay special attention to building and maintaining rapport, and to acknowledging any initial objections or fears of the sharer; e.g., by saying: "This does sound odd, doesn't it, but I've found it useful."

An agreed signal for when the sharer is ready to proceed to the next step, e.g., nodding the head, helps to confirm our own observation of the sharer's nonverbal signals.

The following is a suggested framework:

1. "First, identifying the pattern or behavior that you want to change, and giving it a name."
   (The content, i.e., the specific problem, may be known only to the sharer. The pattern to be changed may be some actual behavior, or perhaps behavior in a dream, the pattern "should," etc).
2. "Now going inside yourself and gently asking

your unconscious, please would it be willing to communicate with you in consciousness about . . . (name), and please would it give you a signal for yes."

(The helper also watches for signals).

"Noticing any change you may be aware of. It may be a picture, a sound, a feeling, a movement or tension in some part of your body. It may be a change in your breathing. Any change, whatever it is for you.

"And if you are uncertain whether the change that you notice is the signal for yes, asking your unconscious to give you time to get more used to attending to it. Asking if it would please intensify the signal so that you can be sure."

"When you have identified a yes signal, thanking your unconscious for its willingness to communicate with you about . . . (name). And asking it gently 'Now please a signal for no.' The no signal may be a separate signal or the absence of the yes signal. Again, asking politely for the no signal to be intensified so that you are sure of it. And thanking your unconscious for these signals."

3. "Now turning to . . . (name), and reassuring it that you do not want to take away from the choices it already has, but that you are wanting to add more choices that are at least as effective and perhaps even more effective, than the choices it already has."

"And thanking . . . (name) for what it has been trying to do for you up till now. You may not like . . . (name), but it may be the only choice you thought you had."

4. "Now turning to your creative self and asking it to generate three new behaviors for . . . (name), and asking it that one be at least as effective, perhaps even more effective, than the choices that . . . (name) already has. Taking all the time you need and asking your creative self to give you the yes signal when it has these three new behaviors. You may get yes for each choice, or just one yes for all three. Your conscious mind may occupy itself with something else; the creative self is capable of generating dozens of possible behaviors, and may not choose even to let you know consciously what the three new behaviors are."

(If the sharer is sceptical of having a creative self or part that creates new ideas, the helper can say "Have you ever had a bright idea or a brainwave and you don't know where it came from?"

The conscious mind may start generating new ideas and get in the way. It may be better to think of something else consciously in order to let the unconscious work more freely.

If the sharer does know the choices consciously, the helper may say, "Great, if your unconscious trusts you like that!"

If the sharer does not know the choices, the purpose may be to avoid the conscious mind blocking them and repressing them. So it may be appropriate to believe in the new behaviors and allow time for the change to become apparent).

5. "When you have got the signal, going back to . . . (name), and asking if it is willing to accept these new behaviors, and to generate them for you in future. (If not, repeat steps 3 and 4). Thanking . . . (name) for being willing to generate them in future.

6. "Asking   (name) if there is any other part that is objecting to these new behaviors."
(If there are objections go back to steps 4 and 5, and repeat until there are no further objecting parts, then again asking . . . (name) if all is well).

7. "Asking your creative self if it would please be willing to let you know in consciousness at any time at least one of the new behaviors, and waiting for the answer.
It may be some time before you realize that you have not been repeating the old pattern and are behaving differently and more appropriately. You may never notice.

8. "Now saying to . . . (name), 'The future is beginning now. Please will you generate this new behavior,' and waiting for the yes signal."

Journaling.

SHARING

It may be appropriate not to talk about the change immediately; some changes need to be slow as they are dramatic and far-reaching, and the sharer may need time to be able to cope with other people's reactions. Discuss whatever seems appropriate.

EXTENSION

The positive purpose and secondary gains behind each behavior pattern vary with each individual. With such things as weight gain, smoking, migraine, it is important to realize that their benefits may be strong. If the three new behaviors later turn out to be less effective, and the original behavior recurs, it is a sign to repeat the exercise. Perhaps at step 3 asking . . . (name) if it will show the creative self what it has been trying to achieve. Then at Step 4, going back to the creative self and thanking it for its new behavior, and asking it to generate three more out of the dozens of possible behaviors that are as effective, and at least one that is more effective than the present behavior.

D. CONCLUSION

RECOLLECTING
Quiet reflection and journaling.

EVALUATION
Brief comment and evaluation of session.

HOME PRACTICE
Explore some of the wealth of our written tradition in hymns and prayers. Practice reorganizing our concepts and changing our behavior by separating the purpose from the behavior in the way we used today.

LOOKING AHEAD
Next time we shall consider praying for ourselves and others, and again practice separating the purpose from our behavior.

AFFIRMATION
Closing praying, silence and the grace.

Praying for Ourselves and Others
Practice in Separating the Purpose
from Our Behavior

A. BECOMING AWARE OF WHERE WE ARE

RECOLLECTING
Being still in the presence of God.
Praying aloud or silently.

RECAP
Last time our theme was praying from the written word; our concepts and beyond; reorganizing and changing our concepts and behavior by separating it from its purpose.

SHARING
Share how we have got on.

TODAY'S THEME
Today we consider praying for ourselves and others, and then again practice separating the purpose from our behavior.

B. and C. BECOMING AWARE IN FORMAL PRAYING AND IN COUNSELING SKILLS

PRACTICE
In the whole group pray silently for a while.
Quietly divide up into twos, again sit quietly, and then in turn share celebrations and needs, and each pray, remembering to stay with the sharer's words.

SHARING
In the whole group share as appropriate.
Discuss: How do we pray for others and ourselves?

What do we think praying for others does?

EXTENSION

Praying for Ourselves and Others

Throughout this program we have thought of prayer as opening: being willing to be opened by God, open to reality, in the depths of our being. Praying opens us and links us to power beyond ourselves, a power as real as the power of nuclear fission.

We ask for ourselves in petition; in intercession we ask for others through ourselves, which is an extension of praying for ourselves. When we pray for ourselves, we may express the desire for the obstacles to our own relationship to God to be diminished or removed; when we pray for others, we may express the desire for the obstacles to be removed in our relationships with others and in both our and their relationship with God through us.

When we pray for others, the answer to our desire for them may often mean attention to blocks in ourselves. We cannot change others, but God may change them through us if we are willing to make the necessary changes in ourselves (session 10; an outcome model). In praying for others, as in the rest of this program about changing and growing, we recognize that although we may neither change others nor change God, change ultimate reality, we may instead change our perception of reality, change our understanding of ourselves, of others and of God. We may do this by easing our attachments and attitudes to the hurts that we perceive God and others have done to us (session 23,24: forgiving others and self; session 25: separating behavior from its purpose). When we are hurt our natural reaction is to withdraw and protect ourselves. When our wounds are healed we may open ourselves and let God's love flow through us to others. As our attitude softens, others in turn may be less protective and respond more openly. This is how forgiveness and reconciliation may work. Nouwen expands this idea in his book *The Wounded Healer* (1972).

Praying for others (intercession) then, involves a willingness on our part to change, to pray and to be the answer to that prayer. So in the helping relationship praying for another, intercession, may mean listening to another in a way that becomes an answer to their loneliness, confusion, grief and pain. It may mean listening in a way that helps the sharer to realize that there may be no immediate solution or immediate positive answer beyond changing their perception of the pain (session 16). Praying for others may involve the appropriate use of any helping skills we have learned, and will certainly draw on our ability to be open to God and God's discerning love in our own depths.

Praying for others involves the ability to be with others in the depths of their situation, but without that loss of perspective which comes from too much attachment. It is important when we are praying for someone else to realize that however crippled they may be, they are loved by God as much as we are, and so deserve our care and respect. "Love one another as I have loved you" (John 15:12). No one is beyond the pale as far as God is concerned. "God so loved the world that he gave his only Son" (John 3:16).

Many people who are experienced in the healing ministry recommend that when we pray for others we sense the other person whole, that we see, hear, feel them and hold them up to God in the way we desire them to be; e.g., if they are ill, not thinking of them and "their" illness, but imagining them well and full of life; if in an unhappy situation, sensing them as happy and vibrant.

We have no way of estimating just how powerful our prayer may be, especially when joined with the prayer of others.

SHARING
Share as appropriate.

Separating Purpose from Our Behavior

SHARING
Brief time for comment before practicing. Refer to last session as needed.

PRACTICE
In twos start with a time of quiet to relax and open ourselves to God's presence, i.e., rapport built with self, the other person and God, remembering that God knows what we do and what we intend.

Practice the same way as last time separating our intention from our behavior in order to substitute more satisfying behavior to achieve the same purpose.

SHARING
Share as appropriate in the whole group.

D. CONCLUDING

RECOLLECTING
Quiet reflecting and journaling.

EVALUATION
Brief evaluation and comments on the session.

HOME PRACTICE
Become more aware in our praying for ourselves and others; practice with at least one more situation changing our behavior by separating it from its purpose. For next time, we may need to revise the procedure of session 19 in separating negative feelings from a memory.

LOOKING AHEAD
Next session we shall continue by praying with one or several others; think about what others may understand by our words; and practice a way of substituting new chosen behavior.

AFFIRMATION
Close with praying and the grace.

SESSION 27

Praying with One Other or a Group
What do Others Understand by Our Words?
Developing New Behavior

A. BECOMING AWARE OF WHERE WE ARE

RECOLLECTING
  Being still in the presence of God.
  Praying silently or aloud.

RECAP
  Last session we prayed for ourselves and others, and practiced reorganizing and changing our concepts and behavior by separating the purpose from the behavior.

SHARING
  Discuss anything arising from last session.

TODAY'S THEME
  Today our theme is praying with one person or a group; what others understand by our words in praying and in general; and a way of substituting new behavior that we have chosen.

B. BECOMING AWARE IN FORMAL PRAYING

PRACTICE
  Praying silently.
  Praying in twos, in small groups, or in the whole group, as appropriate.

SHARING
  Either in the whole group or first in small groups discuss what to us are the most important features of praying

(a) with someone else.
(b) in a group.
  How have our ideas on this praying been affected by what we have learned in this program?
  How are we getting on with encouraging simple open awareness in our own prayer time?

EXTENSION

Praying with One Other or a Group

  Praying is opening, linking ourselves with the power behind and throughout the universe, with the universal energy that we Christians know as love, know as God. When we pray with one or more other persons the effect on us is greatly to strengthen this linking. We are tapping into a source of power and renewal and love that the spiritually discerning have been aware of for millenia. For Christians this power is apparent in the person of Jesus Christ and in our relationship with him.
  This power is the strength behind and in every praying group. Groups where we may prayerfully share our everyday concerns and our deepest desires, as well as groups that meet specifically for group guidance and discernment, have a crucial role in the ongoing renewal of the church in mission, commitment and service. Reinforced by belonging to a caring praying group, we may engage in the helping relationship with a new sense of the importance of praying with those we seek to help. With another person we may dis-

cern when it is appropriate to pray aloud in words of prayer through our personal awareness and sensitive use of listening and helping skills.

Rapport-building and Listening Skills in Prayer

The praying that we may engage in, in twos or in groups, make take many forms and have varied and profound effects, but fundamental to them all are building and maintaining rapport and listening within ourselves, with others and with God. Both in the helping relationship and in peer groups for mutual support and encouragement, reflectors, open questions, sub-summaries and summaries are basic in effectively discerning the participants' needs, hopes and desires, and praying accordingly. A prayer that is directly to the point and which the sharer senses as deeply relevant and full of empathy may be solely a summary of the sharer's words put into the context of a formal prayer.

Other helping skills may also shape the form of our praying. Touch, e.g., holding hands, laying on hands, may be a powerful way of communicating care, and linking the other person with the source of love, the source of care, and with positive attitudes. Holding hands to pray in twos or threes may be an effective way of including and encouraging beginners who are hesitant about praying aloud. We need to remember, however, that touch may also arouse negative feelings (session 4).

Group silence may also be a potent way of linking us with the source of healing and love which undergirds everything.

> Most people who have taken part in group prayer will have sensed the deep interior silence that sometimes enshrouds the whole gathering as though the Spirit were palpably present.
>
> This I believe, is a type of communal contemplation, a form of meditation that is particularly marked in a community of love. Here it is not only the individual but also the group that relishes an obscure sense of enveloping presence (Johnston, 1980, 84).

A time of praying silently, of being quiet at the beginning or during a conversation or prayer time, may be important to help us to relax. It may

remind us who is the great helper, and make us aware of how God may be moving in the exchange, and putting thoughts in our minds that will affect the outcome. This silence is especially useful when we sense that rapport has been lost, or we are confused about the direction in which the conversation is moving.

In praying with others, as in all prayer, being simple is the essence. This is important to remember when we are introducing someone to the practice of praying aloud with another person. One way of starting is to think of something each is thankful for, and to say simply, "Thank you God for. . . ." The next development may be for each to say a one sentence prayer. If more needs to be said, then again making a one sentence prayer, using our own everyday language and speaking to a loving friend who knows all about us.

C. BECOMING AWARE IN COUNSELING SKILLS

What do Others Understand by Our Words?

INTRODUCTION AND SHARING

Comment as appropriate and offer our own examples during the following notes. We may take turns to read the examples given.

When we are praying with others in our own words and with our own content, we are inevitably influencing them. This is true of everything we are or do in the helping relationship.

Although we use words continually, we often are unaware of the actual effect they are having on others. For two people the same word will have a different meaning, however slight, and may evoke widely differing responses. Part of increasing our effectiveness as helpers and in verbal prayer is to increase our awareness of the effect of our words, and to incorporate into our ordinary language ways of using the powerful tool of language with more beneficial and positive effects.

Unspecified Words

In session 15 we considered how specifiers (open questions that usually ask who, what or how about specific words) challenge the sharer to extend their concepts by linking their words more closely to their actual sensory experience. However, if the helper is the one using the words, and wanting the words to link up with the sharer's own unique experience, then the opposite type of words may be appropriate, in order to exclude the helper's experience and leave the sharer as free as possible.

Examples of vague unspecified words in which nearly all specific information is deleted are love, joy, peace, knowledge, experience, prayer. These are vague abstract nouns that enable the other person to search through their own experience for the most appropriate meaning, e.g., "He is a man of prayer." (What, how does he pray?)

Examples of unspecified verbs (session 8) are think, know, understand, learn, experience, remember, be aware of, change; e.g., I know you can learn this. (How? What?)

Linking Words

Linking words help the listener to connect something that is already happening to something they want to happen; e.g., and; as, when, while (time); helps, makes, causes, requires. For example, instead of saying, "Breathe slowly and relax," or even, "You are breathing in and out and beginning to relax," linking it by saying, "As you are breathing in and out, just beginning to relax. Your breathing in and out slowly will be helping you to relax more."

There are two other powerful ways that we may often unconsciously use words, i.e., presupposing and embedded suggestions. If we become aware of these ways we may be able to use them more positively and effectively.

Presupposing

When presupposing, we may appear to give the other person lots of choices, but in fact all the choices may presuppose a certain response.

Time: before, after, during, when, etc. e.g., "Do you want to stand up before we go on?" (We are going on).

Order: first, second, last, or.

e.g., "Which do you want to do first?" (You will do both).

"Do you want to do this before or after we finish?" (You will do it, and we shall finish).

Awareness: realize, know, notice, aware. e.g., "Do you realize that. . .?" (The rest of the sentence is presupposed).

Change of time: begin, end, stop, start, already, yet, still, any more, etc. e.g., "Are you still feeling angry?" (You were). "Have you stopped smoking?" (You were).

Luckily, fortunately, etc.: the rest is presupposed.

Embedded Suggestions

How many of us unwittingly use words negatively as embedded suggestions, and then wonder why we evoked a contrary response! Yet embedded suggestions can be a gentle way of indirectly evoking satisfying behavior.

Notice the following embedded suggestions: "When you are ready you may close your eyes. I wonder how soon you'll feel better. I'm sorry you are so ill." (Close your eyes. Feel better. You are so ill). These embedded suggestions are even more powerful if we mark them in some nonverbal way; e.g., by discreetly pausing, changing our tone or volume, gesturing, etc.

If we make a negative statement or command, the listener usually responds to the positive suggestion as a way of understanding it; e.g., "Don't think about tonight." The listener has to think of tonight in order to find out what to obey, and is also receiving the embedded suggestion: "Think about tonight." So if we do use negative commands, we need to realize that we are in fact commanding the opposite.

A gentle way of making suggestions may be to ask a yes-no question that commonly evokes a response rather than a literal answer; e.g., "Do you know when the bus goes? Can you speak a bit louder?"

A non-threatening way of asking questions when we are seeking information, especially when we are starting to build rapport, is to embed them in an "I" statement; e.g., "I'm wondering what you would like to talk about." (What would you like to talk about?) "I'd be interested to know . . ."

For a more detailed treatment of what others

understand by our words and embedded suggestions see Grinder and Bandler, 1981, 240–50.

Developing New Behavior

INTRODUCTION

In this section of our program we are practicing definite ways of accepting and forgiving ourselves and others, and of enabling specific changes. Pros and cons and R.I.P.A.L.C.A.R.T. were mainly for change in the outer (environment) area. In the inner (emotional) and ultimate (meaning) areas of our lives we have considered systematic associating and affirmations; changing our reactions to our past; separating negative feelings from a memory; loving ourselves as someone else loves us; healing early relationships and memories with Jesus; releasing our repressed emotions harmlessly, forgiving others and ourselves; separating the purpose from our behavior.

A Way of Substituting New Behavior

Today we consider substituting specific new behavior for old behavior. The following framework dissociates seeing and hearing from feeling in the same way as separating negative feelings from a memory. We may substitute behavior at the conscious or unconscious level; if at the unconscious level, we work with the part that knows and establish signals, as with separating purpose and behavior (session 25).

This way of substituting new behavior may help us to change behavior that we are dissatisfied with, either by establishing a pattern which we know we want, or by helping us to select a suitable pattern from our past or from some real or imaginary person.

PRACTICE

The leader may go briefly over the exercise. We then divide into twos and in turn practice this way of substituting new behavior. If necessary refer to session 19 on separating negative feelings from a memory.

Steps when using this way as a helper:

1. Rapport building.
2. Establishing some kind of yes/no signal. We may well observe signals that the sharer is unaware of. But it is useful also to have an agreed signal; e.g., "You may like to indicate yes by nodding your head, or moving a finger." Our questions then need to be closed so that we get a yes/no answer.
3. Identifying the behavior that the sharer is dissatisfied with.
4. As with separating negative feelings from a memory (session 19), establishing strong satisfying links, and then taking time to get the sharer to see and hear, but not feel, themselves behaving in the unwanted way out in front of themselves, as if they were in the projectionist's booth, watching themselves in the middle of the movie theater watching a movie. Remembering to mark the dissociation by touching the sharer. This double dissociation may allow the sharer to watch and listen more comfortably to the behavior. Saying to the sharer "Indicating when you have finished watching and listening comfortably and safely to this behavior that you want to change."
5. "Do you know how you would prefer to behave in this situation?" If they know, continue at 6.
    If they do not know what new response they would prefer to make, help them to identify satisfying behavior in their past, e.g.:
    "Going back, scanning your life. Have you ever behaved, or can you imagine yourself behaving, in another situation in a way that you would like to respond in this one?"
    If they have, get them to relive that situation from the inside, associating strong links, and then continue at 6.
    If they still do not know what response they would like to make, they will need to search for a model. (See end for an expanded procedure for 5 and 6).
6. (a) "So now watching and listening to yourself responding in this new way in the situation that used to be a problem for you. Giving me the yes signal when you have finished."
    (b) "And as you were watching and hearing yourself behaving in a new way in that situation, was that quite satisfactory to you?" If not, going back and choosing more satisfactory behavior (5), and watching and hearing it (6).
7. (a) Reassociating with the dissociated experi-

ence. "Now coming back from the projectionist's booth to being inside yourself as you are sitting here with me in the theater."

Remove your hand, assuring them of God's Spirit with them.

"So that you can replay the same movie, this time being inside it yourself, now going up to the screen and stepping inside the first scene at the beginning of the film. And now experiencing for yourself from the inside what it is actually like to behave in this new way in the situation. Giving me the yes signal when you have finished."

(b) "Was it still satisfactory?"

Make sure that the yes signal is congruent with their answer, because some behaviors are not as satisfactory from the inside as they may have seemed.

If it is not satisfying, replaying it with alterations until it is satisfactory (7a), or choosing another behavior (5).

8. Experiencing the future to ensure that the change transfers to appropriate life situations.

"Now thinking of a similar situation in the future, and experiencing it from the inside. Sensing how it is to be you behaving in your new satisfying way, as you see and hear and feel and smell and taste and behave in this way that is satisfying to you.

"And asking your unconscious to be aware of the cues that will indicate at the beginning of the situation the need for this new behavior, and asking if it will please be responsible for this new behavior actually occurring where the old behavior used to occur.

"Giving me the yes signal when you are ready."

9. "Now taking as much time as you need, thanking your unconscious, and thanking God in whatever way is appropriate for you."

Expanded Procedure for 5 and 6
Using Someone as a Model

5. "Do you know anyone who behaves in this kind of situation in a way that you would like to behave? They may be someone real or imaginary or someone you have seen on T.V. or read about. The fact that you want to change your present behavior shows that you have

some standard for the kind of way you want to respond. So, picking someone you respect and admire, whom you think responds much more effectively and appropriately in this kind of situation, and is an excellent model for you.

"Giving me the yes signal when you have chosen the person with the appropriate response."

5(a) "So now watching and listening to the person you have chosen responding appropriately in the situation that you want to have a new choice about.

"Giving me the yes signal when you have finished."

(b) "And now you have been watching and listening to this other person, is this the way you would like to respond?" If not, either find another model or alter the model's behavior (5a), and then watch and listen to the model again (5b).

When they want to respond in the same way as their model, continue:

6(a) "Now, changing the other person so that they have your looks and voice, watching and listening to yourself in the film responding in this new way in the situation that used to be a problem for you. Giving me the yes signal when you have finished."

(b) "And as you were watching and hearing yourself behaving in this new way, was it effective and satisfying for you? Do you still want to respond in this way?"

If not, go back and choose another model or behavior (5a). If they are satisfied, continue at 7, reassociating with the dissociated experience.

Journaling as desired.

SHARING
Share in the whole group.

EXTENSION

Saints as Models

Christians whom we have known or read about may have a strong formative influence on us. The above procedure is another way of helping to incorporate the qualities that we admire in them into our own lives.

D. CONCLUDING

RECOLLECTING
Quiet reflecting and journaling.

EVALUATING
Brief evaluating and comment.

HOME PRACTICE
Being more aware of the words we are using, their meaning for and effect on other people; at least once practicing today's way of substituting for our unwanted ways specific behavior that we do want.

LOOKING AHEAD
Next session our theme is reading the Bible, and metaphor.

AFFIRMATION
As appropriate, close with silence, a hymn and the grace.

SESSION 28

Reading the Bible
Metaphors

A. BECOMING AWARE OF WHERE WE ARE

RECOLLECTING
Being still in the presence of God.
Praying silently and aloud.

RECAP
Last time we prayed with one person or a group; considered what others may understand by our words, embedded suggestions and negative commands; and practiced a way of substituting new behavior.

SHARING
Comment on anything arising from last session.

TODAY'S THEME
Today we think about ways of reading the Bible, and about metaphor in the Bible, in our daily life and in stories in the helping relationship.

B. AND C. BECOMING AWARE IN FORMAL PRAYING AND IN COUNSELING SKILLS

PRACTICE
Silent praying.
Read and meditate on the parable of the mustard seed, Matthew 13:31–32.
Journaling.

SHARING
Share how this parable spoke to us in the language of analogy and metaphor.

EXTENSION

Reading the Bible

A recurrent theme of this program has been the need for helpers and those being helped to make effective links with reality, and the reality that is God, in terms of their present and past experience. In our last session we emphasized the importance of praying as a means of creating and maintaining these links. We touched on the benefits in praying both individually and corporately. Praying in groups enormously strengthens and confirms the effects of individual action.

There are also other ingredients in the effective linking of our experience. Reading the Bible, like having a specific time for praying, is another proven way of cultivating our relationship with Jesus Christ, who may fulfill all our experience.

For some, reading the Bible is a prerequisite to formal praying. For Max Warren, renowned missionary leader and ecclesiastical statesman, it was an important principle to pray with the Bible in one hand and the newspaper in the other. In this he was reflecting an emphasis of contemplatives down the centuries, that worship of God must go hand in hand with service. Each is a test of the other (see Merton, 1973).

What Makes Bible Reading So Important?

Bible reading is important because it is basic to forming the concepts which determine our relationship to God, and so is the best single aid to learning to pray.

On this matter a note of caution needs to be

sounded. Our view of the Bible, its message and its language needs to be open, not closed. As we have often emphasized, the most that words can do is to point to reality, point to truth. Words, as with any symbols, may never confine or contain reality. Reason tells us that if they could they would rank with God. Plainly neither we nor our words do that, for God remains God.

When we communicate in words or nonverbally, we are still using symbols to communicate our own experience, which is individual, unique and cannot be fully understood by another. The other person of necessity receives an incomplete communication and fills in the gaps from their own representation and perception of reality. All language is symbolic and communicates incompletely, even factual scientific language.

Yet even though neither words nor experience may embrace reality, words may powerfully recall and rekindle our experience, especially in religious and poetic language, including the language of the Bible, which is rich with analogy and metaphor. No language can express the inexpressible, but analogy and metaphor may be the most adequate pointers. If we attach too much significance to the words themselves, reality may elude us. We become deluded (session 24).

The Bible communicates the record and truth of our relationship with reality, with God. It is unique because it is the least ambiguous reflection of our relationship with God, especially through the life of the man Jesus. We do violence to the purpose of the Bible to view it as though it were a repository of truth written in scientific language. As a treasure-store of experience and analogy, as well as of historical fact, the Bible remains one of the most powerful and authentic ways of informing our prayers, of making us aware of God's presence, of developing our relationship with God, i.e., of linking and converting us to reality.

We need to read the Bible regularly, thoughtfully, openly, for it to do its work of transforming us to become like Christ in heart and mind and soul.

SHARING

Comment as appropriate.

Metaphors

INTRODUCTION

Everyday Metaphors

We have recognized that analogy and metaphor in the Bible are essential in forming our concepts and linking us with reality. To some degree, all words are symbols, all words are metaphors. The use of metaphor in a more technical sense, as implying a comparison, is an everyday occurrence; it is not confined to the Bible, to religious writing, to myths and fairy tales, or to poetry. Many of our everyday words are metaphors; e.g., sensory verbs that are not used in a literal sense, e.g., I see (S), I get the hang of it (F), that clicks with me (H), (sessions 8, 9).

Metaphorical Stories

Metaphors may also be a powerful way of making changes in our relationships and behavior. So as helpers we need to be aware of what gentle yet powerful tools metaphors may be, and how they may be used to produce satisfying changes. They are there for our use just as much as for the persuasive exploiters who pervade our society.

Milton Erickson was a past master at telling an amusing or adventurous tale which used metaphor to produce the change that the hearer really wanted. Every story was skillfully designed to match each significant detail of the person's own situation.

How Metaphors are Effective

A metaphorical story conveys some message or learning about a particular problem. In the story a character is confronted by some problem; the way the problem is resolved may provide a solution for others in a similar situation.

We have recognized earlier that all our communication uses symbols to represent our experience, i.e., is to some degree metaphorical of our unique experience, and so is incomplete. The receiver, in trying to make sense of our incomplete communication, fills in the gaps, and represents it in terms of their own experience, their concept of reality which can never be the same as our own.

An appropriate metaphorical story starts the hearer unconsciously or consciously searching for the personal resources and concepts they need to deal with the problem. At the same time it presents a solution which has been effective for someone else in a similar situation with similar relationships and coping patterns. Because we all make sense of communications in terms of our own experience, the hearer naturally links the story with their own situation, and so is free to incorporate and use or to reject the offered solution.

Because a story is non-threatening and often not consciously recognized as being connected to the problem, such metaphors may be effective with problems considered difficult or embarrassing.

So the special advantage of metaphors is that people may respond without trying, unconsciously selecting what they need to know.

A striking example of a healing metaphor constructed to help a woman change in the way she wanted to may be found in *Solutions*, 190–192; many others are in Rosen (1982) and Gordon (1978).

SHARING
Comments.

PRACTICE

Making up a Metaphorical Story

In the whole group enjoy making up a simple metaphor.

INTRODUCTION

*Four S Steps in Making Up
a Metaphorical Story*

1. *Situation and structure:* Identify the problem situation, its essential structure, and its characters.
2. *Similar Situation and Structure:* Imagine a situation with similar details of structure and characters; e.g., tackling a problem is like climbing a mountain.
3. *Solution:* Provide a logical solution which the sharer may transfer and use in their own situation.
4. *Story:* Dream up and tell an entertaining story with a similar structure of situation, relationships and solutions, but which disguises the purpose, in order to avoid conscious resistance, and to free the hearer to make their own choices on a wider base.

PRACTICE
In the whole group suggest simple situations and choose one. Work through the four S steps.

Practice either in the whole group or in smaller groups.

SHARING
Comment and share our experience and metaphors.

EXTENSION
Metaphorical stories, embedded suggestions and negative commands, then, make their impact because we all try to make sense of communications in terms of our own experience.

A type of embedded suggestion with which we often unwittingly and randomly influence people is by using quotes. But we can also use quotes intentionally and effectively. This involves making any statement we want to make to our hearer as though we are reporting in quotation marks what someone else said at another time and place. So we may deliver any message without taking responsibility for it; e.g., "So he said to her, 'I love you!'"

Because we are apparently talking about what someone else said at another time and place, the hearer may well respond to the message without identifying what they are responding to or who is responsible. The characters in our metaphorical stories may say exactly what we want to say and the hearer may get the message.

Metaphors are treated in more detail by Sidney Rosen in *My Voice Will Go with You: The Teaching Tales of Milton H. Erickson* (1982); and David Gordon in *Therapeutic Metaphors* (1978).

Erickson's methods were studied minutely by

Bandler, Grinder and Cameron-Bandler, and lie behind much of their work. In *Solutions*, 189–200, Cameron-Bandler briefly outlines the essentials of constructing metaphorical stories that provide people with conscious or unconscious learning leading to new productive behavior.

D. CONCLUDING

RECOLLECTING
Quiet reflecting and journaling.

EVALUATION
Brief evaluating and comment.

HOME PRACTICE
Becoming more aware of how we use words metaphorically and their impact. Practice thinking up similar situations as settings for metaphorical healing stories, e.g., the family is like a garden. Make up at least one story using the four S steps.

LOOKING AHEAD
Next time we shall consider understanding the Bible as a living two-way relationship; work on a common relating pattern and on a way of maintaining and strengthening a satisfying relationship.

AFFIRMATION
Close by reading the parable of the yeast (Matt. 13:33), and saying the grace.

Understanding the Bible:
A Two-way Relationship
A Relating Pattern
Strengthening a Fulfilling Relationship

A. BECOMING AWARE OF WHERE WE ARE

RECOLLECTING
  Being still in the presence of God.
  Praying silently and aloud.

RECAP
  Last time we thought about reading the Bible, and especially the power of its metaphorical language. We considered how so many of our words are metaphors, and how we may make up stories for healing specific situations.

SHARING
  Share how we have got on with our metaphors.

TODAY'S THEME
  Today we think of understanding the Bible in a living two-way relationship. In this session and the next we shall touch briefly on crisis which specifically affects our relationships with others. Up till now we have considered ourselves as helping an individual. These two sessions involve also knowing or imagining how the other person in a relationship is thinking and feeling.

B. BECOMING AWARE IN FORMAL PRAYING

PRACTICE
  Silent praying.
  Read Matthew 13:9–17,23 or 9–23. The Purpose of Parables (The Sower).

Understanding the Bible:
A Living Two-way Relationship

INTRODUCTION
  In our last session we saw that the Bible and its language may be an important means of linking us with ultimate reality, with God, because it is analogical and metaphorical. Once we recognize its analogical and metaphorical nature we are free to understand the Bible in a new way, and the Bible is freed for its linking role.
  Openness in our approach to the Bible is as important as in any other aspect of our inward and outward journey. Scripture can stand up to the test of critical examination. The language of the Bible is not more sacred than any other language relating to meaning, values and direction, even though what it communicates may be different.
  How then are we to understand the message of the Bible? How may the Bible yield its unique insight into reality?
  When we have perhaps cleared away some of the problems through a critical approach to the text, we are freer to open our whole selves, heart and mind, to the meaning of the Bible. We are free to adopt the prayerful interactive way of reading scripture so that we may not only read scripture but let scripture read us. This two-way reading is the monastic tradition of "lectio divina" in which we allow scripture to become a two-way window. We see, and we allow our-

selves to be seen; we apprehend and are apprehended; we not only embrace but are open to being embraced by reality.

So our search for truth in the scriptures becomes (what the origin of the word suggests) a search for "troth," a search for the commitment of a living relationship. This relationship is with the risen Christ, experienced through the Holy Spirit, the presence of God in us.

> Christianity is not centered around a moral teaching, but around a person. . . . The scripture is the normal way of introducing us gradually to the knowledge and love of this person. This process involves the kind of dynamic that happens in making friends with anyone. You have to spend time together, talk together, listen to each other, and get to know each other. At first you feel a little awkward and strange in one another's company, but as you get better acquainted, and especially as you feel yourself going out to the goodness you perceive in each other, the amount of time spent in conversation begins to diminish. You are at ease to rest in one another's presence with just a happy sense of well-being.

> The process that I have spoken of in terms of human friendship is the way lectio divina works too. In a sense, it is a methodless way of meditation. It does not depend on some particular technique, but on the natural evolution of friendship. . . . It is a personal exchange (Keating, 1981, 45–46).

> To engage in this personal exchange, this friendship, is the highest meaning of "imitating" Jesus Christ. We are not to follow the patterns of his life mechanically or slavishly, that would only make us puppet-forms of our true selves. Instead, we are to follow Jesus in the way we should follow a friend, always alert for the resonances and dissonances of two independent people trying to live in a bond of truth, of mutual fidelity. As we do so, we discover our own lives being inwardly re-formed by a living relationship with one who loves us and wants to set us free (Palmer, 1984, 33).

So, becoming like Christ in heart and mind and soul involves our opening ourselves to him in prayer and silence, opening ourselves in our everyday lives, and opening ourselves to a living two-way relationship. The Bible, especially in its record of Jesus' life on earth, has a unique place in opening us, in encouraging and developing our relationship with the God of love, the source of life.

PRACTICE

In session 13, centering with the body as a base and practicing listening skills, we thought about King Solomon's prayer for an understanding heart, a hearing heart, listening from our centers. Let's hear again 1 Kings 3:9; "Give therefore thy servant an understanding heart, (a hearing heart) to judge thy people, that I may discern between good and bad, for who is able to judge this thy so great people?"

As we open our hearts prayerfully to God let us ask if God will bring a scripture verse to our minds for us to hear and to be open to.

SHARING

Share our scriptures, and discuss them as appropriate.

Silent or vocal praying together.

C. BECOMING AWARE IN COUNSELING SKILLS

Relating with Others

PRACTICE

Each write what we consider are the factors needed to maintain a fulfilling relationship of love, respect or trust.

Share them in the group, and write them up on the board.

EXTENSION

Relating Two-Way with Others

Understanding the Bible is two-way; we read and are read, we live and are lived in. Obviously we relate two-way with others as well as with God.

Relationships have been an implicit part of all that we have covered in this program. Up till now we have mainly considered ourselves as helping an individual. Although it is not the aim of this program to go at greater depth into such areas as couple counseling and family therapy, in this session and the next we shall deal briefly with crisis that specifically concerns the sharer's relating with another. The situations will involve the sharer's knowing or imagining how the other

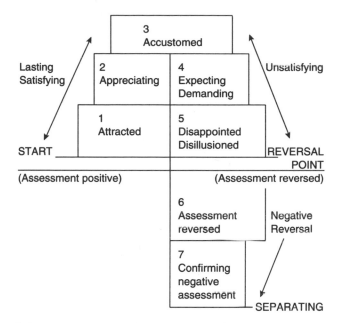

Fig. 10. A relating pattern (based on Cameron-Bandler, 1985, 116–28)

person is thinking and feeling as well as their own position.

A Relating Pattern

INTRODUCTION AND SHARING

Comment briefly as appropriate in going over a common relating pattern:

In diagnosing what stage a person is at in their relationship and what help may be appropriate, it may be useful to consider the stages as a relating pattern. In a relationship crisis people are often at different stages.

Cameron-Bandler has described a common pattern in significant relationships from attraction through to separation as the threshold pattern (Cameron-Bandler, 1985, 116–28). This sequence may occur in any type of significant relating: a relationship of love, of trust, of respect; relating to people, to a situation, to a job, or to an object.

Figure 10 summarizes this common relating pattern, which we shall go on to consider in more detail.

A Satisfying Relationship: Beginning and Lasting

1. Attracted

What attracts us to someone? We each have concepts of what we find attractive. They are probably based partly on innate reactions; e.g., most people soften towards big eyes and round faces which are characteristic of our young; partly on the values of our own culture, and on the relationships we have experienced.

Whether consciously or unconsciously, we establish our values, e.g., which qualities we find attractive in another person. It may be good looks, confidence, warmth, intelligence, money, position. We associate definite sensory perceptions with each of these qualities, e.g., blonde, tall and dark, walking tall and speaking fluently, smiling and soft-bodied, etc. Then we assess whether a person is attractive by whether or not we perceive the behavior and sense impressions that we have associated with the qualities we admire.

We are probably aware how the same sense impressions and behavior may be interpreted differently in different cultures; e.g., what makes a person beautiful; or again, a person looking down in front of an elder may be considered respectful in one society, and shy, dishonest or stupid in another. But we need to be aware that in every relationship, each of us assumes that certain behaviors have a specific meaning, which we respond to without question. Yet the other person may assume the same behavior to have a different meaning, and attach our meaning to quite different behavior, e.g., touching gently, leaving us alone. We may more easily appreciate and understand the other's behavior when we know what it means to them and is intended to mean to us.

When we are first attracted to someone, especially when we fall in love, we are apt to notice only the behavior and sense impressions that we link with desirable qualities.

2. Appreciating

When we are genuinely appreciative, instead of taking each other for granted, we are noticing and responding to what makes us feel loved and loving, and so are increasing our loving feelings.

Our relationship may last and be satisfying if we know which experiences each of us believes are significant and necessary to the relationship, know which behavior gives each of us the significant experiences, and if we are willing and able to elicit and provide them. Put more simply, the key is to know what we each need, what provides it, and how we can get it and give it to each other.

To achieve and maintain this appreciation, we need to be adaptable in ways of getting our needs met and meeting the other person's needs; i.e., in widening our concepts and becoming aware of our choices. A way of maintaining and strengthening a satisfying relationship (R.I.L.L.A.N.C.T.) is set out later this session.

3. Accustomed

Having a secure, familiar relationship may free us to attend to other matters, and if it includes appreciation and some attraction, may be satisfying, comfortable, and safe. However, if we want adventure and find safety boring, we may need to attend again to what there is to appreciate, and to explore new ways of attracting and satisfying each other.

Cameron-Bandler suggests that romantic interludes may make a great difference to apathy with couples. She often prescribes that in the following two months, each partner alone should plan one weekend for both to share, to fulfill his/her fantasies of how s/he wants to spend time with the other, staying within a prescribed budget. After their learning experience she concentrates on integrating into their everyday lives the aspects they both enjoyed, and learning to laugh and adjust to the other aspects (Cameron-Bandler, 1985, 122).

A warning which probably tallies well with our own experience is that such weekends may work wonders for those who are at the accustomed stage, but if they are falling into the unsatisfying stages of the relating pattern, then the weekends may well be disappointing or arouse hostility.

An Unsatisfying Relationship: In Danger, Starting to End?

4. Expecting, demanding—duty instead of pleasure

At this stage we no longer notice what we once appreciated. "Wanting to" is replaced by "should" and duty. We complain instead of complimenting because we are mostly noticing when the behavior we value is not there instead of when it is. We tend to ignore it when it is there, do little to elicit it, and interpret its absence as our being not loved or not wanted.

5. Disappointed, disillusioned

Now that we are feeling unloved because we are attending to our unsatisfied desires, we may respond by deciding that the other person is unlovable, uncaring, etc. We begin to notice behavior that we dislike which may have been there all the time.

As helpers we may be able to guide a person back to being appreciative if they still remember the past as happy and want to get back to better times.

We need to help them:

a. To want to regain the satisfaction that they knew in the past. We may be able to do this by helping them to reexperience those past satisfying feelings and situations, and so revive their former belief that the other person may provide much of what they want and need. We may also help to motivate them by getting them to face the traumatic consequences of separation.

b. To take responsibility for eliciting the behavior that they want from the other person. We may be able to help them to have more choice in bringing about satisfying experiences. Once they want the relationship to be fulfilling again, and will take responsibility for making it satisfying, they are back to appreciating, noticing when the valued behaviors are present and responding to what makes them feel loved and loving.

A Negative Relationship: Ending?

6. Reversal point: assessing reversed to negative

There may come a point when we believe that the relationship is over, not worth having, and that the other person cannot and will not provide what we need. Our initial positive assessment and attraction is reversed to a negative assessment.

Besides noticing only behavior we dislike in the present, we alter our memories, too. We reverse the normal process by hearing and looking at our past satisfying experiences from the outside, and separating our feelings from the memory, but fully associating with and feeling from the inside our past unsatisfying memories. Moreover, unpleasant experiences loom large in the future, and overshadow any possibly satisfying ones.

We may reach the reversal point unexpectedly —a trivial occurrence, an innocent word or gesture may be the last straw. It may suddenly turn us round, switch us off. Other people may have little understanding of what is happening.

7. Confirming the negative assessment

We now perceive everything as confirming our negative beliefs about the relationship and the other person. We interpret their behavior as meaning the opposite of our original interpretation when we were attracted; e.g., the walking tall and speaking fluently may now denote for us not confidence but empty brashness; the smiling, soft-bodied person may now denote not warmth but a vacuous, sloppy person. The attractive soaring helium-filled balloon tugging us upward with its string seems now a prisoner's ball and chain.

8. Separating

Some people remain together in their negative reversal, others have had enough. They disown the other, they outwardly break the relationship, and separate.

As helpers we need to be aware of the signals which lead us to discern which stage of the relationship people are in, especially which side of the reversal point; e.g., How do they respond to satisfying and unpleasant memories? Are they only discouraged, or repulsed by the relationship continuing?

If one person in a relationship has passed the reversal point, it is important for us as helpers to concentrate on their coming back (session 30). Otherwise they may well sabotage whatever is attempted.

The desirable stages in a satisfying relationship are loving and appreciating, backed up by being attracted and accustomed to each other.

A Way of Maintaining and Strengthening A Satisfying Relationship (R.I.L.L.A.N.C.T.)

PRACTICE

After the leader has briefly gone over the following exercise, each of us may work through it ourselves.

1. *Rapport-build,* i.e., become more aware of myself and God.
2. *Identify* the relationship I want to work on.
3. *List* what I want from the relationship and the sensory details of the specific behavior that gives it to me; e.g., "What exactly makes me feel loved, secure, stimulated?"
4. *List* what I think the other person wants and what specifically gives it to them.
   Check this out with the other person now or later, taking good notice of the differences.
5. Be *adaptable* in *acting* specifically:
   a. to meet the other person's desires.
   b. to elicit the responses and behavior that I want.
   Check this with the other person.
6. *Notice* any signs of moving away from being appreciative backed by being attracted and accustomed. Ask myself, "What phase do I think I am in; the other person is in? What sensory messages am I interpreting to lead me to this conclusion?"
7. *Commit* myself to wanting and knowing how to lead either of us back if necessary; e.g., "What steps can I take in this today?"
8. *Thank* God, self, and the other person as appropriate.

SHARING

Share as appropriate in twos, small groups or immediately in the whole group.

D. CONCLUDING

RECOLLECTING

Quiet reflecting and journaling.

EVALUATION

Brief evaluating and comments on the session.

HOME PRACTICE

Becoming more aware of reading our Bibles in a personal relationship with God. Go through today's relating pattern and exercise, and act on any new understanding in our personal relationships. Write our evaluation of the whole program, for sessions 31 and 32, following the guidelines at the end of session 33.

LOOKING AHEAD

Next time our theme is praying the Bible, and reevaluating relationships.

AFFIRMATION

Close with singing one verse of "Be still and know that I am God," silent praying and the grace.

SESSION 30

Praying the Bible
Reevaluating Relationships

A. BECOMING AWARE OF WHERE WE ARE

RECOLLECTING
Being still in the presence of God.
Praying silently or aloud.

RECAP
Last time we thought of our reading the Bible as a two-way relationship; we considered a common relating pattern; and we worked on a way of strengthening one of our own relationships.

SHARING
Brief comment as appropriate.

TODAY'S THEME
Today we shall consider how we may pray the Bible, and two ways of reevaluating our relationships.

B. BECOMING AWARE IN FORMAL PRAYING

PRACTICE
Silent praying.
Thinking of a situation either that you were in this week or that someone you were helping was in. Thinking of the text that came to your mind or that comes to your mind now. And thinking of the prayer that it gave rise to or might give rise to, as you think of Jesus Christ present and active in that situation through the Holy Spirit.

SHARING
Briefly sharing the situation, text and prayer if desired.
Praying together in the group as appropriate, remembering our listening skills.

Praying the Bible

INTRODUCTION
In the last two sessions we have thought about reading and understanding the Bible as a living two-way relationship. Now we consider praying the Bible (session 25: Praying and singing from the written word).

Last session we saw that the key to understanding the Bible lies in recognizing that the Bible is about our relating with God. Crucial to this relating is our relating with Jesus, who uniquely expresses and represents our relationship with God, with ultimate reality. The question that we are addressing in this program is how we may move into and deepen this relationship. We have said that it is a relationship that develops like any other, through spending time talking, listening and getting to know one another. Our rapport-building, centering, listening, attending to process rather than to content, our ways of changing and forgiving may all contribute to our awareness and openness.

There are no guaranteed methods, but there are well-tried ways of encouraging the openness needed to relate more deeply with Jesus. The Bible becomes a resource for relating better with Jesus through our connecting with the inner meaning and feeling of the relationships portrayed there.

To experience the inner meaning, we need to pray the Bible. Wink's *Transforming Bible Study* (1981) provides fascinating glimpses of ways to pray the Bible that may lead to transformation.

The first step is moving in imagination inside the events. For our praying to become alive, we need to share in the action, rather than to get bogged down while looking on at some detail. As we have found repeatedly during this program, we need to experience the events from the inside, as participants rather than observers. We need to sense and experience the sights, sounds, feelings, tastes, and smells of the events we read about in the Bible, especially those relating to Jesus.

The second step is moving in imagination into the meaning of the people portrayed there, into their inside world, into their deepest feelings and values and concepts; especially into those of Jesus who, as we saw earlier, uniquely expresses and represents our relationship with God. Dialoguing with Jesus, as in our prayer journals, is one way of opening ourselves to his meaning and to his inner world.

The paradox is that as we connect in these two ways, moving inside the events and into the inner world of meaning, we also need to ease our attachment, to be gentle, to dissociate from feelings and things related to events, including the events of Jesus' life, in order to discern God's heart, mind, will and purpose for us at any given moment of our lives. Knowing has to give way to unknowing and trusting.

In connecting with the Bible to develop our relationship with Jesus and discern inner meanings, we are guided by the movement of the Spirit in two ways:

1. In the events and people portrayed in the Bible.
2. In the dynamic interplay between the people and events of the Bible on the one hand, and on the other hand the unique situation of our own lives and the lives of those we are attempting to help.

It is by our being open to the movement of the Holy Spirit in this dynamic interplay that our praying becomes alive, in our personal prayers and in our use of the Bible in the helping relationship. Praying and singing from the written word, including scripture, may be a deeply emotive and effective way of linking us with the past, and reassuring us in the present, especially in times of crisis, when we may doubt ourselves, others and God.

Praying using familiar words and scripture may affect us in a way that nothing else can.

Again and again people in extremity in hospital will be roused, challenged or comforted by words and prayers from scripture. They may join in familiar responses when they themselves are beyond putting two words together coherently. The associations may be very deep. The words of scripture may re-link us to a whole world of assurance and peace.

As we learn to pray the Bible more effectively, our relationship develops with God, with Jesus Christ, and we learn through awareness of God's Spirit to develop more effective relationships with others. And because, through praying the Bible, we are coming truly to know ourselves as being repentant, forgiven, freed, accepted and loved by God, we may enable others to experience this reality for themselves.

SHARING
Share our own experiences.

C. BECOMING AWARE IN COUNSELING SKILLS REEVALUATING RELATIONSHIPS

Reversing the Negative Reversal

INTRODUCTION
Having considered how we may develop our relationship with Jesus and how this is linked with praying the Bible, we now go on to further ways of helping people whose relationship is in crisis. Last session we considered relating in terms of a relating pattern (Figure 9) and how to maintain and strengthen a satisfying relationship.

This session we look at two ways of dealing with a relationship that has passed the negative reversal point (Cameron-Bandler, 1985, 201–13). We have passed the negative reversal point when we are associated into painful memories and dissociated from past pleasure, and interpret nearly everything about the other person as negative, even though originally we may have perceived it as satisfying.

Whether or not we separate from someone, a relationship still exists. Our past affects our present. So it is important for our memories to become a satisfying resource that we may draw on, rather than a canker eating us up. One way of turning our tragedies into our jewels is by reassociating with our satisfying experiences, and dissociating from our pain. We may still acknowledge the pain, but we do not have to feel it in the present when we remember past events and people.

A Way of Separating Pain, and Reassociating Satisfying Feelings

PRACTICE

When the leader has gone over the exercise briefly, we may divide into twos and if time take it in turn to reevaluate an unsatisfying or negatively reversed relationship.

As usual, we need to gain and maintain rapport, ensure that the sharer is relaxed, identify the relationship to be worked on, and complete each step before going on.

1. *The present reaction of the sharer, A, to B.*
   A imagines meeting B unexpectedly, at an unusual time or place; e.g., home early: while out. We need to notice A's reaction carefully in order to compare it with their reaction at the end.

2. *A makes satisfying links appreciating themselves*
   A experiences what they most appreciate and cherish about themselves, systematically associating it with touch, and holding on to their self-appreciation throughout, using the systematic links when necessary. At any time they may return to strengthen their self-appreciation.

3. *A sees B and feels self-appreciation*
   A pictures B in a photo as B was when A first met or was attracted to B. While looking at the picture A presses the self-appreciation link.

4. *A sees B as separate*
   After A can both see B and feel self-appreciation, then A sees B over there, separate from A, an independent person with a separate life. If necessary at any stage, we may use dissociation (e.g., separating feeling from a memory in the movies), to enable A to see B's pain, frustration, etc. separately from its effects on A.

5. *A recalls B's positive qualities*
   While still feeling self-appreciation, A re-

members the attributes and qualities that originally attracted A to B and that A valued.

6. *A recalls and keeps a shared satisfying memory*
   While keeping their own sense of self-appreciation and seeing B clearly as separate, A chooses a pleasant shared experience that held more because A and B were together than if either had been alone. A explores it, experiencing and savoring it fully. A realizes that it is their own memory, part of their life treasure, worth holding onto and not letting anything take it away.

7. *A returns to the present*
   A returns to the present, retaining the sense of self-appreciation.

8. *Test: A again unexpectedly meets B*
   A again imagines a surprise meeting with B. We notice any difference in reaction, and ask A how different it is from the first imagined meeting.

SHARING
Share in the whole group.

Reevaluating A Relationship

INTRODUCTION

Reevaluating a relationship is a second much longer way of dealing with a relationship that has passed the reversal point. It may take two or three sessions, and we can only go over it here briefly.

It is a way of helping people to identify their values, behavior, needs and wants in a personal relationship; to reevaluate them, and to develop ways of maintaining a satisfying relationship. After evaluating how far each can fulfill the others' needs, they may either be motivated to return to a satisfying relationship or be surer that separating is a wise choice.

Separating pain and reassociating satisfying feelings (as above) may well be a useful preliminary.

A Way of Reevaluating a Relationship

Note: If B is not doing it, A needs to get information from B about B's wants and needs, and satisfying them in the past, present and future (steps 1–3 for B).

1. *A identifies and explores their own needs and wants*

a. A identifies what they want and need in the relationship now, in the past, and in the future.

b. A explores the differences between these needs, and how their wants and needs naturally change at different stages of their life.

2. *A identifies B's contribution*

a. A identifies how B has satisfied A's needs and wants in the past, and might satisfy A in the future.

b. A discovers what more A got than they expected, how B helped A to develop their own character, and how A will benefit from this in the future.

3. *A creates possible futures*

a. A creates several possible future situations based on B's existing qualities and behavior, and assesses whether B may be able to provide what A needs and wants.

b. A compares one of these situations with a future one based on B's possible future qualities and behavior, and evaluates the difference.

4. *A understands B's and A's past behavior*

a. A identifies B's objectionable behaviors.

b. A senses what would be going on in A in order to behave in the same way as B, and considers the possibilities behind B's behavior which make it understandable.

c. A imagines how different it might have been if A had behaved differently, trying various behaviors in each of various situations, including responding to how B was feeling instead of what B was doing.

d. A considers how B's behavior is an example of a quality that in another situation A enjoys, values, and benefits from.

5. *A tries out satisfying behavior in the past*

A identifies how in the past A's behavior did not reflect all of A's satisfying qualities. A takes one negative past incident with B; considers A's most valued qualities, and how adequately A reflected those qualities in behavior; and also considers B's feelings behind B's behavior. A chooses one of A's most valued qualities which would be appropriate in the context, and tries out different behaviors to

reflect that quality, sensing how the whole interaction is transformed.

This may be repeated several times.

6. *A tries out and assesses satisfying future behavior*

a. A refers back to a possible future situation based on B's existing behavior (3a). A readjusts it by behaving in some of the new ways (just tried out in step 5) that reflect A's valued qualities.

b. A decides whether A is willing to make the present and future different by making the necessary changes in A's behavior.

7. *A tests whether the decision is worth it*

a. *If A is willing to change:*

A sees A behaving in the new way in the future and influencing the course of the relationship, and feels and senses fully what it is like to make a crucial difference in improving the relationship with B.

A sees B, recognizes B's positive attributes and feels appreciation for them.

A imagines the next opportunity to test out the new and different behaviors to influence the direction of A's life and the relationship with B.

If both A and B are willing to be adaptable and to change, each now takes responsibility for making the relationship satisfying, by behaving in ways that exercise their own best qualities, while appreciating and responding to the other's valued qualities. Their greater understanding and commitment to satisfy each other in the future may bring them back to the desirable stage of appreciating, being accustomed, even being attracted to each other.

b. *If A is unwilling to change:*

A asks what A has to lose, what needs and wants will be unfulfilled without B. A asks what A will miss that A is getting now, and how A will satisfy A's needs and wants without B.

If either A or B consider they are unwilling and unable to fulfill each other's needs, each may become more understanding and appreciative of the other person and the relationship, and be affirmed in their decision to separate.

Separating pain/reassociating satisfying feelings and re-evaluating the relationship both aim to reverse the negative reversal and to help people become more aware of the range of their choices and resources.

By associating into satisfying situations, dissociating the automatic painful links, and achieving some understanding of the other's responses, the sharer is starting to polish the rough pebble into a valuable gem which may enhance rather than weigh down any future relationship. This taking hold of the satisfying, and recognizing some value from our pain may be understood as "working through" a situation, seeing the rainbow through the rain, refocusing to a wider perspective, discerning God at work in our lives.

All the ways of accepting and forgiving ourselves and others and enabling change that we have been working on since session 18 aim to enable us to be more open and aware of our choices and total resources, physical, mental, emotional, spiritual. Our whole program has been designed to help us to open ourselves, to be more aware of how God's Spirit is and may be working in our own lives, to discern God's Spirit at work in the lives of others and to help them to become more aware themselves of God's Spirit.

Because our relationship with God deepens in many ways when we are more in touch with God's will and plan for us, our awareness, our perspective and so our range of choices become so much wider and more satisfying. When we enjoy relating more deeply with God, in relating with others we move towards fulfilling our own deepest needs and desires as we move towards fulfilling the deepest needs and desires of others.

Even in crisis, perhaps especially in crisis because we are realizing the lack of our own resources, if we open ourselves to God's resources we may be filled with God's love and light as God's Spirit flows through us to others.

D. CONCLUDING

RECOLLECTING
Quiet reflecting and evaluation of the session.

EVALUATION
Brief comments and evaluation.

HOME PRACTICE
Practice praying the Bible; go through the notes on reevaluating a relationship; act on any new understandings from separating pain and associating satisfying feelings; and complete our written evaluation of the whole program.

AFFIRMATION
Close with the hymn: "Praise to the Living God," and the grace.

PART FOUR

Evaluation and Celebration

Contemplation in Crisis: Maintaining Our Awareness of God A Summary of the Program Evaluation and Personal Progress

A. BECOMING AWARE OF WHERE WE ARE

RECOLLECTING
Being still in the presence of God.
Praying silently or aloud.

RECAP
Last session we thought about praying the Bible, and reevaluating relationships. We were also asked to bring today our written evaluation of the whole program.

SHARING
Share anything arising from last session.

B. and C. BECOMING AWARE IN FORMAL PRAYING AND IN COUNSELING SKILLS

PRACTICE
Silently centering ourselves and becoming more aware of God's presence.
Praying aloud as we are led.
Seeking God's help as we surface and share our responses to the program.

Evaluation

INTRODUCTION AND SUMMARY
In this session and the next we come to the final stage of this *Spiritually Aware Pastoral Care* program. We evaluate the program and consider ways in which we may build on our learning from it. As Christians we are called to grow to maturity in Christ and to love and encourage each other, as Paul reminded us in Ephesians 4:13,16. So all of us have a responsibility to develop and change and to help others to do the same.

All Christian helpers who offer truly pastoral care are involved in spiritual guidance. What we have learned here about seeking the guidance of the Holy Spirit applies to us as helpers, whether in relation to our family, friends or those we seek to help more formally.

While recognizing the importance of psychological understanding and skills, and the feeling and thinking content of a situation, we need to attend to the Holy Spirit; we need actively to seek grace, the help of the Holy Spirit, at the same time as we are helping another person. Then we may experience lightness, a sense of participation, and mutual healing because of our basic orientation.

Being aware of the Holy Spirit is especially necessary for us in a crisis situation, when we as helpers may doubt our ability to cope, while those seeking help are doubting their own ability. It is easy to be overwhelmed by feelings, by the details of the situation, so that we may not surface above them to creative ways of emerging from the crisis. We need to keep asking: "How in fact do we become more aware of the loving Holy Spirit? How do we keep more in touch with God, the source of life and peace and strength; i.e., how do we maintain a contemplative approach to life?"

The great guides of the contemplative tradition, those who have learned to encourage a contemplative view of the whole of life, those who have learned to pray, who aim to open themselves to reality at all times, are those who may teach us how to maintain a sense of God present and active everywhere.

This awareness of God active in and through everything that is happening at the moment is the real clue to all our relating within the cosmos.

The contemplative understanding of prayer as an attitude of the whole person to the whole of life may also free us to appreciate more fully ways in which many of the best insights of the psychological approach to helping people are used by God, and may be used by us, to free our awareness, and to help us to address spiritual issues such as meaning, purpose, value and direction.

So learning from the experience of the great contemplative guides and applying their learnings to ourselves, to our practice as helpers and to the psychological skills we are developing, has been an integral part of each session of our program.

This program has been a mutual learning experience. The framework has been first to establish our basic aims, assumptions, commitment, and what we mean by spiritually aware pastoral care, by contemplation in crisis. Then, closely interwoven with practicing praying, we have set out to learn more about discerning God's Spirit in contemplation; in crisis; in nonverbal awareness skills; in formal and informal meditation and in verbal listening skills; in pain, healing and words, including Biblical words; in our own past and present; and in verbal skills for accepting and forgiving ourselves and others and enabling change.

In evaluating this learning experience we are assessing our perceptions of how far we have each developed our awareness and skills; how far we have incorporated our learnings from a contemplative simple gentle openness to the whole of life into our psychology by praying together, building rapport, encouraging trust and enabling each of us to share out of our own unique story and situation.

We are aiming to recognize and affirm the ways in which we have been:

1. Enabled to make creative links between our own present and past life and traditions.
2. Encouraged and further equipped to discern the continuous presence and action of the Holy Spirit, the whole Spirit, the healing, loving, creative Spirit, in our own lives and in the lives of others.
3. Helped to enable others to make links and to discern the Holy Spirit for themselves in their own lives (session 1: aims).

Many of our learnings are unconscious; they may be recognized by us only later, or only by others.

SHARING
Let's go through our evaluations, continuing next time with what we don't cover today.
Evaluate the program systematically.

D. CONCLUDING

RECOLLECTING
Quiet reflecting and journaling.

EVALUATION
Brief comments and evaluation of the session.

HOME PRACTICE
Continue evaluating and practicing what we have learned.

LOOKING AHEAD
Next time we shall continue our evaluating. We shall also need to plan and prepare for the celebration and Godspeed in the final session. What ideas do we already have about the form that may take, e.g., shared meal, eucharist?

AFFIRMATION
Close with a hymn, praying aloud, and the grace.

SESSION 32

Evaluation and Personal Progress

A. BECOMING AWARE OF WHERE WE ARE

RECOLLECTING
Being still in the presence of God.
Praying silently or aloud.

RECAP
Last session we started evaluating the whole program, and began to plan our final celebration.

SHARING
Share anything arising from last session.

B. and C. BECOMING AWARE IN FORMAL PRAYING AND IN COUNSELING SKILLS

PRACTICE
Silent praying.
Praying aloud.
Becoming more aware of God's help as we share our responses to the program.

Evaluation of The Program and Our Personal Journey

INTRODUCTION
The measure of how far this program has succeeded for each of us is in how much more aware and open we are to God our loving creator, known to us through the Bible, through Jesus and through God's active Holy Spirit; and how much more open we are to ourselves and to others.

SHARING
Make sure that we give everyone time to share, sharing whatever is appropriate for us from our own journey through this program.

D. CONCLUDING

RECOLLECTING
Quiet reflecting and journaling.

EVALUATION
Brief comments and evaluation of the session.

HOME PRACTICE
Continue practicing what we have learned.

LOOKING AHEAD
Next time is our last. What plans and preparations do we need to make for our celebration and Godspeed?

AFFIRMATION
Close with a hymn, praying aloud, and the grace.

SESSION 33

Celebration and Godspeed

Each group will choose to celebrate our journey together in a different way, perhaps with a shared meal and informal eucharist, incorporating some of the learnings from our program.

May the peaceful awareness and openness to the grace and love and fellowship of God our loving Creator, Redeemer and Sanctifier, be with us and increase in us daily. Amen.

EVALUATION GUIDE

Note: This written evaluation is for our personal benefit and for our reference in group discussion.

First read all the sessions, especially the aims and covenant in session 1.

Then ask ourselves:

1. In what ways have I become more aware of the Holy Spirit this term or in this program:
   in my life in general
   in my prayer life
   in developing my counseling skills
   in my helping relationships?
2. How far have I fulfilled my personal covenant?

3. How do I think I shall use and develop what I have learned?
4. What have I found helpful in the program? What have I found unhelpful in the program? How should I like it to be improved:
   in general
   in specific sessions:
   e.g., aim
   structure of sessions
   leadership
   participation of group members
   content
   practice
   journaling
   book table
5. Any other comments.

BIBLIOGRAPHY

Abbott, Eric. 1963. *The Compassion of God and the Passion of Christ.* London: Geoffrey Bles.

Alexander, Frederick M. 1974. *The Alexander Technique.* New York: Thames and Hudson, Dist. by W.W. Norton & Co.

Anderson, J.G. 1978. "Education for Spirituality in CPE." *Journal of Pastoral Care* 32 (September): 155–160.

Assagioli, Roberto. 1973. *The Act of Will.* New York: Viking Press.

———. 1975. *Psychosynthesis: A Manual of Principles and Techniques.* London: Turnstone Books, 1975.

Augustine of Hippo, *Confessions.*

Bandler, Richard, and John Grinder. 1979. *Frogs into Princes: Neuro Linguistic Programming.* Moab, Utah: Real People Press.

Barnhouse, R.T. 1979. "Spiritual Direction and Psychotherapy." *Journal of Pastoral Care* 33 (September): 149–163.

Barrett, C.K. 1962. *From First Adam to Last: a Study in Pauline Theology.* London: A. & C. Black.

Barry, William A., and William J. Connolly. 1982. *The Practice of Spiritual Direction.* New York: The Seabury Press.

Baum, Gregory. 1970. *Man Becoming.* New York: The Seabury Press.

———. 1975. *Religion and Alienation.* New York: Paulist Press.

Becker, Ernest. 1973. *The Denial of Death.* New York: The Free Press.

Blake, William. 1890. "Auguries of Innocence." *Poetical Works of William Blake.* London: George Bell and Sons.

Boisen, Anton T. 1955. *Religion in Crisis and Custom.* New York: Harper and Row.

Bolton, Robert. 1979. *People Skills.* Englewood Cliffs, N.J.: Prentice Hall.

Bondi, Roberta C. 1986. "The Abba and Amma in Early Monasticism: the First Pastoral Counselor?" *Journal of Pastoral Care* 40 (December): 311–20.

Bonthius, Robert. 1967. Pastoral Care for Structures —As Well As Persons. *Pastoral Psychology* 18 (May): 10–19.

Boorstein, Seymour, ed. 1980. *Transpersonal Psychotherapy.* Palo Alto, CA: Science & Behavior Publications.

Briggs-Myers, Isabel and Mary H. McCaulley. 1985. *Manual: A Guide to the Development and Use of the Myers-Briggs Type Indicator.* 2d ed. Palo Alto CA: Consulting Psychologists Press.

Cameron-Bandler, Leslie. 1985. *Solutions: Practical and Effective Antidotes for Sexual and Relationship Problems.* San Raphael: Future Pace.

Caplan, Gerald. 1964. *Principles of Preventive Psychiatry.* New York: Basic Books.

Capps, Donald. 1981. *Biblical Approaches to Pastoral Counseling.* Philadelphia: Westminster Press.

Capra, Fritjof. 1975. *The Tao of Physics.* Berkeley, CA: Shambola.

Carkhuff, R.R. 1972. *The Art of Helping.* Amherst, MA: Human Resource Development Press.

Clebsch, William A., and Charles R. Jaekle. 1967. *Pastoral Care in Historical Perspective.* New York: Harper and Row.

Clinebell, Howard J., Jnr. 1966. *Basic Types of Pastoral Counseling.* New York: Abingdon Press.

———. 1981. *Contemporary Growth Therapies.* Nashville: Abingdon.

———. 1983. "Toward Envisioning the Future of Pastoral Counseling and A.A.P.C." Adapted from a plenary address given at the 20th Anniversary Convention of the American Association of Pastoral Counselors, April 13–16, 1983. *Journal of Pastoral Care* 37 (September): 180–194.

Cobb, John B. 1974. *To Pray or Not to Pray.* Nashville, TN: Upper Room Publications.

———. 1977. *Theology and Pastoral Care.* Creative Pastoral Care and Counseling Series, ed. Howard J. Clinebell, Jnr. Philadelphia: Fortress Press.

Cook, Peter S. 1978. "Childrearing, Culture and Mental Health." *The Medical Journal of Australia Special Supplement,* 12 August.

Dillistone, F.W. 1981. *Religious Experience and Christian Faith.* London: S.C.M. Press.

Doherty, RoseMary. 1986. Lecture. Spiritual Directors' Program. Washington D.C.: Shalem Institute for Spiritual Formation.

Edinger, Edward F. 1973. *Ego and Archetype.* New York: Penguin Books.

Edwards, Tilden. 1977. *Living Simply through the Day: Spiritual Survival in a Complex Age.* New York: Paulist Press.

———. 1980. *Spiritual Friend: Reclaiming the Gift of Spiritual Direction.* New York: Paulist Press.

———. 1982. *Sabbath Time.* New York: The Seabury Press.

———, ed. 1984. *Living with Apocalypse.* San Francisco: Harper & Row.

Egan, Gerard. 1975. *Skilled Helper.* Monterey, CA: Brooks/Cole.

Eno, Brian. 1978. *Music for Airports (Ambient 1).* Polydor, 310647.

Erikson, Erik H. 1963. *Childhood and Society.* New York: W.W. Norton and Co.

Fairchild, Roy W. 1983. "Eight Good Books on Spiritual Guidance." *Pacific Theological Review* (Spring). San Anselmo, California: S.F.T.S.

———. 1985. "The Pastor as Spiritual Director." *Quarterly Review* 5 (Summer). Nashville, TN: United Methodist Publishing House: 25–34.

Feldenkrais, Moshe. 1977. *Awareness through Movement.* New York/London: Harper & Row; Toronto: Fitzhenry and Whiteside, 1972, 1977; Harmondsworth, Middlesex: Penguin Books, 1972, 1977.

Ferruci, Piero. 1982. *What We May Be: The Visions and Techniques of Psychosynthesis.* Wellingborough, Northamptonshire: Turnstone Press.

FitzGerald, Constance. 1984. "Impasse and dark night." In *Living with Apocalypse,* ed. Tilden Edwards, 93–116. San Francisco: Harper and Row.

Fowler, James W. 1981. *Stages of Faith: The Psychology of Human Development and the Quest for Meaning.* San Francisco: Harper and Row.

Frankl, Viktor. 1964. *Man's Search for Meaning.* Translated by Ilse Lasch. Published as *From Death-Camp to Existentialism.* Boston: Beacon Press, 1959; revised and enlarged, Boston: Beacon Press, 1962; London: Hodder and Stoughton, 1964 (page references are to 1964 edition).

———. 1969. *The Will to Meaning.* New York: Simon and Schuster.

———. 1975. *The Unconscious God.* New York: Simon and Schuster.

———. 1979. *The Unheard Cry for Meaning.* New York: Simon and Schuster.

Fromm, Erich. 1947. *Man for Himself.* New York: Holt Rinehart and Winston.

Fry, Christopher. 1951. *A Sleep of Prisoners.* London: Oxford University Press.

Gaulke, Earl H. 1975. *You Can Have a Family Where Everybody Wins.* St Louis: Concordia.

Geering, Lloyd. 1983. *The World of Relation: An Introduction to Martin Buber's I and Thou.* Wellington, New Zealand: Victoria University Press.

Good News Bible: Today's English version. 1976. London: The Bible Societies.

Gordon, David. 1978. *Therapeutic Metaphors.* Cupertino, CA: Meta Publications.

Gordon, Thomas. 1970. *How to be an Effective Parent.* London: Collins. U.S. title, *Parent Effectiveness Training.*

———. 1978. *P.E.T. in Action.* Toronto: Bantam.

Gratton, Carolyn. 1980. *Guidelines for Spiritual Direction.* Denville, NJ: Dimension Books.

Grinder, John, and Richard Bandler. 1981. *Tranceformations.* Moab, Utah: Real People Press.

Hadfield, J.A. 1950. *Psychology and Mental Health.* London: Geoge Allen and Unwin.

Haley, Jay. *Problem Solving Therapy.* 1978. San Francisco: Jossey-Bass Publishers.

Halmos, Paul. 1965. *The Faith of the Counsellors.* London: Constable.

Hart, Thomas N. 1980. *The Art of Christian Listening.* New York: Paulist Press.

Herbert, George. 1950. "The Pulley (or the Gifts of God)." In *A book of English poetry,* Harmondsworth, Middlesex: Penguin Books.

Holmes, Urban T. III. 1971. *The Future Shape of Ministry.* New York: The Seabury Press.

———. 1978. *The Priest in Community.* New York: The Seabury Press.

———. 1981a. *A History of Christian Spirituality.* New York: The Seabury Press.

———. 1981b. *Ministry and Imagination.* New York: The Seabury Press.

———. 1982. *Spirituality for Ministry.* San Francisco: Harper and Row.

Jacobson, Gerald F. 1970. "Crisis Intervention from the Viewpoint of the Mental Health Professional." *Pastoral Psychology* 21 (April): 21–28.

James, William. 1902. *Varieties of Religious Experience: A Study in Human Nature.* London: Longmans, Green and Company.

John of the Cross. 1979. *The Collected Works of St John of the Cross.* Translated by Kieran Kavanaugh and Otilio Rodriguez. *The Ascent of Mount Carmel. The Dark Night.* Washington: Institute of Carmelite Studies.

Johnston, William. 1978. *The Inner Eye of Love.* San Francisco: Harper and Row.

———. 1980. n.p. Quoted in Mark Link, *Breakaway.* Allen, Texas: Argus Communications.

———. 1981. *Silent Music.* Fontana 1976. Fount Paperbacks. First published, London: Collins, 1974.

Jung, Carl. 1933. *Modern Man in Search of a Soul.*

Translated by W.S. Dell and Cary F. Baynes. Reprinted, New York: Harcourt Brace Jovanovich, Harvest/HBJ Book, n.d.

———. 1953–1979. *Collected Works.* Translated by R.F.C. Hull. Edited by Herbert Read et al. 20 vols. Bollingen Series XX. Princeton NJ: Princeton University Press.

Kane, Margaret. 1975. *Theology in an Industrial Society.* London: S.C.M. Press.

Keating, Thomas. 1981. *The Heart of the World.* New York: Crossroad.

Kelsey, Morton T. 1978. "Pastoral Counseling and the Spiritual Quest." *Journal of Pastoral Care* 32 (June): 89–99.

———. 1980. *Adventure Inward.* Minneapolis: Augsburg Publishing House.

———. 1982. *Christo-Psychology.* New York: Crossroad Publishing Company.

Kubler-Ross, Elisabeth. 1978. *On Death and Dying.* London: Tavistock Publications.

Lane, Belden. 1981. "Spirituality and Political Commitment: Notes on a Liberation Theology of Nonviolence." *America,* 13 March, 95.

Lankton, Steve. 1980. *Practical Magic: A Translation of Basic Neurolinguistic Programming into Clinical Psychotherapy.* Cupertino, CA: Meta Publications.

Leech, Kenneth. 1980. *Soul Friend: The Practice of Christian Spirituality.* San Francisco: Harper and Row.

———. 1981. *The Social God.* London: Sheldon Press.

———. 1985. *Experiencing God: Theology as Spirituality.* San Francisco: Harper and Row. British ed. *True God: An Exploration in Spiritual Theology.* London: Sheldon Press, S.P.C.K..

———. 1986. *Spirituality and Pastoral Care.* London: Sheldon Press, S.P.C.K.

Le Shan, Lawrence. 1980. *Clairvoyant Reality: Towards a General Theory of the Paranormal.* Orig. *The Medium, the Mystic and the Physicist.* Wellingborough, Northamptonshire: Turnstone Press, 1974. Paperback.

Lindemann, Erich. 1965. "Symptomatology and Management of Acute Grief." In *Crisis Intervention: Selected Readings,* ed. Howard J. Parad, New York: Family Service Assn. of America.

Link, Mark. 1980. *Breakaway.* Allen, Texas: Argus Communications.

Loder, James E. 1981. *The Transforming Moment.* San Francisco: Harper and Row.

Lossky, Vladimir. 1957. *The Mystical Theology of the Eastern Church.* Crestwood, N.Y.: St Vladimir's Seminary Press.

Louth, Andrew. 1981. *The Origins of the Christian Mystical Tradition.* Oxford: Clarendon Press.

McNamara, William. 1975. n.p. Quoted in May, *Will and Spirit,* 326; San Francisco: Harper and Row, 1982, from Charles Tart. *Transpersonal Psychologies,* 405. New York: Harper and Row, 1975.

McNeill, John T. 1977. *A History of the Cure of Souls.* New York: Harper and Row.

Maloney, George. 1976. *Inward Stillness.* Denver, NJ: Dimension Books.

May, Gerald. 1977. *The Open Way: A Meditation Handbook.* New York: Paulist Press.

———. 1979. *Pilgrimage Home.* New York: Paulist Press.

———. 1982a. *Care of Mind/Care of Spirit.* San Francisco: Harper and Row.

———. 1982b. *Will and Spirit: A Contemplative Psychology.* San Francisco: Harper and Row.

Merton, Thomas. 1951. *Ascent to Truth.* n.p., 177. Quoted in Kenneth Leech. *Soul Friend,* 170. San Francisco: Harper and Row, 1980.

———. 1971. "Is Mysticism Normal?" *Commonweal* 51, (1949–50), cited in J.J. Higgins' *Merton's Theology of Prayer* (1971), 22.

———. 1973. *Contemplation in a World of Action.* New York: Image Books, Doubleday and Co.

Moltmann, Jurgen. 1980. *Experiences of God.* Philadelphia: Fortress Press.

Morley, Wilbur E. 1970. Theory of Crisis Intervention, *Pastoral Psychology* 21 (April): 14–20.

Neufelder, Jerome M. and Mary C. Coelho, ed. 1982. *Writings on Spiritual Direction by Great Christian Masters.* Minneapolis: The Seabury Press.

Nouwen, Henri. 1972. *The Wounded Healer.* New York: Doubleday and Co.

———. 1977. *The Living Reminder: Service and Prayer in Memory of Jesus Christ.* New York: Seabury Press.

———, Donald P. McNeill, and Douglas A. Morrison. 1982. *Compassion.* New York: Doubleday and Co.

Oden, Thomas C. 1980. "Recovering Lost Identity," *Journal of Pastoral Care* 34 (March): 4–19.

Ornstein, Robert. 1977. *The Psychology of Consciousness.* New York: Viking, 1972; New York: Harcourt Brace Jovanovich.

Otto, Rudolf. 1950. *The Idea of the Holy.* 2d ed. Translated by J.W. Harvey. London: Oxford University Press.

Palmer, Parker J. 1984. "The Spiritual Life: Apocalypse Now." In *Living with Apocalypse,* ed. Tilden Edwards, 23–38. San Francisco: Harper and Row.

Parad, Howard J. ed. 1965. *Crisis Intervention: Selected Readings.* New York: Family Service Association of America.

Peck, M. Scott. 1978. *The Road Less Traveled.* New York: Touchstone, Simon and Schuster.

Pruyser Paul W. 1976. *The Minister as Diagnostician:*

Personal Problems in Pastoral Perspective. Philadelphia: Westminster Press.

Ramsay, A.M. 1974. *Canterbury Pilgrim.* London: S.P.C.K.

Reed, Bruce. 1975. *The Task of the Church and the Role of Its Members.* Washington D.C.: Alban Institute.

———. 1978. *The Dynamics of Religion.* London: Darton, Longman and Todd.

Rogers, Carl R. 1951. *Client-Centered Therapy.* Boston: Houghton Mifflin.

Rosen, Sidney. 1982. *My Voice Will Go with You: The Teaching Tales of Milton H. Erickson.* New York: W.W. Norton and Co.

Rutherford, Peter, Rod Mitchell and Elspeth Williams. 1979. *Listening Skills.* Wellington, New Zealand: Community Service Course, Wellington Polytechnic.

Shalem Institute for Spiritual Formation. Spiritual Director's Program. 1986. *Discernment Examen.* Washington D.C.: Shalem Institute for Spiritual Formation.

Shea, John. 1978. *Stories of God.* Chicago: The Thomas More Press.

Soelle, Dorothee. 1975. *Suffering.* Philadelphia: Fortress Press.

Spink, Peter. 1980. *Spiritual Man in a New Age.* London: Darton, Longman and Todd.

Squire, Aelred. 1976. *Asking the Fathers.* 2d U.S.A. ed. New York: Paulist Press and Wilton, Conn.: Morehouse-Barlow, 1976, 19. Quoted in Gerald May. *Will and Spirit,* 32. San Francisco: Harper and Row, 1982.

Stone, Howard W. 1976. *Crisis Counseling.* Creative Pastoral Care and Counseling Series, ed. Howard J. Clinebell, Jnr. Philadelphia: Fortress Press.

Switzer, David K. 1970. "Crisis Intervention Techniques for the Minister." *Pastoral Psychology* 21 (April): 29–36.

Teresa of Avila. *The Interior Castle.* Edited by Fr. John Vernard, Surrey Hills, N.S.W., Australia: Dwyer, 1980.

Thayer, Nelson S.T. 1981. "Merton and Freud: Beyond Oedipal Religion." *Journal of Pastoral Care* 35 (March): 36–41.

———. 1985. *Spirituality and Pastoral Care.* Philadelphia: Fortress Press.

The Cloud of Unknowing. 1961. Translated by Clifton Wolters. Harmondsworth, Middlesex: Penguin Books.

The Jerusalem Bible. 1966. London: Darton, Longman and Todd.

Topping, Wayne. 1985. *Stress Release: Identifying and Releasing Stress through the Use of Muscle Testing.* Bellingham, Washington: Topping International Institute.

Turner, Kathy. 1987. "Pastoral Response to the Person in Community." In *Pastoral Ministry in a Fractured World: Proceedings of the Third International Congress on Pastoral Care and Counselling Held in Melbourne, Australia, August 19–26, 1987,* 41–55. Melbourne: International Council on Pastoral Care and Counselling.

Vaughan, Frances. 1979. *Awakening Intuition.* New York: Anchor Press/Doubleday.

Welch, John. 1982. *Spiritual Pilgrims: Carl Jung and Teresa of Avila.* New York: Paulist Press.

Wesley, Suzanna. 1732. "Letter to Son John," July 24, 1732. In *The Journal of John Wesley* vol. 1, August 1 1742. Everyman's Library 105. London: Dent; New York: Dutton, 1906, 390. Quoted partially in Peter S. Cook. 1978. "Child-Rearing, Culture and Mental Health." *Medical Journal of Australia special supplement,* 12 August 1978, 7.

Whitlock, Glenn E. 1980. "A New Approach to Pastoral Counseling; Pastoral Psychology and Preventive Psychiatry; The Pastor's Use of Crisis Intervention." *Pastoral Psychology* 21 (April): 5–8, 9–13, 37–46.

Wilber, Ken. 1987. Interview by Catherine Ingram. *Yoga Journal* (September–October): 40–49.

Wilson, Michael. 1971. *The Hospital: A Place of Truth.* Birmingham, U.K.: University of Birmingham Institute for the Study of Worship and Religious Architecture.

———. 1975. *Health is for People.* London: Darton, Longman and Todd.

Wink, Walter. 1981. *Transforming Bible Study.* London: S.C.M. Press.

INDEX